World-Class Universities

Global Perspectives on Higher Education

Series Editors

Philip G. Altbach
(Center for International Higher Education, Boston College, USA)
Hans de Wit
(Center for International Higher Education, Boston College, USA)
Laura E. Rumbley
(Center for International Higher Education, Boston College, USA)

This series is co-published with the Center for International Higher Education at Boston College.

VOLUME 42

The titles published in this series are listed at *brill.com/gphe*

World-Class Universities

Towards a Global Common Good and Seeking National and Institutional Contributions

Edited by

Yan Wu, Qi Wang and Nian Cai Liu

BRILL
SENSE

LEIDEN | BOSTON

All chapters in this book have undergone peer review.

The Library of Congress Cataloging-in-Publication Data is available online at http://catalog.loc.gov

Typeface for the Latin, Greek, and Cyrillic scripts: "Brill". See and download: brill.com/brill-typeface.

ISSN 2214-0859
ISBN 978-90-04-38961-8 (paperback)
ISBN 978-90-04-38962-5 (hardback)
ISBN 978-90-04-38963-2 (e-book)

Copyright 2019 by Koninklijke Brill NV, Leiden, The Netherlands.
Koninklijke Brill NV incorporates the imprints Brill, Brill Hes & De Graaf, Brill Nijhoff, Brill Rodopi, Brill Sense, Hotei Publishing, mentis Verlag, Verlag Ferdinand Schöningh and Wilhelm Fink Verlag.
All rights reserved. No part of this publication may be reproduced, translated, stored in a retrieval system, or transmitted in any form or by any means, electronic, mechanical, photocopying, recording or otherwise, without prior written permission from the publisher.
Authorization to photocopy items for internal or personal use is granted by Koninklijke Brill NV provided that the appropriate fees are paid directly to The Copyright Clearance Center, 222 Rosewood Drive, Suite 910, Danvers, MA 01923, USA. Fees are subject to change.

This book is printed on acid-free paper and produced in a sustainable manner.

Contents

Acknowledgements VII
List of Figures and Tables VIII
Notes on Contributors XI

1 World-Class Universities: Towards a Global Common Good and Seeking National and Institutional Contributions 1
   Yan Wu, Qi Wang and Nian Cai Liu

PART 1
Global and Theoretical Perspectives

2 Global Cooperation and National Competition in the World-Class University Sector 13
   Simon Marginson

3 World-Class Universities and Higher Education Differentiation: The Necessity of Systems 56
   Philip G. Altbach

4 World-Class Universities in a Post-Truth World 70
   Pierre de Maret and Jamil Salmi

5 Examining Rankings and Strategic Planning: Variations in Local Commitments 88
   Jenny J. Lee, Hillary Vance and Bjørn Stensaker

6 World-Class Universities: A Dual Identity Related to Global Common Good(s) 102
   Lin Tian

7 The Art of Starting a New University: Lessons of Experience 125
   Jamil Salmi

PART 2
National and Regional Responses

8 The Role of American World-Class Universities in Serving the Global Common Good   141
   Genevieve G. Shaker and William M. Plater

9 Pursuing Excellence in Graduate Education and Research While Serving Regional Development   163
   Rita Karam, Charles A. Goldman, Daniel Basco and Diana Gehlhaus Carew

10 World-Class Universities' Contribution to an Open Society: Chinese Universities on a Mission?   188
   Marijk van der Wende

11 World-Class Universities and the Global Common Good: The Role of China and the US in Addressing Global Inequality   215
   Gerard A. Postiglione and Ailei Xie

12 What Are the Benefits and Risks of Internationalization of Japanese Higher Education?   231
   Futao Huang

13 State and World-Class Universities: Seeking a Balance between International Competitiveness, Local and National Relevance   243
   Isak Froumin and Mikhail Lisyutkin

Acknowledgements

The editors wish to thank John Bennett and Jolanda Karada, Brill | Sense, for their support in the publication of this volume; Professor Philip G. Altbach, research professor and founding director of the Center for International Higher Education at Boston College; Dr Jan Sadlak, President of IREG – International Observatory on Ranking and Academic Excellence; and Dr Paul Deacon for the linguistic editing of the manuscript.

Figures and Tables

Figures

2.1 Worldwide gross tertiary enrolment ratio (%), compared to proportion of people living in cities (%) and proportion of labour in agriculture (%), 1991–2015.   16
2.2 Examples of individualized and collective contributions of higher education.   26
2.3 Proportion (%) of people answering 'yes' to the question 'do you trust others?' OECD nations, 2012 OECD survey of adult skills.   29
2.4 Annual number of published science papers, 2003–2016 United States, China, Germany, United Kingdom, South Korea.   39
2.5 Proportion of all science and engineering papers that were in the top 1 per cent of their field by citation rate: United States, United Kingdom, Netherlands, China, South Korea, Singapore: 1996–2014.   40
2.6 Growth in annual number and proportion of internationally co-authored papers in science and engineering, 2003 to 2016, world and United States.   45
2.7 The rate at which papers by authors from selected countries are cited by papers with authors from United States, compared to the rate that these countries cite United States authors, science and engineering papers, 2014.   50
4.1 Characteristics of world-class universities: Alignment of key factors.   73
6.1 The adapted AGIL scheme for the function system of modern universities.   113
9.1 Logic model.   165
9.2 Occupational groups with highest graduate demand in Texas, 2012–2022.   166
9.3 Graduate degree completions by broad field, 2005 and 2014.   167
9.4 Percentage race/ethnicity distribution of public university graduate degree recipients and general population (18- to 64-years-old) in Texas, 2014.   168
9.5 Graduate and professional degree production, 2005 and 2014.   169
9.6 Per capita graduate and professional degree production, 2005 and 2014.   170
9.7 Percentage of residents, 25- to 64-years-old, holding a graduate degree, 2005 and 2012.   171
9.8 Federal obligations to higher education for R&D, 2013.   171
9.9 Texas R&D expenditures by institution, 2013.   172
9.10 California R&D expenditures by institution, 2013.   173
9.11 Florida R&D expenditures by institution, 2013.   173
9.12 New York R&D expenditures by institution, 2013.   174
9.13 Number of Carnegie research universities (R1, R2, and R3) by state, 2005 and 2015.   175

9.14   Number of institutions ranking in top 500 of ARWU by state, 2005 and 2015. 176
9.15   Institutional motivators for new graduate degree programmes. 178
10.1   China's position in international citations network 1996–2013. 200
12.1   Benefits of internationalization of higher education (%). 235
12.2   Risks of internationalization of higher education (%). 237
13.1   Geographical distribution of the Project 5-100 universities. 249

Tables

2.1   Gross expenditures on R&D (constant 2005 US dollars, PPP), eight leading science countries: Five-year intervals (1990–2015). 18
2.2   Internationally mobile or foreign doctoral students as a proportion (%) of all doctoral students in 2015, OECD systems, Brazil and Russia, compared to number of ARWU top 500 universities in each country in 2015 (number of top 500 universities in brackets). 32
2.3   Recipients of United States doctorates on temporary visas, by country/region of origin (four largest country/regions) by science-based discipline, 1995–2015. 34
2.4   Annual rate of growth in published science papers, 2006–2016, nations producing more than 10,000 papers in 2016. 37
2.5   Growth in the number of published papers in the top 10 per cent of their research field by citation rate, from 2006–2009 to 2012–2015, selected leading Asian universities. 42
2.6   World top universities in (1) physical sciences and engineering, (2) mathematics and complex computing, in published papers in the top 10 per cent of their field by citation rate: 2012–2015. 43
2.7   Proportion of all papers in science and engineering that were internationally co-authored, 2003 and 2016, countries producing more than 10,000 papers in 2016, by region (science includes some social science). 46
2.8   Intensive research collaborations by United States, China and United Kingdom, with rest of the world, in 2016: Rate of international co-authorship in science and engineering papers between named pairs, relative to their rate of international co-authorship with all countries. 49
4.1   Corruption ranking and excellence ranking in Colombia (2017). 75
4.2   Most corrupt professions in Colombia (2017). 75
4.3   Proportion of low-income students in top US universities. 76
4.4   Contribution of universities to the sustainable development goals. 82
5.1   Study sample by institutional regions and rankings. 92
5.2   Global rankings criteria in 2017. 92
5.3   Third mission economic and social/cultural classifications. 93

6.1	WCUs in three major university rankings.	110
6.2	Available documents of WCUs (N = 61).	113
6.3	Keywords related to talent cultivation (simplified version).	115
6.4	Keywords related to scientific research (simplified version).	117
6.5	Keywords related to social service (simplified version).	119
10.1	Subject fields in which China holds number 1 position and >20% of global top 50.	198
10.2	Subject fields in which China holds number 1 position or >20% of global top 50.	199
10.3	Scientific impact per field.	199
12.1	Benefits of internationalization of higher education by sector-level of importance (%) (responses of 'strongly agree and agree').	236
12.2	Benefits of internationalization of HE by type-level of importance (%).	236
12.3	Risks of internationalization of HE by sector-level of importance (responses of 'strongly agree and agree').	238
12.4	Risks of internationalization of higher education by type-level of importance.	239
13.1	The areas of the activities which could be funded by the universities from the Project 5-100 grant (subsidy).	250

Notes on Contributors

Philip G. Altbach
is the Research Professor and Founding Director of the Center for International Higher Education at Boston College, where from 1994 to 2015 he was the Monan University Professor. He is currently guest professor at Peking University and Xiamen University in China and has been an Onwell Fellow at the University of Hong Kong, and a fellow of the National Science Foundation of Taiwan. He was given the Houlihan award for distinguished contributions to international education by NAFSA: Association of International Educators, the Bowen distinguished career award by the Association for the Study of Higher Education, and has been a senior associate of the Carnegie Foundation for the Advancement of Teaching. In 2010, he was Erudite Scholar of the Government of Kerala. He has taught at Harvard University, the University of Wisconsin, and the State University of New York at Buffalo. Dr. Altbach holds the B.A., M.A. and PhD degrees from the University of Chicago. He is author of *Global Perspectives on Higher Education, Turmoil and Transition, Student Politics in America,* among other books. He also co-edited (with Jamil Salmi) *The Road to Academic Excellence,* (with Michael Bastedo and Patricia Gumport) *American Higher Education in the 21st Century,* the *International Handbook of Higher Education, World Class Worldwide: Transforming Research Universities in Asia and Latin America* and other books.

Daniel Basco
is President of Vertex Evaluation and Research, LLC and an Adjunct Policy Researcher at the RAND Corporation. At Vertex, Basco develops innovative metrics for evaluating programs and policies at the intersection of education, R&D, and innovation. At RAND, Basco advises higher education institutions and governments on ways to use better data and evaluation methods to continuously improve programs for undergraduate students. Previously, Basco was a management consultant and researcher supporting the White House Office of Science and Technology Policy, the National Science Foundation, and the National Institutes of Health He earned his BS in Social Policy from Northwestern University and his MPhil and PhD in Public Policy Analysis from the Pardee RAND Graduate School.

Diana G. Carew
is an assistant policy researcher at RAND and a doctoral fellow at the Pardee RAND Graduate School. Her research areas include higher education, human capital strategic planning, workforce development, and regulatory reform.

Prior to joining Pardee RAND, she was an economist and director of the Young American Prosperity Project at the Progressive Policy Institute in Washington, DC.She previously worked for the Export-Import Bank, and for the US Bureau of Labor Statistics.

Isak Froumin
is a Head of the Institute of Education at the National Research University Higher School of Economics in Moscow (Russia) – the first education graduate school in Russia. His responsibilities also include advising the university strategic planning and international cooperation and he is co-leader of the research project 'China-Russia Comparative Research Project on Educational Modernization Towards 2030' (jointly with the China Institute for Educational Science). Between 2012 and 2016, he was an advisor to the Minister of Education and Science of Russia Federation. He led the World Bank education programme in Russia from 1999 to 2011. His World Bank experience also extends to the projects in Kazakhstan, Kyrgyzstan, Afghanistan, Nepal, Turkmenistan and India. He has edited or authored more than 250 publications, including articles and books.

Charles A. Goldman
is a senior economist at the RAND Corporation and a professor of economics at the Pardee RAND Graduate School, and he sits on the advisory board of the Shanghai Academic Rankings of World Universities. He specializes in the economics of education, skills and workforce needs, strategic planning for education systems, and organization and performance of schools, universities, and systems. He is conducting a series of projects in Texas, all aimed at improving the match between higher education and workforce needs. Building on this work, he is conducting a study of how Australia's education, training, and workforce development systems can meet the demands of the country's rapid increase in naval shipbuilding. His work in skills also examines occupational competency requirements and military members' transitions from active duty to the civilian labour market. He has studied policy and implementation of both basic and higher education in the United States, Australia, Europe, Asia, and the Middle East..

Futao Huang
is currently Professor of the Research Institute for Higher Education, Hiroshima University, Japan. His major research fields include university curricular development, internationalization of higher education, and a comparative study of higher education in East Asia. Since the late 1990s, he has published widely in Chinese, English and Japanese in many international

peer-reviewed journals, including Higher Education, Higher Education Policy, Higher Education Policy and Management, Journal of Studies in International Education. In recent years, he has been invited to speak at various international conferences organized by the UNESCO, OECD, EUA, DAAD, German Rectors Conference, Nuffic, NSF and many universities in North America, Europe, and Asia.

Rita Karam

is a Senior Policy Researcher at the RAND Corporation. She specializes in educational policies, educational equity and programme improvement. Currently, she leads two studies investigating the effectiveness of technical programmes, as well as the efficacy of technology-based tool designed to facilitate program planning, advising and job-matching with under-represented youth. For over 15 years, she has been investigating school reform, science, engineering and technology (STEM) education, and post-secondary education and workforce preparation using experimental and quasi-experimental methods. She has examined the implementation of such initiatives and their effects on academic outcomes and employment. In her research, she considers various factors such as the complexity of programmes and their coherence with local policies as well as other government policies, and their alignment with cultural values..

Jenny J. Lee

is a professor in the Center for the Study of Higher Education at the University of Arizona in the US. She is also a visiting scholar in the Centre of Higher Education Development at the University of Cape Town in South Africa. Her research encompasses a range of key higher education issues that centre on the internationalization of higher education, including her latest work on international student mobility and their experiences.

Mikhail Lisyutkin

is a lecturer and a head of the universities management studies at the Institute of Education, National Research University Higher School of Economics. His current research interests include the dynamics of the universities' development and decline, universities' international competitiveness and excellence initiatives in higher education, the development of the higher education systems.

Nian Cai Liu

is currently the Director of the Center for World-Class Universities and Dean of the Graduate School of Education at Shanghai Jiao Tong University. He is one of the vice-presidents of 'IREG Observatory on Academic Ranking and Excellence'. His research interests include world-class universities and research universities, university evaluation and academic ranking, research evaluation and science policy, globalization and internationalization of higher education. He moved to the field of educational research in 1999, before which he was a professor in polymer science and engineering. He did his undergraduate study in chemistry at Lanzhou University of China and obtained his doctoral degree in polymer science and engineering from Queen's University at Kingston, Canada. He is on the editorial/advisory boards of several international and national journals

Pierre de Maret

served as Rector of the Université libre de Bruxelles (ULB) from 2000 to 2006 and was President of the Belgian French-speaking Conference of Rectors, and of the National Fund for Scientific Research in Belgium.He is Honorary Professor at University College London and was President of the Society of African Archaeologists (US) and from 2005 until 2009, he was a member of the Board of the European University Association (EUA). In 1990, he conceived and launched the UNICA network, the consortium of the Universities of the Capital Cities of Europe. A member of the Belgian Royal Academy, he holds Honorary Degrees from the Universities of Montreal, Lubumbashi, Tubingen, La Republica (Santiago-Chile), Lyon II and Chisinau. Involved in the early stages of the European Higher Education integration process, he has been actively contributing to it, organising several programmes and serving on the Erasmus Academic Advisory Board for the European Commission.

Simon Marginson

is Professor of International Higher Education at the University College of London's Institute of Education, Joint Editor-in-Chief of the journal Higher Education and a research leader for The UK in a Changing Europe. Simon has worked at the UCL Institute of Education since October 2013. Prior to that he was Professor of Higher Education at the University of Melbourne (2006–2013), and Professor of Education at Monash University (2000–2006). He was the Clark Kerr Lecturer on Higher Education at the University of California, Berkeley in 2014, and in the same year received the Distinguished Research Award from the Association for Studies of Higher Education in the United States. He is a member of Academia Europaea, a Lifetime Fellow of the Society for Research into Higher Education in the UK, and a Fellow of the Academy of Social Sciences Australia. He is currently researching the public good contributions of higher education, and completing a book with colleagues on the implications of the worldwide trend of high-participation higher education systems.

William M. Plater

currently serves as Research Director for Community Engagement and Civic Learning for the Global Common Good at Laureate Education, Inc., a global network of more than 70 campus-based and online universities in 25 countries, and as Senior Scholar at The Quality Assurance Commons for Postsecondary and Higher Education.Plater is Executive Vice Chancellor and Dean of the Faculties Emeritus at Indiana University Purdue University Indianapolis (IUPUI) and Indiana University Chancellor's Professor Emeritus of Public Affairs, Philanthropic Studies and English. From 2012 to 2014, he was Senior Advisor for International Affairs of the WASC Senior Colleges and Universities Commission, where he served as a Commissioner from 2005 through 2011. Heserved as the Indiana University Dean of the School of Liberal Arts (1983–1987), Executive Vice Chancellor and Dean of the Faculties (1987–2006), Acting Chancellor (2003), and Director of the Workshop on International Community Development (2006–2010) at IUPUI until his retirement in 2010. Before joining IUPUI, he was Associate Director of the School of Humanities at the University of Illinois at Urbana-Champaign, where he earned BA, MA and PhD degrees in English.

Jamil Salmi

is a global tertiary education expert providing policy advice to governments, universities, professional associations, multilateral development banks and bilateral cooperation agencies. Until January 2012, he was the World Bank's tertiary education coordinator. In the past twenty-five years, Dr. Salmi has provided advice on tertiary education development, financing reforms and strategic planning to governments and university leaders in about 100 countries all over the world. Dr. Salmi is Emeritus Professor of higher education policy at Diego Portales University in Chile and Research Fellow at Boston College's Center for Higher Education. Dr. Salmi's 2009 book addresses the *Challenge of Establishing World-Class Universities*. His 2011 book, co-edited with Professor Phil Altbach, was entitled *The Road to Academic Excellence: the Making of World-Class Research Universities*. His latest book, *Tertiary Education and the Sustainable Development Goals*, was published in August 2017.

Genevieve G. Shaker

is associate professor of philanthropic studies in the Indiana University Lilly Family School of Philanthropy at IUPUI and adjunct professor of liberal arts and women's studies and she is a fellow of the TIAA Institute. She was an advancement officer for 20 years, most recently as associate dean for development and external affairs for the Indiana University School of Liberal Arts, where she facilitated fundraising, communications, alumni programming, and public events. In 2015 she was recognized nationally as the year's outstanding scholar/practitioner by the Association for Fundraising Professionals with its 'Emerging Scholar' award. She is the editor of *Faculty work and the Public Good: Philanthropy, Engagement, and Academic Professionalism* (Teachers College Press, 2015), which engaged scholars of higher education and philanthropy to explore the intersection of academic work and philanthropic values. She serves as associate editor of Philanthropy and Education, a journal dedicated to building new understandings in an under-researched area.

Bjørn Stensaker
is a professor of higher education, working at the Faculty of Education at University of Oslo, Norway. He has a special research interest in studies of governance, leadership and organizational change in higher education, and he has published widely on these subjects in international journal and books

Lin Tian
is a PhD candidate in the Center for World-Class Universities (CWCU) at Shanghai Jiao Tong University. Currently, her research interests include functions of world-class universities and internationalization of higher education. She is also a Research Associate on CGHE's global higher education engagement research programme. After graduating from the University of Edinburgh, she worked in Shanghai Jiao Tong University as a research assistant (2014–2015) and then began to pursue her doctoral degree there from 2016. Currently, her research interests include functions of world-class universities and internationalization of higher education.

Hillary Vance
is the Director of Southeast Asia Programs and a PhD candidate in Higher Education at the University of Arizona. She oversees the development of University of Arizona micro-campuses across the Southeast Asia region. Her doctoral research is focused on politics and transnational higher education in Cambodia and Southeast Asia. She is based in Phnom Penh, Cambodia and has experience researching and working in student and programme mobility in international higher education and international education NGOs.

Qi Wang
is an assistant professor at the Graduate School of Education (GSE), Shanghai Jiao Tong University (SJTU) and research fellow at the Center for International Higher Education, Boston College. She also works as Associate Director for Administration and Research at the ALLEX Foundation (Alliance for Language

Learning and Education Exchange), focusing on developing strategy for Mainland China operations. She completed her MA and PhD studies at the Department of Education, University of Bath, UK, from September 2002 to November 2008. She joined SJTU in May 2009 and works at the Center for World-Class Universities. Her research interests include building world-class universities, employability management and skills training, and globalization and education development. In particular, her current research focuses on building world-class research universities from a theoretical and comparative perspective, and how different governments and universities in East Asia and Europe adopt policies to implement this global aspiration.

Marijk van der Wende
is Distinguished Professor of Higher Education at Utrecht University's Faculty of Law, Economics and Governance. Her research focuses on the impact of globalization and internationalization on higher education. She has published widely on the impact of these processes on higher education systems, institutions, curricula, and teaching and learning arrangements. She is also an affiliate faculty and research associate at the Center for Studies in Higher Education (CSHE) at the University of California Berkeley and member of the Academia Europaea (the Academy of Europe, behavioural sciences section). She is currently a member of the Supervisory Board of the Open University of the Netherlands, the Board of the Rathenau Institute for Science and Technology in Society, theInternational Advisory Board of the Centre for the Study of World Class Universities, Shanghai Jiao Tong University, the Graduate Campus Advisory Board of the University of Zurich, the Board of the Amsterdam University College Scholarship Fund (ASF Foundation), and Member of the European Science Foundation's College of Expert Reviewers.

Yan Wu
is an Assistant Professor at the Center for World-Class Universities (CWCU) of Shanghai Jiao Tong University (SJTU). She has been in the ranking team at CWCU since 2005. Since 2016, she has been responsible for organizing the biennial International Conference on World-Class Universities. Her primary research interests include the ranking and evaluation of universities. She had been responsible for the Global Research University Profiles (GRUP) project, which started in 2011 and has been developing a database on the facts and figures of around 1200 research universities in the world. The database has been or will be used to produce much more comprehensive and customized comparisons of research universities at a global level. She obtained her bachelor's (2000) and master's degree (2003) both in Philosophy from East China Normal Universities.

Ailei Xie
is an Associate Professor at Guangzhou University and the Executive Director of Bay Area Education Policy Institute for Social Development. His main area of research is on social development and education policy, education and social justice. The current focus of his study is on parental involvement in rural schools, and rural students and their success in China's elite universities. Before joining Guangzhou University in 2017, he was an Assistant Professor at Shanghai Jiao Tong University, postdoctoral research fellow at The University of Hong Kong and visiting fellow at Cambridge University. He graduated from the University of Hong Kong with a PhD in sociology of education in the year of 2012.

CHAPTER 1

World-Class Universities: Towards a Global Common Good and Seeking National and Institutional Contributions

Yan Wu, Qi Wang and Nian Cai Liu

Abstract

The Seventh International Conference on World-Class Universities was held in November 2017. The conference theme was 'World-Class Universities: Towards a Global Common Good and Seeking National and Institutional Contributions'.

In the era marked by globalization and its profound impacts on individuals, society, state and market, world-class universities need to position themselves in the forefront of seeking conceptual and practical solutions to daunting challenges by paying greater attention to their roles in serving local society and contributing to global common goods. This volume provides updated insights and debates on how world-class universities will contribute to the global common good and balance their global, national and local roles in doing so.

Keywords

World-class universities – research universities – global common good(s) – national and institutional

1   Introduction

World-class universities, often used interchangeably to refer to research universities or flagship universities, are regarded as cornerstone institutions of any academic system and imperative to develop a nation's competitiveness in the global knowledge economy. It is widely agreed that world-class universities are committed to creating and disseminating knowledge in a range of disciplines and fields; delivering elite education at all levels; serving national and local needs; and contributing public goods at both the global and national levels (Altbach, 2009; Liu, 2009; van der Wende, 2009). The development of world-class universities is high on the policy agenda of various stakeholders across the globe in the past decades. World-class universities' roles and contributions to economic, social and cultural development respectively are indispensable. Such a 'world-class' movement has been further intensified and manifested by the proliferation of university rankings (Salmi, 2009; Hazelkorn, 2011).

It was in this context that Graduate School of Education at Shanghai Jiao Tong University initiated the biennial International Conference on World-Class Universities in 2005. Previous conferences have gathered university administrators, government officials, leading scholars and policy researchers from around the world to discuss the various issues and topics related to world-class universities. These timely topics include: strategies and challenges of developing academic excellence from global, national and institutional perspectives; the influences and roles of WCUs in affecting global higher education; and issues on balancing and integrating visibility and performance.

The Seventh International Conference on World-Class Universities was held in November 2017. The conference theme was 'World-Class Universities: Towards a Global Common Good and Seeking National and Institutional Contributions'. This volume provides updates, insights and debates on how world-class universities will contribute to the global common good and balance their global, national and local roles in doing so.

2 World-Class Universities and Global Common Good(s): The Context

The choice of the conference theme reflects the propositions of the UNESCO report 'Rethinking Education: Towards a Global Common Good' – in an era marked by globalization and its profound impacts on individuals, society, state and market, and there is a need to consider and to understand education as 'a global common good'.

2.1 Higher Education Repositioned as a Global Common Good

With the increasing complexity of changes in the world, the long uncontested view that higher education is a public good has been challenged. Higher education is often referred to as disseminating knowledge and producing social and public benefits to all human beings. However, the changing landscape of higher education is blurring the simplistic dichotomy between public and private. The meaning of 'public' is contested by a range of factors, including increasing marketization and privatization, rising calls to cut public funding, greater diversification of stakeholders and engagement from non-state actors, and emerging forms of global governance (UNESCO, 2015; Marginson, 2018). Also, internationalization – growing collaboration and interaction between/ among universities, faculties and students across the globe – has weakened the concept of the nation-state and thus makes the concept of public good(s) 'in which human well-being is framed by individualistic socio-economic theory' (UNESCO, 2015, p. 78) difficult to apply to higher education.

The UNESCO report proposes the notion of a 'global common good', as a 'constructive alternative' to the public good; and suggests that education and knowledge be considered global common goods. This notion of a global common good takes a participatory process in defining the nature of education and places emphasis on the collective and inclusive dimension of education as a shared social action, responsibility and commitment to solidarity; and values 'the diversity of contexts, worldviews and knowledge systems, while respecting fundamental rights' for all people (ibid.). Only with such approach can we cope with global challenges, such as technological transformation and shifting employment patterns, new information and communication technologies, environmental concerns and climate change, social and cultural transformation.

Chapters in this volume provide an in-depth review and analysis on these notions in relation to higher education, especially world-class universities (Chapters 2, 6, 8, 10 and 11).

2.2   *World-Class Universities Serving as a Global Common Good*

In the current context of global higher education transformation, universities are facing risks, and their civic roles and social responsibilities are largely challenged. Researchers raised the concern higher education is becoming a marketplace 'with customers and stakeholders'. World-class universities are no exception to.

The quest for academic excellence has spread across the globe in the last two decades. Governments in both developed and developing countries have been actively engaged in building world-class universities and seeking a global reputation and visibility. However, it has been argued that this world-class movement raises problems and issues. These leading universities are driven by market forces, constantly searching for additional funds (due to severely reduced public funding in recent years), trapped by the proliferation of ranking games (Chapter 5) and to some extent creating 'the Ivory Tower Syndrome' (Chapter 4). The battle for excellence and global status is criticised for reinforcing pre-existing hierarchies (Rhoads, Li, & Ilano, 2014). Further, world-class universities are considered to have kept themselves away from the broader post-secondary environment and are thus questioned for compromising their social responsibilities, their roles and contributions to the local communities (Chapter 3, 4).

Nevertheless, world-class universities are considered to be in a unique position as 'the open global space' (Chapter 2) and to serve as a global common good. With a concentration of talent, abundant resources and favourable governance, these leading universities are believed to be able to embrace opportunities, confront challenges and enhance sustainable development for the benefit of the whole world, and should nurture world-class education and research, and serve both local society and global imperatives (Chapter 7).

2.3 Sustaining an Ecosystem in Seeking Academic Excellence

Related to the concern of world-class universities drifting from the rest of the higher education system, recent literature stresses an increasing emphasis on the importance of developing a differentiated world-class university system. This point is reflected throughout the current volume. Higher education expansion involves all postsecondary institutions from all missions – research, teaching, social services – but with different foci.

Altbach and Salmi (2011) also reminds us that education reform and changes do not happen in a vacuum, and a complete analysis of operating a world-class university needs to take into consideration the ecosystem within which institutions evolve. That ecosystem includes elements of the macro environment, leadership at the national level, governance and regulatory frameworks, quality assurance frameworks, financial resources and incentives, articulation mechanisms, access to information, location, and digital and telecommunications infrastructure. Some of these factors might be absolute requisites and others might not be entirely indispensable, due to each country's cultural, socio-economic and political context. However, all these factors are certainly significant (ibid.). Countries and those overseeing their higher education systems need to carefully assess their needs, resources and long-term interests, and design their strategies based on their national and institutional models. There is no universal model or recipe for academic excellence (Salmi, 2009).

3 Contributions to This Volume

Reflecting the above points and perspectives, this volume intends to stimulate an important and timely discussion from a comparative perspective on the following topics: the ultimate goals, missions and roles of world-class universities; mechanisms to identify, regulate, measure and finance global common goods in education and knowledge for world-class universities to create; and the strategies and approaches to balance world-class universities' roles in developing global common goods, national contributions and local engagement to achieve global sustainability. This volume is composed of two parts: 'Global and Theoretical Perspectives', and 'National and Regional Responses'.

3.1 Global and Theoretical Perspectives

The first part, from a 'Global and Theoretical Perspectives', explores and defines the importance of global common goods in higher education. This part also extends the discussion on opportunities and challenges facing higher education, particularly the world-class university sector, in the face of socio-economic, political and technological transformation around the world, and addresses how universities can serve and contribute to global common goods.

Marginson (Chapter 2) leads the discussion on the actual and potential contributions of world-class universities to the global common good. Reviewing the definitions of public good(s) and common good(s), he argues that the most important global common goods associated with world-class and research-intensive universities are research, communication and people mobility. Through analysing and mapping patterns of scientific production and cooperation of world research system in the past two decades, Marginson stresses that world-class universities are increasingly integrated as a single collective networked whole and operates as positive sum through collaborative research work, in spite of serious problems (e.g. brain drain, unequal use of English and non-English languages, etc.) yet to be adequately addressed. This emerging global science system is going beyond the notion of nation-states, and is forming a single global but diverse society. However, one critical challenge for world-class universities is to strengthen their local relations and contributions, as well as moving forward with the common global agenda.

Altbach (Chapter 3) sets his discussion in the context of the global massification of higher education. Higher education systems around the globe are becoming increasingly complex. It is true that world-class universities, as a small part of any higher education system, produce the largest share of research, and are the most internationalized institutions and cultivate talents, but they tend to neglect the fact that they exist in a diverse higher education system and that they have a special responsibility to the rest of academe. Altbach reminds us that education reform and changes do not happen in a vacuum, and a complete analysis of operating a world-class university needs to take into consideration the ecosystem within which institutions evolve.

De Maret and Salmi (Chapter 4) explore how world-class universities can impact higher education landscape and contribute to the global common good in a post-truth world. They argue that these leading universities should commit themselves to tackling the issues including 'inclusion and diversity, preparation of ethical professionals and committed citizens, relevant research, improved communication channels, engagement with society and the world, and environmental responsibility'. Echoing Marginson, De Maret and Salmi emphasise the importance of such universities working as a network for the common good and reiterate the 'Shanghai Principles' of 'inclusiveness, ethics, objectivity, relevance and global collaboration'.

Taking the perspective of third mission (social services) reflected in university strategic plans and examining more than 70 universities' documents from over 30 countries, Lee, Vance and Stensaker (Chapter 5) investigate and compare these strategies between ranked and unranked institutions. Their finding suggests a differentiated pattern between ranked and unranked universities – ranked universities lay their strategic plans in a more global and regional context, while those of unranked universities are more locally oriented. The authors suggest that third mission activities should go beyond the market and not be excluded while evaluating and measuring university performance and quality.

Tian (Chapter 6) conducts a discourse analysis of four official documents (president's message, mission statement, vision statement and strategic plan) of world-class universities, to investigate the role of world-class universities in serving the global common good. This chapter starts by reviewing the conceptual shift from public to common goods in higher education. Its findings reveal the dual roles of world-class universities in relation to global common goods: these leading universities serve as a global common good in their emphasis of global/international development and the well-being of the global communities on the one hand, and contribute global common goods by conducting global science and emphasising human development, global interconnectedness and well-being.

One of the important strategies to build academic excellence is to establish a university from scratch (Salmi, 2009). Based on one of their latest projects on accelerated universities, Salmi (Chapter 7) takes a comparative approach to examine the features, opportunities and challenges of eight selected universities. In addition to the three common features of world-class universities (namely the concentration of talent, abundant resources and favourable governance), other prevalent characteristics include strong leadership, international partnership, sustainable financial support, and a well-balanced role between the local/national and the global. Salmi reiterates the importance of an ecosystem while building academic excellence.

3.2 National and Regional Responses

The second part, 'National and Regional Responses' reflecting on policy trends and changes in national and regional context, provides in-depth case analysis and examines implications for both national/regional governments and higher education institutions in balancing their roles in global engagement and local commitment.

The first chapters in this part focus on issues in higher education in the United Sates. Shaker and Plater (Chapter 8) review how leading universities in the US serve a civic role from a historical point of view and argue that a commitment to the global common good is intertwined with the concept 'world-class', and that leading universities need to sustain their commitment to the public. Though the current political environment in the US cause significant concern as well as increasing uncertainty, the authors believe that, among all the stakeholders, individual faculty are the key force to effectively fulfil this public commitment and thus contribute to society.

Focusing on the US state of Texas, Karam et al. (Chapter 9), analyse its opportunities and challenges in becoming a competitive state. It is argued that, having developed an increasing number of research universities, Texas has few universities which can compete at the international level, and tends to attract less federal funding. Texas should have the desire to make additional public investment in research competitiveness so as to allow the state to enhance the quality of graduate education and research while serving local labour market needs.

The next two chapters by van der Wende (Chapter 10) and Postiglione and Xie (Chapter 11) shed light on China and its increasing global role in higher education, particularly in relation to its peers in the West. Van der Wende sets her chapter in the context of the current political climate around the world – the backlash against globalisation, growing inequalities resulting from globalization and the rise of China – and discusses the implications for world-class universities and for European higher education and research; Postiglione and Xie discuss the bilateral relationship and links between China and the US. These two chapters share common views. Both chapters argue that the current discourse on university reform has shifted to a notion of 'the common good', and productive collaboration and a relationship with China and its world-class universities is of great importance to address global problems and challenges. The recent development of Chinese higher education can be seen as both a follower with policy focus strongly oriented on the West (widening and diversifying), and a leader with its impact on World-Class University Movement and more importantly in the New Skill Road project. This raises ongoing questions for future research and calls for an understanding of the similarities and differences between globalization in the East and West. Postiglione and Xie also suggest that China and the US should pay much more attention to the growth in social and economic inequality as well as unequal access and equity in their own institutions.

Huang (Chapter 12) depicts vice presidents' perceptions and views on public goods of internationalization in Japanese higher education. The vice presidents' views on the benefits and risks of internationalization show some differences among different types of institution, namely, national, local and private universities. However, a general consensus is revealed – the internationalization of Japanese higher education is highly valued and academically prioritized to advance their global competitiveness. Internationalization is viewed as public goods to raise student/staff international awareness and enhancing international collaboration and partnership in research and knowledge creation, which shows significant differences from the 'revenue generation' view of their counterparts in the west. Based on the findings, Huang provides implications for research, policy and institutional practices.

Launching national initiatives to develop academic excellence is one of the strategies frequently adopted by national governments around the world. Despite positive results, such approach is often questioned or challenged for its trade-off between governmental accountability and institutional autonomy, and between its objectives and foci on global competitiveness and local commitment. Froumin and Lisyutkin (Chapter 13) take a close look at Russia and its national excellence initiative 'Project 5-100' to reflect on and respond to these questions. They argue that, while being pushed by the government towards the global research university model, these funded higher education institutions have also become more responsive to local and national needs, forming a 'multiversity' model. The authors suggest that this multiversity model ensures a relatively long-term sustainable growth of the university, as well as providing great local support, thus creating an ecosystem for academic excellence.

This book not only represents a contribution to ongoing discussions on the topic of building world-class universities, but also a continuation of the previous six volumes on this topic – 'World-Class Universities and Ranking: Aiming beyond Status', 'The World-Class University as Part of a New Higher Education Paradigm: From Institutional Qualities to Systemic Excellence', 'Paths to a World-Class University', 'Building World-Class Universities: Different Approaches to a Shared Goal', 'Global Influences and Responses: How World-Class Universities Affect Higher Education Systems' and 'Matching Visibility and Performance: A Standing Challenge for World-Class Universities'.

References

Altbach, P. G. (2009). Peripheries and centers: Research universities in developing countries. *Asia Pacific Education Review, 10*, 15–27.

Hazelkorn, E. (2011). *Rankings and the reshaping of higher education: The battle for world-class excellence.* London: Palgrave.

Liu, N. C. (2009, February). *Building up world-class universities: A comparison.* Presentation at 2008–2009, Research Institute for Higher Education, Hiroshima University, Higashihiroshima.

Marginson, S. (2018). Public/private in higher education: A synthesis of economic and political approaches. *Studies in Higher Education, 43*(2), 322–337.

Rhoads, R. A., Li, S., & Ilano, L. (2014). The global quest to build world-class universities: Toward a social justice agenda. *New Directions for Higher Education, 2014*(168), 27–39.

Salmi, J. (2009). *The challenge of establishing world-class universities.* Washington, DC: The World Bank.

United Nations Educational, Social and Cultural Organization, UNESCO. (2015). *Rethinking education: Towards a global common good.* Paris: United Nations Educational, Social and Cultural Organization. Retrieved January 28, 2017, from http://unesdoc.unesco.org/images/0023/002325/232555e.pdf

van der Wende, M. C. (2009). *European responses to global competitiveness in higher education* (Research and Occasional Paper Series, No. 7). Berkeley, CA: Center for Studies in Higher Education, University of California.

PART 1

Global and Theoretical Perspectives

CHAPTER 2

Global Cooperation and National Competition in the World-Class University Sector

Simon Marginson

Abstract

Institutions of higher education generate many individual and collective benefits, on both the local/national and the global planes. World-class universities operate as a single network, one that is increasingly integrated and also operates as a positive sum, with the leading research nations fostering emerging science countries through collaboration. While world-class universities mostly function as exclusive social institutions in local/national contexts, subject to middle class capture and often implicated in growing income inequalities, on the global scale they have more freedom to pursue solidaristic and collective approaches. 'Flat' cooperative science works differently to markets or corporate command structures. The most important global common goods associated with world-class universities are research itself and the systems of communications and people mobility associated with networked activity. The last two decades have seen explosive growth in both total science outputs and joint international papers, an increasing proportion of output. Many more nations are entering the open global system. World science power is more plural, with remarkable growth and improvement in China, South Korea and Singapore (though the main achievements are confined to physical sciences of STEM) and developments in parts of Europe and Latin America. While nation-states mostly invest in research to secure national competitive advantage, global relations in higher education and research are primarily cooperative and the global science system evolves according to its own logic. However, global/national tensions can destabilize cross-border activities, though less in science than in global people mobility and communications. It is becoming more essential for world-class universities to strengthen their local relations and contributions, as well as advance global agendas.

Keywords

Globalization – higher education – research – science – international collaboration – networks – China – Singapore

1 Introduction

Since the early 1990s and the advent of the internet and communicative globalization, the size, scope and contributions of higher education and science have been transformed. The larger socially engaged kind of higher education that emerged in the United States (US) in the 1950s–1970s – a national system with more institutions, larger institutions and growing institutions, and a distributed (albeit uneven) research capacity, a system that creates a very broad range of individualized and collective goods and readily connects across borders – has spread on the planetary scale. The first mover US American templates for higher education and science have been influential, even hegemonic in domains such as language of use and the organizational forms of the research university, but have not been wholly determining. Standard global templates are hybridized with local structures and agents. The logic of global higher education and science is more that of an open collaborative network (Castells, 2000) than a vertical command system, a closed oligopoly of market share, or an arms race in technological advantage (though from time to time, universities and science are annexed in unstable fashion to national or commercial projects in each of these categories).

This collaborative global network is continually fed by cross-border research exchange and people mobility, the global common goods integral to research-based higher education. A principal aspect has been the emergence of a more pluralized set of science nations and research-intensive or 'World-Class' universities (WCUS),[1] facilitated not only by the network growth typical of knowledge-based flows but by the global dispersal of national economic capacity.

1.1 *Participation*

From 1995 to 2015 the world Gross Tertiary Enrolment Ratio (GTER) as measured by the United Nations Educational Social and Cultural Organization's (UNESCO's) Institute of Statistics, rose from 15.6 to 35.7 per cent, with four fifths of the 215.9 million tertiary students enrolled in full degree programmes.[2] In more than 60 education systems the GTER now exceeds 50 per cent (UNESCO, 2018a). The quality of mass higher education, and rates of completion, vary by country. In the poorest 30 per cent of systems participation mostly remains very low (Marginson, 2016a). Nevertheless, by any measure the world is undergoing a great growth of educated 'capability', to use Amartya Sen's term (Sen, 2000).

The growth of higher education and of science are driven by the globally pervasive dynamics of modernization and development. The process is social and cultural as well as political and economic, and larger than the drive for capital accumulation, which is the most obvious motor. It is also highly uneven, within and between nations. Rajani Naidoo (2014) refers to 'combined and uneven development'. Conditions for building higher education vary, in terms of economic resources, the coherence of policy and state agencies, inherited learning cultures and the size of the middle class. Regardless, in emerging nations the ten thousand-year-old Neolithic world, the world of semi-subsistence agriculture edged by villages and small towns, is being swallowed up by the spread of cities and the manufacturing and service economy. Meanwhile, in countries like the United States, industrialized at an earlier time, regional towns and cities are partly displaced by globally connected metropolises absorbing a growing share of capital and people. Universal communications quicken development. Between 1995 and 2017, the estimated number of worldwide internet users grew from 16 million to 4,157 million, moving from 0.4 per cent of the global population to 54.4 per cent (Internet World Stats, 2018).

Above all, urbanization, growth in the proportion of the population that lives in cities, especially growth in the urban middle classes, sustains the growth of tertiary enrolments. Between 1970 and 2016 the urban share of world population rose from 36.5 to 54.3 per cent (World Bank, 2018) (Figure 2.1). As families move to the cities and into the wage and mass market economy their measured income expands and aspirations for advanced education grow and become realizable. Cities incubate family demand for upper secondary and tertiary education, concentrate political pressure on governments to expand provision, and enable economies of scale: comprehensive colleges and universities are really sustainable only in cities or in sites nearby to them. Growth of educational infrastructure further funnels and magnifies aspirations for education, triggering the supply of more places and more institutions in a continuing process. Higher education comes within sight of the whole urban population, not just the middle class, pushing social demand/supply of colleges and universities to 50 per cent and beyond in all high-income and middle-income countries.

Global demand for higher education will expand much further. For Brookings, Homi Kharas (2017) states that the global middle class reached 3.2 billion persons in 2016, half a billion more than previously projected. (The middle

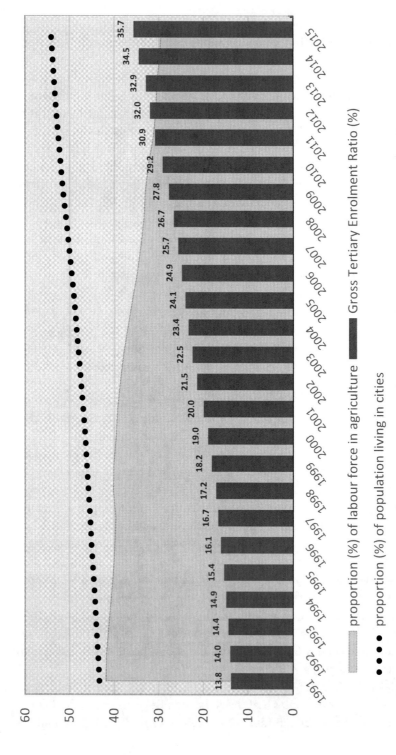

FIGURE 2.1 Worldwide gross tertiary enrolment ratio (%), compared to proportion of people living in cities (%) and proportion of labour in agriculture (%), 1991–2015

class is defined as persons with incomes of US$10–100 a day in 2005 purchasing power parity values). Kharas finds that 'within two or three years' the majority of the world's inhabitants will be middle class (Kharas, 2017, p. 2). The growth of the middle class is principally sustained by three of the world's four most populated nations: Mainland China (hereafter China), India and Indonesia (the other is the US). In China, participation in tertiary education reached 43.4 per cent in 2015, in India 26.9 per cent, and in Indonesia it was 31.1 per cent in 2014 (World Bank, 2018).

Gert Biesta (2009) defines the three purposes of higher education as 'qualification, socialization and subjectification'. 'Qualification' includes not just the formal certification of graduates but their acquisition of knowledge and skills for work and living. 'Socialization' refers to the preparation of citizens in the sensibilities and attributes necessary to functioning members of a larger collectivity. 'Subjectification' refers to the formation of distinctive self-determining or self-forming persons making their own pathway through the world (Biesta, 2009, pp. 39–41; Marginson, 2018a). The explosive growth of higher education brings with it growth in the number of qualified persons, in persons socialised as citizens, and in persons with agency freedom. Whether there will be a concurrent expansion in social opportunities to utilize these freedoms, severally and together, is less apparent (Cantwell, Marginson, & Smolentseva, 2018, Chapter 16). All the same, higher education's potential contribution to the common good is being enlarged worldwide at a rapid rate.

1.2 Research

At the same time, in high participation countries and in some other systems, there is equally rapid growth in the stock of knowledge in the form of published science. The 1990s internet sealed the establishment of a dominant world system of English-language journals. This coincided with growth in knowledge-intensive industrial production, which was also catalysed by information and communications technologies. Together these developments set in motion today's accelerated growth and spread of scientific capacity and outputs.

The role now played by global science makes it more necessary to develop national scientific capacity. To access global science, nations need their own trained people, not just as users but as producers of research who interact effectively with researchers abroad. In a growing number of countries research science has moved from the margins of policy to the normal business of state. Most high-income and many middle-income countries now want their own science system, alongside clean water, viable banking and stable governance. Increasingly also, the WCU is seen as the optimal institution for housing

TABLE 2.1 Gross expenditures on R&D (constant 2005 US dollars, PPP), eight leading science countries: Five-year intervals (1990–2015)

	1990 $s billion	1995 $s billion	2000 $s billion	2005 $s billion	2010 $s billion	2015 $s billion	R&D as proportion of GDP 2015 %
United States	152.4	184.1	268.6	326.2	408.5	496.6	2.74
China	n.a.	12.8	33.0	86.8	213.5	408.8	2.07
Japan	64.9	76.6	98.8	128.7	140.6	170.0	3.29
Germany	36.0	41.0	53.6	63.9	87.1	114.8	2.93
South Korea	n.a.	13.2	18.5	30.6	52.2	74.1	4.23
France	23.4	27.7	33.2	39.5	51.0	60.8	2.22
India	n.a.	n.a.	15.7	26.5	43.7	50.3	0.63
United Kingdom	18.7	19.6	25.1	30.6	37.6	46.3	1.70

n.a. indicates data not available. PPP = Purchasing Power Parity data to enable cross-country comparability.
SOURCE: DATA FROM NSB (2018, TABLE A4-12)

researchers and facilitating the cross-border circulation of knowledge and people normal to global science.

Together this package of tendencies, assumptions and goals has been transformative. There has been rapid growth in the nations actively investing in research and development (R&D), the proportion of Gross Domestic Product (GDP) devoted to R&D in emerging science systems, in total R&D investment, and in total scientific output. Table 2.1 demonstrates the spectacular change in China and South Korea. Between 1991 and 2015 the share of GDP allocated to research increased from 0.72 to 2.07 per cent in China, and from 1.83 to 4.23 per cent in South Korea, the highest level of any country in the world. The mature research system in Japan also increased its GDP commitment to R&D over that period, from 2.68 to 3.29 per cent. East Asia now spends much more in total on research than does either Europe/UK or North America (NSB, 2018, table A4-12). The data are for all investment in R&D, including industry spending. Direct investment in universities varies between 5 and 30 per cent of R&D, depending on country, but the universities' role is larger than this suggests: in most countries part of industry R&D is conducted in universities, and universities train most researchers with PhDs, wherever they work.

Between 1990 and 2015 all the science nations in Table 2.1 more than doubled their research spending in constant dollars. The United States research system tripled its spending over 25 year period. China grew its R&D outlay from only US$12.8 billion in 1995 to US$408.8 billion (32 times larger) 20 years later, moving close to the US total (NSB, 2018). At the same time, research in Northeast Asia and Singapore, the Chinese civilizational zone, also made major advances in quality, as is discussed below.

In sum, the total world output of science papers, most of them by university researchers and many of them fed into knowledge-intensive industries, rose from 1.19 million in 2003, to 2.30 million in 2016, representing growth of 92.5 per cent (NSB, 2018). The 2003–2016 period also saw worldwide tertiary enrolments increase by 72.1 per cent (UNESCO, 2018a). Each of mass teaching/learning in higher education, science, and research universities, are growing at unprecedented rates and becoming more central to society.

This multiplication of students and research, both at the same time, drives growth in the status, number and size of globally networked WCUs. Multi-disciplinary research universities have expanded their roles, size and status within nations, at the same time as they are building activity as global players. The contribution of WCUs to the common good is not fixed but open in historical terms. On one hand, *the common good is inherent in the globalized higher education and knowledge system.* This is a function of open, expanding global networks, to the extent that their core substance is knowledge and information, which are global public goods in economic terms, rather than capital. Networked WCUs are disposed to secure mutual positive sum benefits and in a common manner. On the other hand, the contributions of WCUs to the common good are the subject of contestation (and varying interpretations) and are articulated by nation-state policies and by the missions and strategies of WCUs themselves. Within the common good there are many interests in play.

1.3 *Contents of the Chapter*

This chapter focuses on the WCU sector, especially its globally networked research activities. Though WCUs house only a small proportion of students – the top 1000 research universities enrol about 7–8 per cent of the world tertiary population – they generate many collective and individual benefits, in both the national and global dimensions. The question addressed here is: 'What are the contributions of World-Class Universities to the common good, especially the global common good?' The joined-up potential of WCUs is much larger than is suggested by the neoliberal model of university as self-serving firm with customers/students and a 'brand value' (proxy for equity price) that is determined by ranking position. Consider the robust capacity and drive of WCUs to sustain international relations in a world of nation-states. This drive cannot be explained in terms of individualized profit motives: most cross-border activity has to be subsidized. While there is competition within the networked global system, on the whole systemic relations and benefits are aggregative, not zero-sum. The emergence of a larger group of high science countries matters not only because it signifies a multi-polar world in power terms, though that is important, but also because it expands the scope of the shared network in which all nodes are enhanced. The chapter focuses not just on individual WCUs and their global distribution but also on the combined effects of science/WCUs as a collectively networked whole.

Section 2 of this chapter reviews the definitions of public goods and common goods, and the various global common goods produced by WCUs, in the context of the larger set of individualized and collective contributions that they make. Section 3 expands on the workings of the worldwide research system, which arguably is the most important part of that WCU contribution to global common goods, mapping patterns of scientific production and cooperation. Section 4 is a brief conclusion.

2   Public and Common Good(s) in WCUs

2.1   *Public Good(s) in Higher Education*

Public Good (Singular). The term 'public good' normally refers to the broadly distributed general welfare or condition of virtue of the public, meaning society as a whole. 'Public good' can be highly normative. It is sometimes equated with the European feudal metaphor of the 'commons', a shared resource that all can utilize, not subject to scarcity or contaminated by congestion, such as a river or a pasture where all can graze their animals (Mansbridge, 1998). Here it moves toward 'common good' (see below). It is also associated with notions of democratic forms, openness, transparency and popular sovereignty.

Public Goods (Plural). This term is used more precisely than the singular public good, but has two different meanings (political, and economic) that only partly overlap.

In the political definition, public goods are outcomes produced in the state sector or otherwise controlled by government/state. Matters become public because they are of broad concern or effect and so must be resolved by the state (Dewey, 1926).

In the economic definition, public goods cannot be produced profitably in a market because they are non-rivalrous and/or non-excludable (Samuelson, 1954). Goods are non-excludable when the benefits cannot be confined to single buyers, such as clean air regulation. Goods are non-rivalrous when consumed by any number of people without being depleted, such as a mathematical theorem, which sustains its value as knowledge indefinitely and on a global basis. Private goods are neither non-rivalrous nor non-excludable and may be produced and sold in markets. Economic public goods and part-public goods require at least some state funding or philanthropic support. For example, knowledge is a natural economic public good (Stiglitz, 1999). It can be artificially privatized at the point of creation (e.g. by patent or copyright), and control of the artefacts in which it is embodied may be enforced by law, but once knowledge is revealed, its non-rivalrous and non-excludable qualities become dominant. The knowledge itself is readily duplicated without cost and its artefacts are freely reverse engineered and pirate-copied.

The economic definition of public goods is influential in policy because the problem of market failure appears to provide a rationale for the public/private division of costs. Using this formula, the state funds up to the point where market failure ends, after that the individual pays. The state pays only for people who cannot pay for themselves. But this formula carries two problems. One is the assumption that the distinction between public and private goods is always based on natural qualities. While some economic public goods, like knowledge or street lighting, are intrinsically public as Samuelson imagined, this does not exhaust the potential for public goods. There are other public goods that are determined by social relations and state policy. Education and health become turned into economic public goods when they are produced on a universal basis without distinctions of value, so becoming non-rivalrous and non-excludable.

The second problem in Samuelson's formula is that of zero-sum, the idea that if a good is more public it is less private, and vice versa. This drives the policy assumption that the private share of costs should be proportional to the private share of benefits. But this makes no sense in relation to policy-created public goods – for example, when society deliberately chooses not to provide education on a market basis, because this has perverse outcomes (e.g. restricted access and distributional inequalities) and there are additional public benefits to be gained from a shared, cooperative, universal approach, which requires non-market financing.

Rather than the intrinsic character of higher education (public or private) determining its source of finance, financing is one of the factors that determines the public or private (i.e. non-market or market) character of the activity. Teaching and student places can be organized either as economic public or private goods. Systems with full cost private tuition fees at the point of access tend to be more hierarchical in value, in the manner of all market-produced goods, dividing between high value and low value student places. High value places, attached to prestigious institutions and high-income degrees, are scarce, subject to fierce social competition, and targeted by affluent families for private investment. The families that access those places, and the educational institutions that house them, focus on higher education as private individual goods rather than collective (common or joint) public goods. However, in most countries, government funding extends more broadly than just the market failure problem. Most national populations expect governments to treat student places as non-market goods, for political reasons, to expand citizen rights and secure a measure of social equity.

When policy moves away from the minimalist naturalistic approach to public goods and the zero-sum idea of public/private goods, the rationale for a zero-sum public/private split of financing collapses. It should be emphasized that in higher education and research, public and private goods are not alternatives but additive. An expansion of each kind of good can augment the other. When graduates gain enhanced 'qualification' in Biesta's (2009) sense they also gain 'socialization', a capability in more developed and productive social, political and economic relationships. This is a collective, mutual and public benefit. When there is more qualification there is also more socialization. It is not zero-sum. The public financing of research in universities that connect to industry and government directly and indirectly generates many other public and private goods, with no zero-sum choices in sight.

In sum, there are two contrary ideas of the public/private boundary, based respectively on the state/non-state divide and the non-market/market divide. Rather than choosing one against the other, or compressing them into a single market/state dichotomy (highly misleading), it is better to retain the two different clear-cut definitions of public/private goods. Both tell us something useful. Arguably, by using both definitions together within one framework higher education is more effectively explained. This idea has been developed elsewhere (Marginson, 2018b).

2.2 *Common Good(s) in Higher Education*

Common Good (Singular). The singular 'common good' is mostly understood as a shared condition of well-being and freedom, or virtue, at the level of society as a whole.

Common Goods (Plural). The term 'public goods' does not necessarily mean goods that are beneficial to people. An aggressive national war is technically a 'public good' in both the economic and political sense but it may not be good for people in the nation. In contrast, common goods are beneficial in a humanistic sense, and broadly beneficial (Marginson, 2016b). They contribute to shared social welfare, relations of solidarity, inclusion, tolerance, universal freedoms, equality, human rights and/or broadly distributed individual capability (Sen, 2000). Equality of opportunity in education is an example of a collective common good. In Mandarin Chinese lexicon, common goods are social goods that contribute to broad humanity (人类, Ren Lei). UNESCO (2015) has developed a notion of common goods in education, which can be provided by either public or private sector institutions. Another example is the British National Health Service, providing universal care free of charge, and deploying scarce resources so as to prioritize people in greatest need because of serious illness or accident. In Nordic countries, equal and solidaristic society is an end in itself and state policy emphasizes policies designed to secure common goods (Valimaa & Muhonen, 2018).

Common goods are collective public goods in the economic sense as they are necessarily non-market in character. As in the UNESCO definition, they are not always public goods in the political sense. Epistemologically, 'public' and 'common' have differing statuses. First, as noted, 'public goods' is a technical term for non-market goods, or state determined goods, that has no necessary normative meaning. The term 'common goods' refers to material relations and practices, that can be tracked empirically, but these practices also have a normative element. 'Common' is what people practice as joint, mutual, shared, to their common benefit. What is 'beneficial' is determined by the receivers of those benefits, working collectively. Second, and related to this, while many public goods are open to observation, regardless of viewpoint, common goods are more difficult to pin down and require further definition. Whether a good is state-produced or controlled, and whether or not goods are produced outside of markets, are not defined by values. But what is valued as 'common' is open to both interpretation and historical-political variation. While it is possible to devise an agreed list of indicators, the identification of indicators is (at least in part) a political and not solely technical process.

Locatelli (2018), working in the framework of the UNESCO discussion, states that 'the concept of education as a common good highlights the purposes of education as a collective social endeavour' (p. 11). She remarks that 'common good' can be understood as broader than 'public good'. While public goods are mostly 'linked to the functions and role of the state' (p. 3), with government provision and/or financing, this is not always true of common goods. Because 'common' is defined by the normative content of the activity, both government and non-government organization, including voluntary local cooperation (Ostrom, 1990), can contribute to common goods. However, 'some kinds of private participation are more defensible than others' (Locatelli, 2018, p. 8); and partial state funding and regulation ('public') may be needed to ensure commonality (p. 13).

2.3 Global Public and Common Good(s)

'Global' as used in this chapter refers not to the whole world and everything in it, but to phenomena, systems and relations that are planetary in scale, such as world ecology, or knowledge in mathematics (Marginson, 2010). 'Globalization' in higher education and other sectors refers to partial convergence and integration on the planetary or large regional (e.g. European Union) scale – from world markets and cross-border supply chains in industry; to networked banking and transport; to worldwide expansion of systems in communications, information and research; to cross-border migration of people; to open flows of ideas and knowledge.

Global Public Goods. In the late 1990s the United Nations Development Programme (UNDP), starting from issues of global ecology, defined global public goods as:

> ...goods that have a significant element of non-rivalry and/or non-excludability and made broadly available across populations on a global scale. They affect more than one group of countries, are broadly available within countries, and are inter-generational; that is, they meet needs in the present generation without jeopardizing future generations. (Kaul et al., 1999, pp. 2–3)

UNESCO (2018c) includes as global public goods in education 'internationally comparative data and statistics', research on improvements in learning outcomes, and cross-border professional networks. It also notes that these goods are 'in short supply, poorly funded and rarely coordinated'. For the most part, global public goods are goods that are not adequately addressed by individual countries acting alone but require coordinated action. In the above quote, the UNDP emphasis on distributional equity ('broadly available') indicates a normative political rather than strictly economic definition of global public goods, taking the notion towards global common goods. Note that because there is no global state, only the economic definition of public goods is relevant. However, international agencies such the United Nations, the OECD and World Bank, operating as quasi global state organizations, attempt to shape values-based notions of the collective global interest.

Global Common Good (Singular). By global common good is meant the combined well-being and freedoms of humanity (人, Ren in Mandarin Chinese); that is, of human society and nations in the world as a whole. In Mandarin Chinese, the combined well-being might translate as 人类福祉 (Ren Lei Fu Zhi), though the combined well-being and freedoms might be better understood if spelled out in full as 人类福祉与自由 (Ren Lei Fu Zhi Yu Zi You).[3]

Global Common Goods (Plural). The term global common goods, plural, refers to shared relationships and benefits arising from higher education and research in cross-border relations, and at the level of the world as a whole, that are broadly accessible to different countries and people. For example, knowledge in mathematics, or the safety and security of mobile students. Global common goods are a sub-set of (non-market economic) public goods, that arise in the global sphere, in the combined global systems that make cross-border relations possible. As discussed in relation to common goods above, global common goods are more specific than collective public goods, in that they contribute to sociability, mutual capability, agency, freedoms, equality and rights. This commonality can be expressed in cross-border relations between countries or regions, between cities, between higher education institutions, and between individuals at any time.

Norms of commonality and their instruments, such as the climate change accords, the Universal Declaration of Human Rights, and the Sustainable Development Goals, which include commitments on tertiary education, are discursive global common goods. For UNESCO, education is not just a common good but a global common good (Locatelli, 2018). As discussed extensively below, the worldwide system of publicly accessible scientific knowledge is one of the most important of all global common goods, one that incubates many particular common goods, including the specific networks and knowledge in each academic discipline. Open communications and systems of free mobility between national higher education systems are other global common goods that establish a generic framework of global relations, with the capacity to foster many particular common goods. In a world in which networked inclusion continually expands (Castells, 2000), joining once separated localities together, people are more engaged with others and this creates an expanding potential for common goods in global civil society. Platform capitalist networks such as Google can facilitate – and distort – the evolution of collaborative common goods.

2.4 *Common Goods in Higher Education*

What common goods are produced in research-intensive universities?

Individual and Collective Benefits. Figure 2.2 provides a way of comprehending all of the contributions of higher education – a map of the contributions of WCUs, individualized and collective, in the national/local and global dimensions. Higher education contributes to relational society in many ways. All four categories include potential common goods (in bold type) that contribute to shared social welfare, solidarity, inclusion, tolerance, equality, universal freedoms, human rights and/or the broad advance of capability. Only some of the possible common goods are listed: higher education also augments intercultural relations, foster tolerance of difference, widens political participation, and so on (McMahon, 2009).

The global collective benefits of higher education in Cell 3, generated in common through relationships than span the different national borders, include the knowledge system, disciplinary cultures, communications, mobility and cross-cultural exchange. Research collaboration on common global challenges lifts WCUs above their more localised and captured functions as engines of national and individual prosperity, advantage and prestige. As remarked by Patrick Aebischer, President of the École Polytechnique Fédérale de Lausanne:

> Universities have become institutions of a global world, in addition to assuming their traditional local and national roles. The answers to global challenges (energy, water and food security, urbanization, climate change, etc.) are increasingly dependent on technological innovation and the sound scientific advice brokered to decision-makers. The findings contributed by research institutes and universities to the reports of the Intergovernmental Panel on Climate Change and the Consensus for Action statement illustrate the decisive role these institutions are playing in world affairs. (Aebischer, 2015, p. 3)

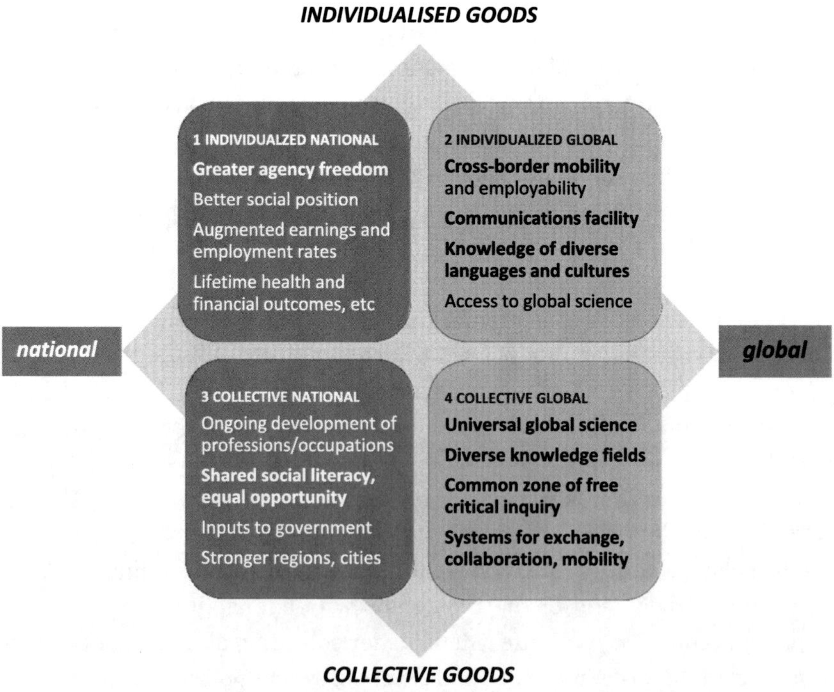

INDIVIDUALISED GOODS

national ⇄ *global*

1 INDIVIDUALZED NATIONAL
Greater agency freedom
Better social position
Augmented earnings and employment rates
Lifetime health and financial outcomes, etc

2 INDIVIDUALIZED GLOBAL
Cross-border mobility and employability
Communications facility
Knowledge of diverse languages and cultures
Access to global science

3 COLLECTIVE NATIONAL
Ongoing development of professions/occupations
Shared social literacy, equal opportunity
Inputs to government
Stronger regions, cities

4 COLLECTIVE GLOBAL
Universal global science
Diverse knowledge fields
Common zone of free critical inquiry
Systems for exchange, collaboration, mobility

COLLECTIVE GOODS

FIGURE 2.2   Examples of individualized and collective contributions of higher education

The same WCUs that compete against each other in vertical rankings also work together horizontally. This does not mean that competition and collaboration (or national and global activities) join neatly in seamless fashion. There are synergies, but also tensions and closures. In global higher education and research, the common good is by no means always uppermost. Nevertheless, the expansion of worldwide research networks means that the potential global commons has been fundamentally expanded.

Discussion of the benefits of higher education often focuses on Cell 1, the individualized national goods, especially the graduate employment rates and lifetime salary benefits associated with degree-holding. Cross-border individualized benefits (Cell 2) are mostly treated as marginal to the national benefits; and the collective benefits of higher education (Cells 3 and 4), which are more difficult to observe and measure, are even less recognized. It is true that higher education is a process of self-formation (Marginson, 2018a) that augments a person's capabilities and opportunities. This includes career and financial benefits. But Cell 1 also includes many more individualized effects, most of them non-pecuniary, as is suggested by Biesta's (2009) trio of qualification, socialization and subjectification. And moving beyond Cell 1 there is much more to higher education than its direct effects for students. The direct effects on graduates indirectly affect the people with whom graduates live and work, and flow into the institutions, systems and languages of complex societies. Education forms people in social relations on a large scale. It is both formative of society and continually formed by society. Individual people develop and exist only on a relational social basis. The individual *always* presumes the social, and vice versa (Vygotsky, 1978; Dewey, 1927). In social science it is absurd to model higher education as if it produces only autarkic individuals. Yet that is what is suggested by the economic policy focus that confines higher education to individual economic benefits.

Here the normative dimension of common goods matters. It affects behaviour. If students, graduates and families are told by political leaders and public media that the main (if not the sole) goal of higher education is their own socio-economic benefit as individuals, all else being equal those graduates will be less community minded – less committed to the common good – than if they are told their higher education should and does benefit the whole society. Further, if higher education's sole purpose is graduates' private advantage, non-graduates outside higher education have no stake in it. This opens up higher education to a populist challenge. If the purpose of higher education institutions is simply to generate the highest possible graduate rates of return, then all its institutions, especially WCUs, are rightly charged with elitism. On the other hand, if higher education is seen as the source of a range of common goods, and graduates are expected to contribute to the betterment of society, as in the Kantian/Humboldtian idea of the university, then WCUs will be held to account for those common goods, in which whole populations have a stake. In short, if WCUs are treated as a shared resource in which all have a stake, then common goods are more likely to result.

Global Common Goods in Higher Education. WCUs produce three kinds of global common goods. First, they help people to form global relational competences – knowledge, skills and sensibilities enabling them to act across national and cultural boundaries. Second, they are a fecund zone of cross-border mobility and mixing of people, particularly research-intensive faculty, doctoral students and university leaders. Third, as 'thickly' networked institutions they constitute a space for conversations of two kinds: knowledge-forming conversations in the academic disciplines, and more generic conversations on matters of the day. In of all these ways WCUs are more globalized than the national-local societies in which they sit.

Global Attributes of Individuals. Learning and work in higher education are associated with enhanced individual capacity to travel, in two respects: capability in physical travel, and capability in information and communications technologies (ICT), cross-border electronic sociability, the capacity to travel electronically across the earth. The extent to which these attributes are engendered by higher education or due to other individual characteristics such as cognitive capability, geographic location, or family income or social capital, cannot be settled here. But it is safe to assume that higher education matters. There is marked variation between graduate and non-graduates in the capacity to travel, in both respects.

For example, in its 2012 Survey of Adult Skills the OECD generated data on ICT-related skills according to educational qualification. Of 25–64 year-olds with tertiary qualifications, 52 per cent had 'good ICT and problem-solving skills'. Only 7 per cent had 'no computer experience' or refused an ICT skill test. Of those with upper secondary or non-tertiary post-school education, 25 per cent had good skills while 21 per cent had no experience or refused the test. Among those with lower secondary or below, seven per cent had good skills and 47 per cent had no experience or refused the test. These patterns held across the 22 countries and parts of countries that supplied survey data (OECD, 2015, pp. 46–47).

Likewise, the average graduate is more at ease than is the non-graduate with physical cross-border mobility. In *Perspectives on Global Development 2017: International migration in a shifting world* (OECD, 2016, p. 32) the OECD compares migration among people with, and without, university degrees. For those without degrees the tendency to migrate is correlated to income. As income

GLOBAL COOPERATION AND NATIONAL COMPETITION IN WCU SECTOR 29

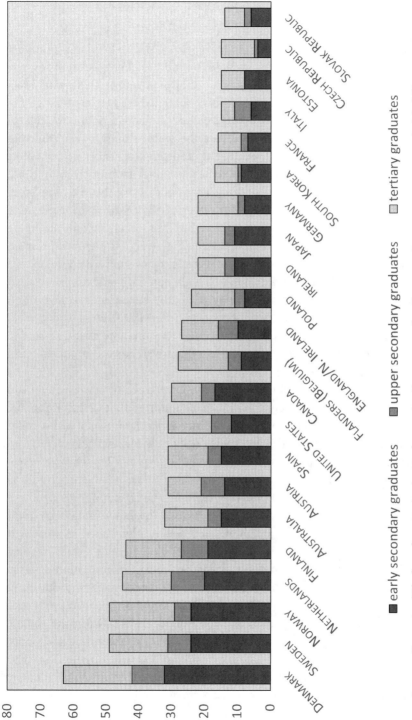

FIGURE 2.3 Proportion (%) of people answering 'yes' to the question 'do you trust others?' OECD nations, 2012 OECD survey of adult skills

rises people are more likely to move. Among those with degrees the pattern is different. As income rises, once a modest threshold level is reached there is little change in mobility. It becomes income inelastic. In helping graduates to greater personal agency in this domain, mobility, higher education weakens the effects of economic determinism on their imaginings, choices and decisions. Here as in other ways degree level education directly constitutes greater personal freedoms. If mobility across borders is a human right – the right to control where one's body moves across the earth – then higher education enhances access to that right. Further, in boosting the capacity for mobility, higher education expands relational society, which is another common good.

One reason that graduates find it easier to travel is that they are more confident in dealing with others. The OECD Survey of Adult Skills also includes data on the proportion of people who said that they 'trust others'. As education level rises people are more likely to trust others (Figure 2.3). In Denmark, Norway, Sweden and Finland, which have a solidaristic social model, the level of trust is relatively high for all people but much higher among graduates: almost half of all Nordic tertiary graduates say they 'trust others' compared to a quarter of those who left school in the early secondary years (OECD, 2015, p. 163). While the OECD survey did not ask directly about trusting foreigners, these data again suggest that graduates may have comparatively advanced capabilities in cross-border social relations.

In both the formal curriculum and the experience of cosmopolitan university settings, higher education also helps to form other Cell 2 (Figure 2.2) relational attributes that facilitate global mobility, communication and understanding, such as language skills, knowledge of other countries, and cultural tolerance. These attributes are enhanced by actual cross-border experiences, 'internationalization' abroad and at home, as testified in an extensive literature (e.g. of many Deardorff, de Wit, Heyl, & Adams, 2012). Prolonged and varied experiences abroad quicken the person's flexibility in the face of difference and change. They heighten confidence, proactivity, awareness of one's identity – or in other words, reflexive self-determining 'agency freedom' (Marginson, 2014). Cross-border mobility and internationalization at home tend to be more prevalent in WCUs than other higher education institutions. This is a function of the institutional resources of WCUs, the socially elite character of many of their students, and the extent to which WCUs are globally networked in research and partnerships and subsidized for inward and/or outward travel.

In the Erasmus programme in Europe, WCUs provide many of their students with cross-border experience, though with a small number of exceptions (e.g. the National University of Singapore) WCU student mobility outside

Europe is lower. Overall, with some exceptions, WCUs have more cosmopolitan faculty populations than other institutions. In certain leading English-speaking WCUs, half or more of faculty are foreign born.

Global Mobility System. Networked higher education institutions and national administrations form a common informal system facilitating ease of academic movement across borders. This mobility system (Cell 3 in Figure 2.2) enables students and staff to acquire individualized global goods (Cell 2), not only global attributes and greater agency freedom but often, better career opportunities and incomes. Mobility is facilitated by a complex, evolving lattice of one-to-one and multilateral cooperative agreements; partnerships and university consortia; multi-country and localized mobility schemes for students and faculty, as noted (e.g. Erasmus, the China Scholarship Council programmes); and accreditation and recognition protocols, including interlocking quality assurance arrangements. The only comprehensive data on cross-border mobility are for student stays of one year or more (UNESCO, 2018a). Some countries, including China and the US, collect data on shorter incoming student stays. Many countries track outward student stays. Data on long-term faculty movement are patchy. Some countries collect data on foreign staff recruitment – one indicator of the global openness of national higher education systems – but there is no global compilation.

Between 1995 and 2011, the worldwide number of cross-border students increased rapidly, from 1.7 to 4.4 million. After 2011 growth slowed to 4.6 million in 2015, though there were also 13 million cross-border online students (OECD, 2017, p. 295). One driver of growth is commercial international education in the UK, Australia and New Zealand. This fosters some instances in WCUs of very large cross-border student enrolment. These WCUs use surplus generated from international students to part-finance research. For example, the University of Melbourne in Australia, which was positioned at 39th in the ARWU in 2017, had 13,200 effective full-time international students in 2014 – 29.1 per cent of student load – who paid US$224.5 million in fees (DET, 2018). In the UK, University College London enrolled 4,470 full-fee non-European Union international students in 2016–2017, 11.8 per cent of all students (HESA, 2018). In the United States, international education in WCUs is less commercial, and WCUs mostly have lower international student volumes, but in 2015–2016, there were 13,340 international students (8.2 per cent) at the University of Southern California (IIE, 2017). China is becoming a major provider for international students (OECD, 2017), with growth of student numbers, as in the US, driven more by foreign policy objectives and university internationalization strategies rather than by revenues. China is currently expanding scholarship aid to 'Belt and Road' emerging countries in Asia and Africa.

International students constitute 4.3 per cent of all first-degree students in OECD countries and 11.5 per cent at Masters level but a large 25.7 per cent at doctoral level (OECD, 2017, p. 300). 'Mobile students gain tacit knowledge that is often shared through direct personal interactions and that enables their home country to integrate into global knowledge networks…students' mobility appears to more deeply shape future internal scientific cooperation networks than a common language, or geographical or scientific proximity' (p. 287). Mobile doctoral students and researchers augment the reputations and revenues of WCUs. At the same time rankings articulate the global competition for talent, magnifying the attractiveness of strong systems and WCUs. Talent flows are skewed in favour of the leading countries with WCUs, though as Table 2.2 shows, mobile doctoral students play a varying role in those countries – large in the United Kingdom, United States and Netherlands; more modest

TABLE 2.2 Internationally mobile or foreign doctoral students as a proportion (%) of all doctoral students in 2015, OECD systems, Brazil and Russia, compared to number of ARWU top 500 universities in each country in 2015 (number of top 500 universities in brackets)

Country	Proportion international or foreign %	Country	Proportion international or foreign %	Country	Proportion international or foreign %
Luxembourg (0)	87.0	Austria (6)	27.0	Slovak R.[a] (0)	9.1
Switzerland (7)	54.3	OECD average	25.7	Latvia (0)	8.8
New Zealand (2)	46.2	Ireland (3)	25.4	S. Korea[a] (12)	8.7
UK (37)	42.9	Canada (20)	24.4	Slovenia (1)	8.5
Belgium (7)	42.3	Brazil[a] (6)	22.4	Chile (2)	8.4
France (22)	40.1	Portugal (3)	21.2	Hungary (2)	7.2
US (146)	37.8	Norway (3)	20.5	Turkey[a] (1)	6.5
Netherlands (12)	36.2	Finland (6)	19.9	Israel[a] (6)	5.5
Sweden (11)	34.0	Japan (18)	18.2	Russian F.[a] (2)	4.5
Australia (20)	33.8	Czech R.[a] (1)	14.8	Mexico (1)	2.6
Denmark (5)	32.1	Estonia (0)	10.7	Poland (2)	1.9
Iceland (0)	31.6	Germany (39)	9.1		

[a]Foreign citizen students (including long-term residents) and not just internationally mobile students.

SOURCE: AUTHOR USING DATA FROM OECD (2017, P. 300) AND ARWU (2018)

in Canada and Japan; relatively minor in Germany, Israel and Korea. Switzerland has more international doctoral students than nationals. The STEM disciplines play the largest part in doctoral mobility. In 2015, 28 per cent of mobile doctoral students were working in natural sciences and mathematics; 25 per cent were in engineering, manufacturing and construction; and 6 per cent in ICTs research (p. 289).

The United States, where 37.8 per cent of all doctoral students are international, takes in much the largest group in quantity terms (OECD, 2017, p. 288). US research in STEM is highly dependent on internationally mobile doctoral students, especially from Asia. National Science Board (NSB) data shows that between 1995 and 2015 there were 166,920 Asian recipients of doctorates in the United States who studied on temporary visas, including 68,379 from China, 63,576 (93.0 per cent) of them in STEM fields; and 32,737 from India, 30,251 (92.4 per cent) in STEM (Table 2.3) (NSB, 2018, tables 2-14 and 2-15). Many student source countries have a net loss of talent. PhD graduates often stay where they are educated, especially the US with its large pool of work opportunities – though these graduates often maintain networks in their home countries and many return or circulate later in their careers. Of American doctoral recipients in 2012–2015 from China, 83.4 per cent had plans to stay and 49.4 per cent had definite plans. The stay rate was highest in mathematics and computer science (NSB, 2018, table A3-21).

The United States, where 37.8 per cent of all doctoral students are international, takes in much the largest group in quantity terms (OECD, 2017, p. 288). US research in STEM is highly dependent on internationally mobile doctoral students, especially from Asia. National Science Board (NSB) data shows that between 1995 and 2015 there were 166,920 Asian recipients of doctorates in the United States who studied on temporary visas, including 68,379 from China, 63,576 (93.0 per cent) of them in STEM fields; and 32,737 from India, 30,251 (92.4 per cent) in STEM (Table 2.3) (NSB, 2018, tables 2-14 and 2-15). Many student source countries have a net loss of talent. PhD graduates often stay where they are educated, especially the US with its large pool of work opportunities – though these graduates often maintain networks in their home countries and many return or circulate later in their careers. Of American doctoral recipients in 2012–2015 from China, 83.4 per cent had plans to stay and 49.4 per cent had definite plans. The stay rate was highest in mathematics and computer science (NSB, 2018, table A3-21).

Networked Global Research and Free Inquiry. As noted, WCUs sustain an expanding worldwide space for research inquiry, other academically codified thought, and the dissemination of scholarship. Wagner, Park, and Leydesdorff (2015, p. 1) find 'science has become increasingly collaborative and team based', and 'a growing percentage of these collaborations happen at the international level'. The global science, data storage/transfer and publishing systems; official national and WCU strategies that foster internationalization (a goal in itself for most national systems and almost every WCU) (Altbach & Salmi, 2011); the culture of collaboration, that fosters bottom-up disciplinary exchanges in each science and non-science – together they constitute not only a vast joined up machine for intellectual production, but a shared space for free inquiry on the global scale, a world mind, free to inquire collaboratively, that spreads and deepens along with the spread of WCUs.

Global Civil Society. Networked WCUs also support a larger joined up conversation, unevenly rooted from place to place but with its own discernible global character, in which the emblematic modes of communication are reasoned argument and evidence-based truth. Again with some local variation, there is a shared commitment to the virtues of free discussion, reflexive social criticism, balanced modernization, poverty alleviation, ecological sustainability, universal education, cosmopolitanism and human rights. This university-orchestrated public culture – one this is critically opposed to the ubiquitous marketing discourse, to fake political news and to other forms of 'post-truth' – draws definition from global science and the widely understood Humboldtian

TABLE 2.3   Recipients of United States doctorates on temporary visas, by country/region of origin (four largest country/regions) by science-based discipline, 1995–2015

Disciplinary field	China Mainland & Hong Kong SAR	India	South Korea	Taiwan
Engineering	23,101	13,208	8274	5045
Physical sciences	10,816	3516	2216	1305
Computer sciences	4229	2477	1015	597
Mathematics	4493	805	967	503
Earth, atmospheric and ocean sciences	1563	357	338	228
Biological sciences	12,202	5654	2459	2374
Medical and health sciences	1368	1371	672	878
Agricultural sciences	1745	823	720	441
Psychology	530	277	481	320
Social sciences	3529	1763	3484	1310
All other fields	4803	2486	3484	3618
Total	68,379	32,737	26,630	16,619

SOURCE: DATA FROM NSB (2018, TABLE 2-15)

idea of the university, including notions of university autonomy and academic freedom (Rohstock, 2012). Blending into national and global civil society, this kind of public culture takes in a large population of the university-educated and university-touched, though societies and polities vary in the extent to which they encourage public forms of intellectualism.

3 Global Science, Network Logic and WCUs

The key to explaining the development of the world research system, its rapid growth, pluralization and patterns of collaboration, is the dynamics of network formation. As Wagner and colleagues note: 'Given the growth of connections at the international level, it is helpful to examine the phenomenon as a communications network and to consider the network as a new organization on the world stage that adds to and complements national systems…The network has features [of] an open system, attracting productive scientists to participate in intellectual projects' (Wagner et al., 2015, p. 1).

Open network structure. In a network structure, new agents freely join the network at negligible cost. Each existing node gains from the addition of each new node, and the potential linkages continually multiply, so that productivity advances continually and the network tends towards universal coverage (Castells, 2000). In higher education and research, there is a continuing multiplication of projects, collaborations and synergies. Cross-border people mobility in higher education, and WCUs' intrinsic contributions to international engagement, tolerance and understanding, also augment the potential for collaboration.

In their study of the development of the global science network after 1990, Wagner and colleagues (2015) state that they 'expected to find a tight core group – meaning a group of frequently interacting countries – with less developed countries falling into a periphery around a core', as found in earlier studies of the global network. They also 'expected high betweenness measures – meaning that some countries have greater visibility and power within the network to attract others into collaborative relationships' (p. 5). What they found instead was a vast expansion of the number of countries in the 'dense centre of the network'. The 35 countries in 1990 expanded to 64 in 2005 and 114 in 2011, 'with many developing countries also joining the core group [...] new members find it relatively easy to join' (p. 6). This coincided with a doubling in the number of countries investing in R&D at scale (p. 7). 'This growth suggests that most nations have scientists who are participating actively in international collaborative networks [...] capacity building has enabled researchers in many more countries to collaborate' (pp. 6–7).

Despite growth in total network size the average distance between countries has diminished and network diameter remains at three. The whole network is traversed in three steps, from a node on one edge of the network to a node on the other edge. Further, 'the average betweenness among nations has dropped', substantially, 'suggesting fewer nodes dominate the network, or, in other words, power is more diffused throughout the network in 2011 than was the case in 1990' (p. 6).

Importantly, 'new entrants are not clustering around the scientific 'leaders', suggesting 'a more open network than was found in 1990' (Wagner et al., 2015, p. 6). 'Many nodes operate effectively in the network' (p. 7). 'New entrants are able to find collaborators without having to pass first through a core of highly powerful (or central) nodes'. Science 'may be operating as an open system' (p. 8). The more open system of global science is also more pluralized. Network structure and agency both facilitate this. 'Many more connections have been forged by more partners [...] The increase in links is disproportionately large compared to the growth in the number of addresses in the file' (p. 6), consistent with the numerical growth in co-authored papers (p. 6). The science network 'has grown denser but not more clustered, meaning there are many more connections, but they are not grouped together in exclusive "cliques"' (p. 1). Relations of power within global science are 'not recreating political or geographic structures' (pp. 1, 6). 'Power is being dispersed throughout the network' (p. 6). This in turn has implications for the relationship between science, the WCUs that house it, and the nation-state:

> As international collaboration has grown, it is possible to argue that the shift towards the global challenges the relationship between science and the state. Collaboration has grown for reasons independent of the needs and policies of the state. Reasons for the growth of collaboration appear to be related more to factors endogenous to science. (Wagner, Park, & Leydesdorff, 2015, p. 1)

3.1 *Growth of Published Science*

Table 2.4 lists all of the countries that produced more than 10,000 papers in 2016. Between 2000 and 2016 published science grew by 3.9 per cent per annum at world level. Most of the mature research systems are on the right side of the table, with slower growth. On the left side, China had annual growth of 8.4 per cent and India 11.1 per cent. Iran moved from 10,703 to 40,974 papers, annual growth of 15.1 per cent. Malaysia achieved 20,332 papers in 2016, and exceptional 20.2 per cent annual growth, though from a low base. Just below 10,000 is Saudi Arabia (9232 papers, 17.1 per cent annual growth). In the

TABLE 2.4 Annual rate of growth in published science papers, 2006–2016, nations producing more than 10,000 papers in 2016

System	Papers 2006	Papers 2016	Annual growth %	System	Papers 2006	Papers 2016	Annual growth %
Malaysia	3230	20,332	20.2	Italy	50,159	69,125	3.3
Iran	10,073	40,974	15.1	Singapore	8205	11,254	3.2
Romania	3523	10,194	11.2	Austria	9155	12,366	3.1
India	38,590	110,320	11.1	Spain	39,271	52,821	3.0
Egypt	3958	10,807	10.6	Switzerland	16,385	21,128	2.6
Mainland China	189,760	426,165	8.4	Belgium	13,036	16,394	2.3
South Africa	5636	11,881	7.7	Germany	84,434	103,122	2.0
Russia	29,369	59,134	7.2	Netherlands	24,461	29,949	2.0
Portugal	7136	13,773	6.8	Sweden	16,634	19,937	1.8
Brazil	28,160	53,607	6.6	Canada	49,259	57,356	1.5
Czech Republic	8839	15,963	6.1	Finland	9204	10,545	1.4
South Korea	36,747	63,063	5.5	France	62,448	69,431	1.1
Denmark	8536	13,471	4.7	United Kingdom	88,061	97,527	1.0
Poland	21,267	32,978	4.5	Taiwan	25,246	27,385	0.8
Mexico	9322	14,529	4.5	United States	383,115	408,395	0.7
Australia	33,100	51,068	4.4	Israel	11,040	11,893	0.7
Norway	7093	10,726	4.2	Greece	10,684	10,725	0.0
World	1,567,422	2,295,608	3.9	Japan	110,503	96,536	−1.3

SOURCE: BASED ON NSB (2018, TABLE 5-22)

world's fourth largest country by population, Indonesia, now a middle-middle income country, science has begun a long upward climb, moving from 619 to 7729 papers (an annual growth rate of 28.7 per cent) (NSB, 2018, table 5–22).

More productive WCUs. Between 2009 and 2015, the number of individual universities producing more than 1,000 science papers in the previous four years rose from 685 to 903. The number producing over 5,000 papers rose from 126 to 190. The number of very large science engines publishing over 10,000 papers doubled from 25 to 50. The number of universities producing high citation science also grew, as did the average number of high citation papers produced by the leading universities. (The number of papers in the top 10 per cent of their field by citation rate grows automatically in proportion to total output.) In 2009, 138 WCUs had more than 500 papers in the preceding four years that were in the top 10 per cent category. By 2015 that number had risen to 211 WCUs (Leiden University, 2018).

3.2   Pluralization of Science

Between 2006 and 2012 there was a modest pluralization of WCUs in national terms. Using a relative definition of WCU, from 2004 to 2017 systems with top 500 universities increased from 37 to 46 (ARWU, 2017). Using an absolute definition of WCU, the number of countries with universities producing over 5,000 science papers in the previous four years rose from 23 countries in 2009 to 27 in 2015. Universities with more than 5,000 papers not from the US or UK rose from 54.0 to 62.1 per cent. There was also greater plurality of high quality papers.

Rise of East Asia and Singapore. Within the overall global pattern of growth and dispersion of research capacity, the most important trend is the rise of East Asia and Singapore (the geographical outlier of the Chinese civilizational zone) to third major R&D region, joining North America and Western Europe/UK. In 2003, China produced less than 30 per cent of US scientific output but it reached first place in 2016 (Figure 2.4). China's number of papers multiplied by 4.9 in 13 years, South Korea's output by 2.7. Meanwhile the number of ARWU-defined WCUs in mainland China grew from eight of the top 500 in 2005, to 45 in 2017 (ARWU, 2017). (China's and Singapore's WCUs would be more highly placed if the ARWU did not use Nobel Prizes as an indicator). The pipeline effects of current national investments ensure that in China and Singapore, and probably in South Korea, scientific output will continue to grow rapidly for years to come, even if budgets stopped increasing tomorrow (they won't). China's science will be twice further boosted, by the 'Double World-Class' project and activity with the 'One Belt One Road' initiative.

Turning from quantity indicators to quality, Figure 2.5 traces changes in six countries from 1996 to 2014 in the proportion of all science and engineering papers that were in the top one per cent of their disciplinary field on the basis of citation rate. In all countries shown there was growth in the weight of the top one per cent papers. The US, the world leader in 1996, moved from 1.75 to 1.90 per cent. In 2005, it was passed by the Netherlands, one of the small-to-medium-size high quality science systems in north-western Europe. In 2011 the US was passed by the UK, which has concentrated research excellence in leading universities through successive iterations of the Research Assessment Exercise/Research Excellent Framework. Over the period European countries, including the UK, benefitted from the collaborative building of research

GLOBAL COOPERATION AND NATIONAL COMPETITION IN WCU SECTOR 39

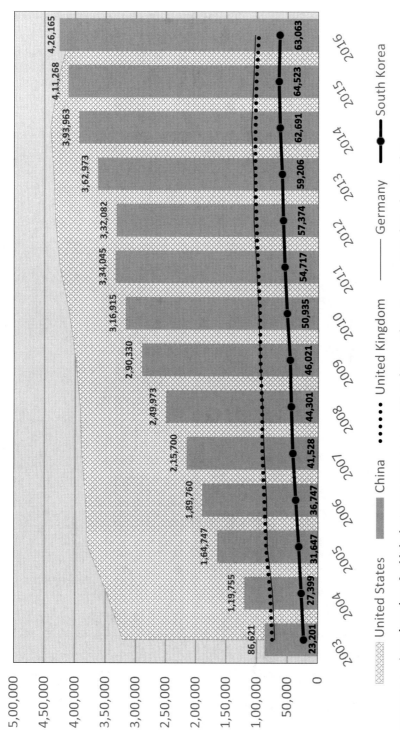

FIGURE 2.4 Annual number of published science papers, 2003–2016 United States, China, Germany, United Kingdom, South Korea

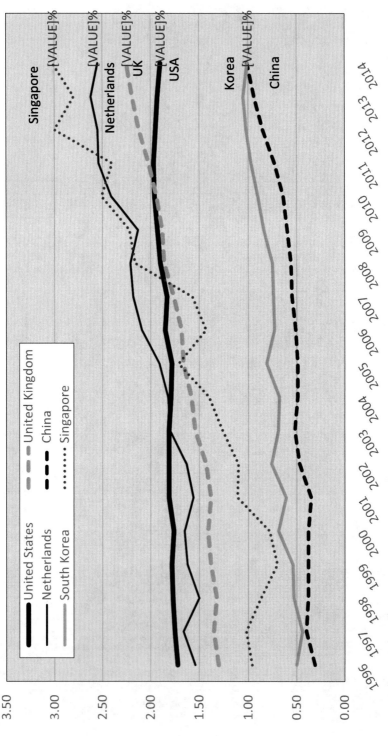

FIGURE 2.5 Proportion of all science and engineering papers that were in the top 1 per cent of their field by citation rate: United States, United Kingdom, Netherlands, China, South Korea, Singapore: 1996–2014

in European Research Area joint programmes. Many smaller European countries, with a cluster of WCUs and nuanced specializations, had more than 1.90 per cent of their 2014 papers in the top one per cent: Austria, Belgium, Cyprus, Denmark, Estonia, Finland, Greece, Iceland, Ireland, Norway, Sweden, Switzerland. In larger Germany the proportion was 1.76 per cent, in France 1.61 per cent (NSB, 2018, A5-51).

The other story in Figure 2.5 is the improvement of quality in East Asia. As in the English-speaking countries, qualitative improvement shows more strongly in the form of increases in top one per cent science, than in increases in average citations to all papers, indicating WCU concentration policies at work. Tiny Singapore with less than six million people lifted the proportion of its papers that were in the top one per cent from 0.70 per cent in 1999 to 3.02 per cent in 2014, three times the world average. South Korea reached world average level in 2012; China with 1.3 billion people climbed from only 0.31 per cent in 1996 to reach world average in 2014. Science in China is still well below the average quality of Western Europe and the US but the massive scale of the national system, coupled with rapid growth in high citation work in some disciplines, means that a large proportion of the world's future knowledge will come from that country.

Physical sciences STEM in East Asia. What about individual WCUs? Table 2.5 summarizes the growth of top 10 per cent papers in leading WCUs in East Asia and Singapore, compared to MIT and Cambridge. At Zhejiang, Peking, Fudan and Huazhong in China, and Nanyang in Singapore, the dynamism is obvious. The performance of smaller Nanyang is approaching that of NUS in Singapore.

Table 2.6 lists the world's top 15 WCUs in physical sciences STEM, in terms of papers in the top 10 per cent by citation rate in 2012–2015. China had eight of the leading 15 universities in mathematics and computing. Tsinghua was far ahead as world number 1 with Nanyang in Singapore in second place. In the larger physical sciences and engineering group, Berkeley and MIT were the top two. US and China both had five of the top 15. Combining the two columns in Table 11, Tsinghua with 1,421 papers just shades MIT with 1,420 papers as the world's top physical sciences STEM university – though the US still had four of the top seven WCUs. If the measure is switched to the much smaller group of top one per cent papers, MIT is top in combined physical sciences STEM, followed by Stanford, Berkeley, Harvard and Nanyang, all ahead of Tsinghua. However, Tsinghua is clear world number one in top one per cent papers in mathematics and computing alone (Leiden University, 2018).

Discipline imbalance. However, when all disciplines are included in the comparison, American WCUs as a group are well ahead of the world in the quantity of high quality work, and like European universities more balanced

TABLE 2.5   Growth in the number of published papers in the top 10 per cent of their research field by citation rate, from 2006–2009 to 2012–2015, selected leading Asian universities

University	System	Top 10% papers 2006–2009	Top 10% papers 2012–2015	Growth 2006–2009 to 2012–2015 2006–2009 = 1.00
Tsinghua U	Mainland China	819	1768	2.15
Zhejiang U	Mainland China	730	1762	2.42
Peking U	Mainland China	622	1538	2.47
Shanghai Jiao Tong U	Mainland China	644	1403	2.11
Fudan U	Mainland China	469	1224	2.61
Huazhong UST	Mainland China	241	1045	4.37
National U Singapore	Singapore	1042	1597	1.53
Nanyang Technological U	Singapore	568	1413	2.49
Tokyo U	Japan	1323	1333	1.01
Kyoto U	Japan	968	932	0.96
U Hong Kong	Hong Kong SAR	558	741	1.33
Seoul National U	South Korea	742	1182	1.59
National Taiwan U	Taiwan	604	786	1.30
MIT	US	2091	2565	1.23
U Cambridge	UK	1796	2274	1.27

SOURCE: BASED ON LEIDEN UNIVERSITY (2018) DATA

than their newly emerged East Asian counterparts. Research systems in China, Singapore, Korea and Japan are skewed to physical sciences STEM, less strong in biological sciences and weak in medical sciences, and (less surprisingly) in English language social sciences and humanities. In the last disciplines the global comparison means less because most work is in national languages. China is an extreme case of the discipline skew. In 2016, 49.6 per cent of all papers by researchers from the United States were in medical sciences biological and other life sciences, excluding agriculture (29.3 per cent in medical research alone). In the European Union (EU) the combined proportion in medical, biological and other life sciences was 40.7 per cent. In China, the combined proportion in those disciplines was 27.5 per cent. Only 13.3 per cent of all papers were in medical research, less than half the US level. In the United States 10.7 per cent of papers were in quantitative social sciences and psychology, in the EU 10.1 per cent but China 1.3 per cent (NSB, 2018, table 5–23).

TABLE 2.6 World top universities in (1) physical sciences and engineering, (2) mathematics and complex computing, in published papers in the top 10 per cent of their field by citation rate: 2012–2015

	University	System	Top 10% papers in Physical Sciences & Engineering 2012–2015		University	System	Top 10% papers in Maths & Complex Computing 2012–2015
1	UC Berkeley	US	1176	1	Tsinghua U	Mainland China	367
2	Massachusetts IT	US	1175	2	Nanyang TU	Singapore	259
3	Tsinghua U	Mainland China	1054	3	Zhejiang U	Mainland China	256
4	Stanford U	US	976	4	Huazhong US	Mainland China	250
5	Nanyang TU	Singapore	931	5	Massachusetts IT	US	245
6	Harvard U	US	875	6	Harbin IT	Mainland China	236
7	Zhejiang U	Mainland China	857	7	NU Singapore	Singapore	226
8	U Cambridge	UK	801	8	Stanford U	US	208
9	NU Singapore	Singapore	749	9	Xidian U	Mainland China	205
10	U S & T	Mainland China	720	10	Shanghai Jiao TU	Mainland China	196
11	ETH Zurich	Switzerland	678	11	City U Hong Kong	HK SAR	188
12	U Tokyo	Japan	649	12	U Texas, Austin	US	187
13	Shanghai JT U	Mainland China	638	13	South East U	Mainland China	184
14	Peking U	Mainland China	636	14	UC Berkeley	US	184
15	Caltech	US	635	15	Beihang U	Mainland China	177

SOURCE: BASED ON LEIDEN UNIVERSITY (2018) DATA

Leiden University (2018) data show that in the number of top 10 per cent papers in biomedical and health sciences in 2012–2015, the highest ranked Chinese university was Shanghai Jiao Tong at 117th. The leader, Harvard, had 726 high citation papers in biomedical and health sciences. Shanghai Jiao Tong had just 30.

3.3 Global Collaboration in Research

Cross-border collaboration can be examined in terms of both national level data on cross-border collaboration and citation, and data on collaborative publication by individual WCUs.

The world picture. The number of jointly authored publications is expanding rapidly (see Figure 2.6), and their proportion of all published science also grows (Figure 2.6, Table 2.7). Cross-national citation of papers is also increasing, suggesting that on average, published research in each country has a growing influence on researchers in other countries. Nevertheless, the patterns of cross-border collaboration in publications and cross-border border citation are uneven between disciplinary fields and vary between countries.

The disciplines vary in the extent to which work is internationally authored. Collaboration increases where there are formal programmes, especially when necessary equipment is cost shared (e.g., telescopes, synchrotrons) or subject matter is intrinsically global (e.g., climate change, water management, energy security, epidemic disease). In 2016, cross-border authorship was 54.0 per cent of published papers in astronomy and exceeded 20 per cent in the geosciences, biological sciences, mathematics, physics and chemistry. Between 2006 and 2016 it rose in every discipline, including engineering from 13.7 to 17.7 per cent and social sciences from 11.4 to 15.4 per cent (NSB, 2018, p. 122).

Using Web of Science data, Wagner and colleagues (2015) find that at world level the proportion of all papers that had international co-authors rose from 10.1 per cent in 1990 to 19.5 per cent in 2000 and 24.6 per cent in 2011. Jointly-authored papers 'account for all the growth in output among the scientifically advanced countries', and emerging countries are playing a growing role in collaboration (p. 1). Using the Scopus data set, the US National Science Board (NSB) finds that the number of internationally co-authored papers rose from 194,398 in 2003 to 498,465 in 2016, moving from 16.3 to 21.7 per cent (Figure 2.6). Domestic-only collaboration held steady and there was a proportional decline in single authored papers. Cross-border papers multiplied by 2.6 while total papers multiplied by 1.9. American internationalization followed the world trend. US Papers with international collaborators advanced from 23.3 to 37.1 per cent (Table 2.7) (NSB, 2018, table A5-42).

GLOBAL COOPERATION AND NATIONAL COMPETITION IN WCU SECTOR 45

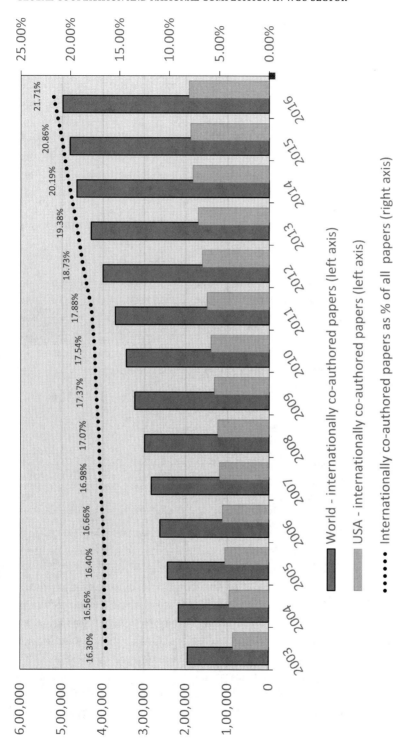

FIGURE 2.6 Growth in annual number and proportion of internationally co-authored papers in science and engineering, 2003 to 2016, world and United States

TABLE 2.7 Proportion of all papers in science and engineering that were internationally co-authored, 2003 and 2016, countries producing more than 10,000 papers in 2016, by region (science includes some social science)

Europe	2003 %	2016 %	Anglosphere	2003 %	2016 %	Asia	2003 %	2016 %
Switzerland	54.5	69.2	New Zealand	44.5	58.2	Singapore	35.0	62.8
Belgium	49.0	66.1	United Kingdom	36.9	57.1	Pakistan	28.2	49.3
Austria	46.3	64.8	Australia	36.9	54.9	Thailand	48.7	40.7
Sweden	45.7	64.3	Canada	39.0	53.0	Malaysia	36.6	38.4
Denmark	47.7	63.3	United States	23.3	37.1	Taiwan	17.5	29.8
Netherlands	44.7	61.8	**Latin America**	**2003 %**	**2016 %**	Japan	18.9	27.9
Norway	45.6	61.4				South Korea	25.1	27.0
Ireland	46.1	60.9	Chile	52.7	61.7	Mainland China	15.3	20.3
Finland	41.2	60.4	Argentina	39.2	45.3	India	18.1	17.4
France	39.6	54.8	Mexico	39.6	42.3	**Sub-Saharan**	**2003**	**2016**
Portugal	45.0	54.2	Brazil	27.2	32.5	**Africa**	**%**	**%**
Greece	35.5	52.3	**Middle East &**	**2003**	**2016**	South Africa	40.0	52.1
Germany	39.4	51.0	**North Africa**	**%**	**%**			
Spain	33.2	50.7	Saudi Arabia	34.5	76.8			
Italy	33.1	47.3	Egypt	32.7	51.7			
Czech Republic	35.8	41.9	Israel	39.9	50.7			
Poland	29.9	31.3	Turkey	16.3	22.2			
Russia	26.9	25.1	Iran	24.2	20.8			

SOURCE: BASED ON DATA FROM NSF (2018, TABLE A5-42)

National and WCU collaboration data. Table 2.7 shows relatively low rates of co-authorship in China, the United States, Russia, India and Brazil. 'Countries with large populations or communities of researchers may have high rates of domestic coauthorship because of the large pool of potential domestic coauthors in their field. Researchers in smaller countries have a lower chance of finding a potential partner within national borders, so collaborators are more likely beyond their national borders'. In addition, 'the EU programme Horizon 2020 (like its predecessor, the 7th Framework Programme for Research and Technological Development) actively promotes and funds international collaboration within the EU' (NSB, 2018, p. 122). Many projects require at least three EU member countries as a condition of funding. Cross-border publishing is high in Singapore and smaller high quality European research systems like Switzerland, Netherlands, Belgium and the Nordic countries, followed by the Anglophone zone, aside from the US, and most other European countries. Co-publication is lower in East Asia. Saudi Arabian universities (76.8 per cent) employ large numbers of foreign faculty on a part-time basis, boosting their global ranking position.

Examining trends in the twenty WCUs with the highest level of total research output, in the six years from 2009, all of these universities experienced a substantial increase in the number and proportion of papers with international co-authors, averaging at nine per cent. The rate of increase was slower in China, Korea and Japan than Europe, the English-speaking countries and at the University of Sao Paulo in Brazil (Leiden University, 2018).

3.4 Patterns within the Network

Networks are flat but are not always symmetrical. Some nodes are bigger than others, and some partnerships are worked more intensely. Lines of influence may be mutual or one way. The United States is the 'largest contributor of partners' (Wagner et al., 2015, p. 7): US-based authors appeared in 38.6 per cent of all co-published articles in 2016 (NSB, 2018, table A5-42). They are directly linked to most countries and indirectly linked to all countries in the global network (Wagner et al., 2015, p. 7). However, in a network setting US leadership is necessarily dominant rather than hegemonic. It is not exercised in zero-sum fashion by excluding other players from entering the network or accumulating connections.

Favoured partners. Within the thickening connections of every nation with other nations, and each WCU with others, some relationships are especially strong because of cultural similarity, historic links, and/or policy and funding drivers. Collaboration index data compare collaboration between the named countries in the pair, relative to the rate of collaboration by both countries with all others. A collaboration index of 1.00 indicates that joint publication is at the level expected on the basis of the two countries' overall patterns; 0.50 indicates weak collaboration intensity and 2.00 indicates unusually strong intensity. The collaborative index is the same for both partners.

Among English-speaking countries, the intense collaboration between Australia and New Zealand (3.38, 1977 joint papers in 2016) reflects the fact they are geographic and cultural neighbours, like Canada and the US (1.13, 19,704 papers in 2016, 43.5 per cent of all joint papers of Canadian authors). Canada was the only Anglophone nation with which US researchers collaborated above 1.00. The US collaboration index with the UK was just 0.77, albeit representing 25,858 papers and 29.5 per cent of joint UK work, because both countries were more intensively engaged elsewhere. Australian co-publication with the UK (8838 in

2016) was less than with the US (12,127) but the UK-Australia index was higher at 1.19 than the US-Australia index of 0.75 (NSB, 2018, tables A5-43 and A5-44).

There is intense collaboration between the three Spanish-speaking Latin American nations with the strongest science systems – Argentina, Chile and Mexico – and between Argentina and its Portuguese-speaking neighbour Brazil. There is another intensive regional collaboration, on a larger scale, between Denmark, Finland, Norway and Sweden. They share geographical location, historic ties and common social systems, and university cooperation in the Association of Nordic University Rectors Conferences (NordForsk, 2018). The six pairings between the four nations had collaborative indexes of 3.16–4.54. There were 9865 collaborative papers across the region in 2016. Nevertheless this was only about 60 per cent of the volume that Nordic researchers co-published with US researchers and 70 per cent of the volume of their joint work with UK researchers. The largest research countries dominate networking activity in absolute terms, even while other connections are more intense.

Table 2.8 shows that both the US and China have only a small number of pairings with above average intensity. US science was intensely focused on neighbours Canada and Mexico, a special tie with Israel (1.33, 4533 papers), and relations with South Korea and Taiwan where the US has played a major role in doctoral training (often the source of co-publication) since the 1950s. In 2016 the US shared 47.6 per cent of all internationally co-published papers involving authors from South Korea, 32.7 per cent in relation to Japan, 32.0 per cent in India, 29.8 per cent in Netherlands, 28.5 per cent in Germany and 25.3 per cent in France (NSB 2018, tables A5-43 and A5-44). Researchers in China had a close relationship with Singapore (2.03, 4413 papers), though intensity has diminished since 2006 (3.02). There was also relatively intensive collaboration with Taiwan and a growing link to regional neighbour Pakistan. The index of collaboration with researchers in Japan declined from 1.51 in 2006 to 1.09 in 2016: the number of Japan-China collaborative papers had multiplied by more than 2.5 but amid the overall growth of research in China the relative importance of collaboration with Japanese researchers has declined sharply. China also sustained intensive links with Australia (9246 papers in 2016) and the US.

The US-China index of 1.19 in 2016 represented 43,968 joint Sino-American papers in 2016, compared to 5406 papers in 2006. This is an immense volume of collaborative science, much the largest nation-to-nation linkage in the world. In total 22.9 per cent of all US co-publishing in 2016 was with researchers from China, and 46.1 per cent of all China's international co-publishing was with researchers from the US (NSB, 2018, tables 5-26, A5-43, A5-44). The collaboration intensified between 2006 and 2016. *This might suggest that the primary China-US relationship in science is collaborative, not competitive.*

Table 2.8 also shows that European science systems like the UK placed each other on high priority, and this may have precluded more intensive relations elsewhere. The UK had indexes above 1.00 for all European countries in the NSB data except the Czech Republic and Russia, but only one intensive relationship

TABLE 2.8   Intensive research collaborations by United States, China and United Kingdom, with rest of the world, in 2016: Rate of international co-authorship in science[a] and engineering papers between named pairs, relative to their rate of international co-authorship with all countries[b]

United States and...		Mainland China and...		United Kingdom and...	
Israel	1.33	Singapore (-)	2.03	Ireland	2.16
South Korea	1.23	Taiwan	1.73	Greece	1.74
Mainland China (+)	1.19	Pakistan (+)	1.23	Netherlands	1.50
Canada	1.13	United States (+)	1.19	Denmark	1.43
Taiwan (-)	1.05	Australia	1.15	Hungary (+)	1.43
Mexico	1.04	Japan (-)	1.09	Norway	1.40
				Finland	1.28
				Hungary (+)	1.50
				Turkey (+)	1.26
				Czech Republic (+)	1.18
				Switzerland	1.21
				Ireland (+)	1.11
				Poland (+)	1.11
				Egypt (+)	1.08
				Russia (+)	1.07
				Austria (+)	1.03
				France	1.01
				Outside Europe	
				New Zealand	1.35
				South Africa	1.33
				Australia	1.19
				Chile	1.01

a. Science includes some social science.
b. 1.00 = expected rate of collaboration, 2.00 = intensive relationship within the global network.

(+) indicates significant increase in rate of collaboration since 2006.
(-) indicates significant decrease in rate of collaboration since 2006.
SOURCE: DATA FROM NSB (2018, TABLE A5-43)

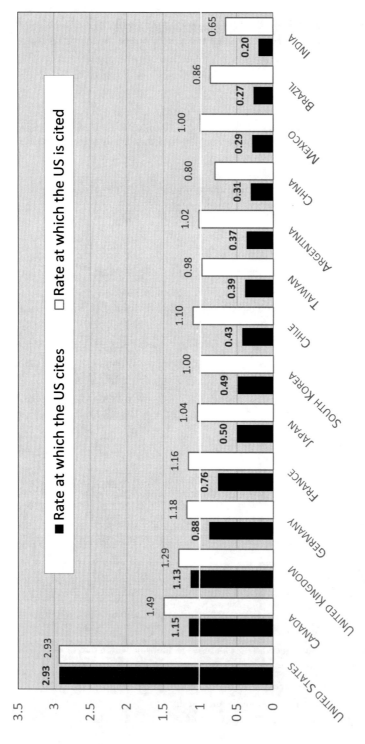

FIGURE 2.7 The rate at which papers by authors from selected countries are cited by papers with authors from United States, compared to the rate that these countries cite United States authors, science and engineering papers, 2014

outside Europe and the Anglophone zone, 1222 papers with Chile in 2016 (1.01). The NSB data show that Germany had collaborative indexes above 1.00 in 2016 for every European country in the data and in most cases the intensity had increased since 2016 (NSB, 2018, tables A5-43 and A5-44). Other European countries have similar European-centred collaboration patterns.

Who cites whom. Another way of mapping cross-border relationships is via data on international citations. As with the co-publication data, the 'expected' or world average position is 1.00 and 2.00 indicates very intensive citation. Unlike co-publication data, the citation data are not necessarily identical for both parties – researchers from country A may cite research from country B more often than vice versa. This contrast enables the mapping of the apparent direction of intellectual influence. Figure 2.7 shows that in every nation US researchers are cited by researchers from that other nation more than US researchers cite them. Americans have a large and strong domestic science system and cite each other intensively (2.93). There is no system of equivalent size in other nations, except in China. Notably, Americans cite research in China at the low rate of 0.37, whereas researchers in China cite US researchers at 0.80. This suggests that Americans influence Chinese researchers more than vice versa. The relationship is collaborative but not yet based on parity of esteem. Whether this is due to different levels of quality, or different levels of cultural closure, or both, cannot be judged from the data. Researchers in only two countries are cited by US researchers at a rate above 1.00, Canada and the United Kingdom. UK researchers come closest to parity of esteem, citing US researchers at 1.29 and being cited at 1.13 (NSB, 2018, table 5–28).

4   Conclusion

Global and international relations have mixed benefits in finance and trade, where there are both winners and losers. However, in higher education and research, cross-border activity can be configured to benefit all parties, provided that relations are conducted on the basis of equality of respect. Brain drain, and the tendency to marginalize non-English language knowledge, are serious problems that have not been adequately addressed.

Looking through a solely national lens, the cross-border activity of WCUs may seem marginal, or an instrument of national competition. Yet global science, communications and mobility are core activities in WCUs across the world. WCUs have established a networked zone of inquiry on the world scale, supported by and formative of traditions of academic freedom that take in a growing number of countries. Cross-border work is attractive to WCUs. In a global space they operate as global civil society actors with fewer constraints on them than at home. In the open global dimension of action, the 'commonness' of WCUs is more developed and they are less bound by the discipline of competition than states imagine.

This chapter has focused on the actual and potential contributions of World-Class Universities (WCUs) to common goods, especially global common goods. The main empirical focus has been global science, with some attention to global mobility. Research and mobility are key aspects of globalization in WCUs and areas of potential national/global tensions. Nation-states can control people mobility, though this is politically difficult, but they do not have the tools to control global research and information (outside military-related research), because of the public good nature of knowledge. The secular trend is to ever-increasing 'flat' research collaboration, between an ever-increasing number and range of national systems and WCUs. The global science system evolves according its own logic (Wagner et al., 2015). *It is becoming more detached from nation-states.* Hence research collaboration between WCUs has a larger meaning. It feeds the slow historical process whereby different national societies, without ceasing to be diverse, are moving towards a one-world society.

Nevertheless, national/global tensions (Rodrik, 2017) pose challenges for WCUs, for example the barriers to academic people mobility amid migration resistance in the US and UK, and the barriers to the full flow of global information in China. And most WCUs will need to more effectively address local/national political imperatives if those universities are to flourish in future. The challenge is to embed higher education and science in a myriad of differing local domains, and to tick the national political boxes, while continuing to move forward with the development of a common global agenda.

Notes

1 This chapter defines 'World-Class University' or 'WCU' not in relative terms (e.g. ranked in a top 100 or top 500) but in absolute terms. A definition based on, say, the comparative top 500 conceals improvement in the absolute level of institutions, and growth in the number of institutions at a fixed level of quantity or quality of scientific output. One simple absolute indicator of a WCU is 1000 published papers over the previous four years, as measured by Clarivate Analytics or Scopus. In the Leiden University ranking, based on Clarivate data, there were 903 such universities at the end of 2015, based on 2012–2015 output.

2 UNESCO's (2018b) term 'tertiary education' is identical to 'higher education' in only some systems. 'Tertiary education' refers to programme, not institution, and includes all programmes at ISCED Levels 5–8, that is, from two-year equivalent academic diplomas (Level 5) to first degrees at Bachelor level (Level 6), Masters programmes (Level 7) and doctoral programmes (Level 8). In many countries, all Level 5–8 activity is classified 'higher education' but in others the term is confined to Levels 6–8 only, or to activity in designated institutions.
3 We thankfully acknowledge Lili Yang for the development of these translated concepts.

References

Academic Ranking of World Universities. (2017). Retrieved March 2, 2018, from http://www.shanghairanking.com/index.html

Aebischer, P. (2016). *Universities: Increasingly global players*. In United Nations Educational, Social and Cultural Organization (Ed.), *UNESCO science report* (pp. 3–5). Paris: United Nations Educational, Social and Cultural Organization (UNESCO).

Altbach, P. G., & Salmi, J. (Eds.). (2011). *The road to academic excellence: The making of world-class research universities*. Washington, DC: The World Bank.

Biesta, G. (2009). Good education in an age of measurement: On the need to reconnect with the question of purpose in education. *Educational Assessment, Evaluation and Accountability, 21*(1), 33–46.

Cantwell, B., Marginson, S., & Smolentseva, A. (Eds.). (2018). *High participation systems of higher education*. Oxford: Oxford University Press.

Castells, M. (2000). *Rise of the network society* (2nd ed.). Oxford: Blackwell.

Deardorff, D., de Wit, H., Heyl, J., & Adams, T. (Eds.). (2012). *The Sage handbook of international higher education*. Los Angeles, CA: Sage Publications.

Department of Education and Training, Australia (DET). (2018). *Selected higher education statistics*. Retrieved March 2, 2018, from https://www.education.gov.au/selected-higher-education-statistics-2015-student-data

Dewey, J. (1927). *The public and its problems*. New York, NY: H. Holt.

Higher Education Statistics Agency, United Kingdom (HESA). (2018). *Student data*. Retrieved March 2, 2018, from https://www.hesa.ac.uk/data-and-analysis/students

Institute for International Education (IIE). (2017). *Open doors: Data on international education*. Retrieved October 6, 2017, from https://www.iie.org/en/Research-and-Insights/Open-Doors/Data/International-Students

Internet World Stats. (2018). Retrieved March 2, 2018, from https://www.internetworldstats.com/emarketing.htm

Kaul, I., Grunberg, I., & Stern, M. (Eds.). (1999). *Global public goods: International cooperation in the 21st century*. New York, NY: Oxford University Press.

Kharas, H. (2017, February). *The unprecedented expansion of the global middle class: An update*. Washington, DC: Brookings Institute.

Leiden University. (2017). *CWTS Leiden ranking 2017: Centre for Science and Technology Studies, CWTS*. Retrieved October 3, 2017, from http://www.leidenranking.com

Locatelli, R. (2018, February 22). *Education as a public and common good: Reframing the governance of education in a changing context*. Retrieved March 17, 2018, from http://unesdoc.unesco.org/images/0026/002616/261614E.pdf

Mansbridge, J. (1998). On the contested nature of the public good. In W. Powell & E. Clemens (Eds.), *Private action and the public good*. New Haven, CT: Yale University Press.

Marginson, S. (2010). Space, mobility and synchrony in the knowledge economy. In S. Marginson, P. Murphy, & M. Peters (Eds.), *Global creation: Space, mobility and synchrony in the age of the knowledge economy*. New York, NY: Peter Lang.

Marginson, S. (2014). Student self-formation in international education. *Journal of Studies in International Education, 18*(1), 6–22.

Marginson, S. (2016a). The worldwide trend to high participation higher education: Dynamics of social stratification in inclusive systems. *Higher Education, 72*(4), 413–435. Retrieved March 2, 2018, from http://rdcu.be/kf7P

Marginson, S. (2016b). *Higher education and the common good*. Melbourne: Melbourne University Press.

Marginson, S. (2018a). *Higher education as self-formation: Inaugural professorial lecture at the UCL institute of education*. Retrieved March 2, 2018, from https://www.ucl-ioe-press.com/books/higher-education-and-lifelong-learning/higher-education-as-a-process-of-self-formation/

Marginson, S. (2018b). Private/public in higher education: A synthesis of economic and political approaches. *Studies in Higher Education, 43*(2), 322–337.

McMahon, W. (2009). *Higher learning greater good*. Baltimore, MD: The Johns Hopkins University Press.

Naidoo, R. (2014, October 24). *Speech to IOE/UKFIET forum on higher education and international development*. London: Institute of Education.

National Science Board (NSB). (2018). *Science and engineering indicators 2018*. Retrieved April 2, 2018, from https://www.nsf.gov/statistics/2018/nsb20181/assets/nsb20181.pdf

NordForsk. (2018). *Research collaboration at university and institutional level*. Retrieved April 2, 2018, from https://www.nordforsk.org/en/policy/norden/forskningssam-arbeid-pa-universitets-og-institusjonsniva

OECD. (2016). *Perspectives on global development 2017: International migration in a shifting world*. Retrieved April 2, 2018, from http://www.keepeek.com/Digital-Asset-Management/oecd/development/perspectives-on-global-development-2017_persp_glob_dev-2017-en#page1

OECD. (2017). *Education at a glance, 2017.* Paris: OECD.
Organization for Economic Cooperation and Development (OECD). (2015). *Education at a glance, 2015.* Paris: OECD.
Ostrom, E. (1990). *Governing the commons: The evolution of institutions for collective action.* Cambridge: Cambridge University Press.
Rhostock, A. (2012). Some things never change: The invention of Humboldt in western higher education systems. In P. Siljander, A. Kivela, & A. Sutinen (Eds.), *Theories of building and growth: Connections and controversies between continental educational thinking and American pragmatism.* Rotterdam, The Netherlands: Sense Publishers.
Rodrik, D. (2017). *Populism and the economics of globalization.* Retrieved October 6, 2017, from https://drodrik.scholar.harvard.edu/files/dani-rodrik/files/populism_and_the_economics_of_globalization.pdf
Samuelson, P. (1954). The pure theory of public expenditure. *Review of Economics and Statistics, 36*(4), 387–389.
Sen, A. (2000). *Development as freedom.* New York, NY: Anchor Books.
Stiglitz, J. (1999). Knowledge as a global public good. In I. Kaul, I. Grunberg, & M. Stern (Eds.), *Global public goods: International cooperation in the 21st century.* New York, NY: Oxford University Press.
UNESCO. (2018a). *UNESCO institute for statistics data on education.* Retrieved April 2, 2018, from http://data.uis.unesco.org
UNESCO. (2018b). *International Standard Classification of Education, ISCED 2011.* Retrieved April 2, 2018, from http://uis.unesco.org/sites/default/files/documents/international-standard-classification-of-education-isced-2011-en.pdf
UNESCO. (2018c). *Fulfilling our collective responsibilities: Financing global public goods in education.* Retrieved March 17, 2018, from https://en.unesco.org/gem-report/node/2333
United Nations Educational, Social and Cultural Organization (UNESCO). (2015). *Rethinking education: Towards a global common good.* Paris: United Nations Educational, Social and Cultural Organization. Retrieved April 2, 2018, from http://unesdoc.unesco.org/images/0023/002325/232555e.pdf
Välimaa, J., & Muhonen, R. (2018). Reproducing social equality across the generations: The Nordic model of high participation higher education in Finland. In B. Cantwell, S. Marginson, & A. Smolentseva (Eds.), *High participation systems of higher education.* Oxford: Oxford University Press.
Vygotsky, L. S. (1978). *Mind in society: The development of higher psychological processes.* Cambridge, MA: Harvard University Press.
Wagner, C., Park, H., & Leydesdorff, L. (2015). The continuing growth of global cooperation networks in research: A conundrum for national governments. *PLoS ONE, 10*(7), e0131816. doi:10.1371/journal.pone.0131816
World Bank. (2018). *Data and statistics.* Retrieved April 2, 2018, from http://data.worldbank.org

CHAPTER 3

World-Class Universities and Higher Education Differentiation: The Necessity of Systems

Philip G. Altbach

Abstract

Research universities are at the apex of any academic system. They produce the largest share of research in every country, are the most internationalized institutions, and educate both future academics and a significant share of society's leaders. They are elite institutions in the best sense of that term providing excellence in teaching and research. Although they are only a small part of any higher education system, these universities have a special responsibility to the rest of academe: they are academic leaders but also educate academics and others who serve in other academic institutions. Research universities too often neglect their academic ecosystem. There needs to be a recognition of the importance of all segments of increasingly complex systems in the context of the global massification of higher education.

Keywords

Research universities – academic systems – global knowledge economy – massification of higher education

1   Introduction

World-class research-intensive universities everywhere exist in an 'ivory tower' in terms of their relationships to the broader post-secondary environment of which they are a part. They tend to see themselves as 'institutions apart' with little interaction and no responsibility for the rest of post-secondary education. While it is the case that research universities are special institutions and require special attention, funding, autonomy and the recognition by society of their key role, they have a responsibility to both society and to the increasingly diverse post-secondary environment that has emerged globally. Research universities can no longer exist in an ivory tower – they must be integrated into coherent higher education systems.

This chapter is concerned with differentiation in post-secondary education and the development of systems to cope with differentiation (Clark, 1983). Differentiation means the increasingly different functions and expanding roles that post-secondary education plays in all countries, and the institutions, systems and organizational structures that are set up to coordinate and govern the expanding and increasingly complex post-secondary reality (Teichler, 2002). All countries experience diversification, but many do not deal effectively with the new realities, often permitting a vast and frequently disorganized array of institutions to haphazardly grow. On the positive side, today's academic anarchy has produced an immense amount of innovation and change in the organization and delivery of teaching and learning, as well as an incipient revolution in the distance delivery of academic programmes, along with entirely new forms of post-secondary institutions.

Post-secondary education has become a massive enterprise everywhere. Globally, more than 200 million students are studying in more than 22,000 universities and untold other post-secondary institutions. In most developed countries, 60 per cent or more of the age group studies in some kind of post-secondary institution – and many countries have reached 80 per cent. The global tertiary-enrolment ratio went up from 14 per cent to 32 per cent in the two decades up to 2012; in that time, the number of countries with access rates of more than half rose from five to 54. Expansion will continue, especially in developing and middle-income countries. Sub-Saharan Africa, which enrolled only seven to eight per cent in 2016, is at the beginning of massification. China and India, which enrol 37 per cent and 27 per cent respectively, will account for more than half of the student growth in the coming decade. The world has experienced a revolution in higher education access in the 21st century (Altbach, Reisberg, & Rumbley, 2010).

At the same time, post-secondary education has assumed a much more central role in the global knowledge economy. Universities continue their central role in educating the professions and others at the top of their societies (Ben-David & Zloczower, 1962). Post-secondary education is necessary for the much larger numbers now required for the now sophisticated knowledge-based economy, and even for jobs that at one time needed only lower levels of training. Further, the nature of skilled labour is rapidly changing as well. University based research is central for economic development. Academic institutions are key points of global communication in the digital age, and are central to the increasingly international scientific and research communities. Post-secondary education qualifications have become key to social mobility in much of the world, placing even greater pressures for the expansion of access.

Thus, post-secondary education globally has been affected by the two tidal waves of massification and the global knowledge economy. These factors have placed unprecedented pressures on the bottom sector – the mass access institutions – and at the top in the research-intensive universities that are central to the global knowledge economy. It is fair to say that no country – with the partial exceptions of the United States and Canada, the first nations to experience massification – have successfully built a coherent and effective academic system to manage the challenges of the 21st century. It is paradoxical that the world is dealing with the twin revolutions but has not managed to organize systems to effectively manage them.

Post-secondary education is central to 21st century societies in ways that far exceed earlier periods, when higher education, particularly at the university level, was the preserve of small elites. Indeed, post-secondary education is central to the success of contemporary economies – and the unrelenting demand of an expanding middle-class everywhere. It imparts necessary skills, is the central driver of the research on which much of contemporary society depends, and is a central requirement for social mobility.

2   The Role of the Research University

Our concern in this chapter is to understand the role of research-intensive universities in the complex array of post-secondary institutions. The traditional universities, at one time the only post-secondary institutions, are now only a small proportion of post-secondary institutions in any country. It is important to point out that the university sector itself has diversified, with research universities constituting only a minority of universities. Most institutions, even most universities, mainly focus on teaching, and there is a need to define the roles for different categories of universities as there is for the entire panoply of post-secondary institutions.

It is worth keeping in mind that the prominent research role for universities now prevalent emerged in the 19th century with von Humboldt's reforms at the University of Berlin (Shils, 1997). The top universities retain their prestige and centrality in educating elites and providing a large proportion of post-baccalaureate education. The university, as the oldest, most prestigious, and arguably most important post-secondary institution, has a special place in the expanding firmament of post-secondary education (Kerr, 2001). Research universities, in every country, sit on the top of the academic hierarchy and provide important services for the entire post-secondary system. They are the primary research institutions, typically the most selective in terms of both students and academic staff, are generally the largest institutions, and they have the biggest budgets.

Universities, and particularly the top research-intensive schools, are the post-secondary institutions that relate most directly to the global knowledge economy, and are the 'world-class' institutions in their countries, and recognized as such in international rankings (Altbach & Salmi, 2011). It is important to recognize that universities which emphasize research are a very small subset not only of universities but of all post-secondary institutions. For example, there may be approximately 250 research-intensive universities in the United States, out of a total of more than 4,000 academic institutions. The large proportion of research – 80 per cent or more – is produced by the small number of research universities that obtain the bulk of funding for research. The 39 Chinese universities that are part of the government-funded 985 project comprise only two per cent of all Chinese universities, but produce half of the total research output (Wang, 2017).

Similar situations exist in other countries, although relatively few have clearly identified these research-intensive institutions and funded them appropriately. In Germany and many other countries, for example, all universities by tradition have a research mission, receive funding for research and compete for additional research support. And in some nations – France, Russia and to a lesser extent Germany are examples – non-university research institutions separate from universities account for a significant proportion of research output. In the global innovation economy, universities produce a large proportion of new ideas. And, of course, their basic research leads not only to Nobel prizes but to fundamental breakthroughs in all areas.

Many countries without a clearly differentiated academic system and where most universities have a research mission have moved to create some kind of arrangement that recognizes a key research-oriented role for a small number of universities. The many excellence initiatives that have been implemented around the world have been one way to recognize and support top-tier universities. The programmes have been in part stimulated by a desire to be better represented in the global rankings, as indicated by the Russian government's support for the '5-100 Russian Academic Excellence Project', designed to help five Russian universities join the top 100 of the rankings. Similar initiatives have been undertaken in at least 37 countries, including China, Germany, France, Australia and Ireland (Salmi, 2016). These programmes have also helped to differentiate the universities chosen to participate from the others and to provide them with resources to enhance their research capacity, while limiting research funding to other institutions.

Other countries have moved to differentiate in other ways. The British government, for example, in 1992 abolished the polytechnics and gave them university status – and then slowly created a hierarchy of all the universities, recognizing the top institutions as research-intensive.

Research universities are often referred to as 'flagship universities' – a term that signifies that they provide leadership to the rest of the academic system (Douglass, 2016). This term is especially common in the United States, where most of the state systems of higher education have one or more designated flagships that receive the most research funds and are the most prestigious universities in their respective state systems. Other countries are beginning to designate flagships, often as part of various excellence initiatives (Salmi, 2016). In most cases, however, the flagship provides little systematic leadership. Rather, they are at the head of a flotilla in which the other smaller ships are aimlessly sailing, and some of which themselves seek to become flagships.

Universities, of course, are also teaching institutions. Even the most distinguished research universities offer instruction at all levels to students. The research universities produce the bulk of doctoral degrees in most countries, and are thus responsible for training the next generation of the academic profession as well as research cadres for industry and government. They also, with few exceptions, teach undergraduates. The fact is that most universities, except for the top research institutions, are mainly teaching institutions, and this must be recognized by both governments and the universities themselves. Because universities are at the top of the hierarchy of any academic system, they must provide leadership for the rest of post-secondary institutions.

Generally, research-intensive universities have no direct or even peripheral relationships with other segments of post-secondary system, although in a few countries, such as the Netherlands, there have been largely unsuccessful efforts to link research universities with other post-secondary institutions. Universities need to recognize the important roles of other post-secondary institutions and work with them to provide system-wide legitimacy, training for academic cadres for the entire academic community, and innovative ideas concerning teaching and learning. In short, universities must recognize that they are part of a linked system providing a range of educational experiences and certification in a wide range of fields and for many aspects of a modern economy and society.

3 A Key Challenge

A key challenge of the 21st century is how to organize the increasingly complex set of post-secondary institutions and to ensure that the ever more diversified needs of post-secondary education are satisfied (Task Force on Higher Education and Society, 2000; Teichler, 2002). Traditionally, when post-secondary education was largely the preserve of the elite with only a small percentage of the age group attending universities, and a larger but still modest number participating in other post-secondary vocational schools, there was little need for a complex arrangement of post-secondary institutions. Universities, in most countries, were public and funded mainly by governments. Most had considerable autonomy and most, following the Humboldtian idea, focused at least to some extent on research. Vocationally oriented institutions did not offer academic degrees but rather certificates of various kinds. In a few countries, such as Germany, the vocational sector was well integrated with industry and an integral part of the post-secondary landscape. Similarly, community colleges in the United States and polytechnics in the United Kingdom had a clear but subordinate role in post-secondary education. However, the polytechnics were abolished in the UK in 1992 and American community colleges are increasingly taking on a more academic orientation. Similarly, the universities of applied sciences in Germany, the Netherlands, Scandinavia, and elsewhere, are taking on increasing academic roles. In these cases, there has been a blurring of the distinctions between different segments of post-secondary education. In much of the world, however, vocational institutions were, and in many cases remain either quite weak or non-existent and seldom integrated into a broader post-secondary system.

With the advent of massification, enrolments and academic institutions of all kinds expanded rapidly. In much of the world, a significant part of that expansion was in the private sector. There is, in post-secondary education, immense and largely uncharted diversity – with many different kinds of institutions serving many needs. There is, however, little coordination or rational organization of these diverse institutions to meet the needs either of massification, the economy, or the requirements and goals of the millions of students, who invest their time and money in post-secondary education. Indeed, it is possible to argue that post-secondary education has become less well-organized than in the past. The incorporation of the vocationally-focused polytechnics into the British university sector, and the end of what the British referred to as the 'binary divide', actually replaced rational organization with ambiguity about the roles and missions of different post-secondary institutions.

4   Diversification – A Plethora of Providers

Post-secondary education in every country is, in the era of massification, inevitably differentiated. In other words, there are a range of different kinds of institutions offering education and training in a vast array of specializations that require some kind of advanced education. This array of institutions offers access to a growing and diverse population demanding post-secondary qualifications. In much of the world, expansion of post-secondary education occurred without any serious planning or concern for the development of a logical or integrated 'system' of post-secondary education. The jumble of institutions with different funding patterns, different goals and purposes, varying curricular and pedagogical approaches and other aspects created, in much of the world, post-secondary education anarchy – a situation that continues in many countries and does not serve either individual students or society well. Most governments are trying to catch up with expansion with quality assurance schemes, testing programmes and new regulations – but few if any have thought seriously about a rational and cost-effective organization of the entire post-secondary sector. Now, with many countries stressing 'workforce development' as a key responsibility of post-secondary education in many countries, the need to integrate all levels of post-secondary education to serve an increasingly diverse constituency is more important than ever.

In fact, it is by now quite difficult to even categorize the various elements of post-secondary institutions – and that dilemma is becoming more problematic with the expansion of online and distance providers. Traditional universities are increasingly offering distance programmes and degrees. For-profit universities are active as well. High-profile online initiatives, such as edX and Coursera, offer many courses in the MOOC (Massive Open Online Course) format, often sponsored by traditional universities. While the 'MOOC revolution', predicted by many has been slow to take off, MOOCs and other online programmes have expanded rapidly.

New actors have emerged that seek to package online and other educational experiences into degrees or certificates that provide credentials for the job market, often bypassing traditional academic institutions. Universities delivering instruction and providing certification and degrees mainly or exclusively through distance education, such as the Open University in the UK, the University of South Africa, Indira Gandhi Open University in India, and many others, are now teaching millions of students throughout the world. Yet, the distance providers are seldom fully integrated into national higher education arrangements.

5 The Revolution of the Private Sector

The private sector is now the fastest growing segment of post-secondary education worldwide. This is not the case in western Europe or North America, but is the reality in many parts of the world. For example, in Latin America, public higher education along with a small number of elite denominational private universities dominated most countries for much of the 20th century. Now, in most of the region, private sector enrolments are close to half of the total and in some cases more than half. In Japan, South Korea, Taiwan, the Philippines and several others, private institutions enrol 80 per cent of students. Private institutions are expanding rapidly in Africa and have become a significant part of the higher education sector in Europe, particularly central and eastern Europe. Private universities and other institutions can be found among all segments of post-secondary providers in many countries, but only a few have a significant number of private non-profit research universities. In almost all countries, the bulk of the private sector is 'demand absorbing', existing at the bottom of post-secondary systems and educating students who cannot gain access to more competitive and prestigious public institutions. Private institutions tend to offer programmes, such as management, information technology and many others, that link directly to the labour market and which are in demand from students.

Many new private post-secondary institutions are for-profit, either officially or de facto in countries that may not permit formal for-profit schools. The for-profit sector has been especially problematic in terms of offering quality programmes and providing adequate services to students at a fair cost. Scandals, criticism of low quality, and other problems are common in the for-profit higher education sphere. In a large number of developing countries, private 'garage universities', as they informally are called in Latin America, offer substandard qualifications of little value in the employment market. Even in the United States, some private for-profit providers have been closed by the government for low standards, financial abuses and other malfeasance. Yet, the sector continues to expand – in the US, 11 per cent of graduate students are enrolled in the for-profit sector, up from three per cent fifteen years ago, as a result, in part, of lower entrance requirements and standards.

Private post-secondary education often faces fewer restrictions in offering specific specializations, providing qualifications, or establishing institutions than is the case for public universities and colleges. However, in some countries, including Argentina, Japan and South Korea, regulations are strong and supervision tight. Private institutions must participate in local quality assurance schemes, but in many places these agencies have limited resources and authority to address problems in this sector, often finding themselves confronting powerful lobbies with political clout.

The challenge in most countries is how the private sector might contribute to the demand for higher education but regulated in a way that the public interest is protected.

6   The Crisis of Quality Assurance and Accreditation

Most countries today have mechanisms for quality assurance or accreditation to provide some measure of supervision to post-secondary education. It is, however, fair to say that in the context of mass enrolments and a wide range of institutions serving so many different needs that these arrangements are in almost all cases inadequate. These programmes reflect the global demand for accountability, originally to measure the efficiency and appropriateness of budgetary expenditures, but recently also to assess learning outcomes by students and other academic 'outputs' to demonstrate impact and effectiveness.

Accreditation and quality assurance are, of course, quite different. The former provides certification and approval for academic institutions or faculties/programmes to operate, usually but not always granted by governmental authorities. Quality assurance monitors and evaluates academic performance with the purpose of assuring students, government and wider society that institutions are providing value. Few accreditation schemes operating today operate without criticism or controversy. Massification and the resulting number, complexity and diversification of academic institutions have made quality assurance mechanisms progressively difficult to create. Worse still, the definition of quality amid so much diversity is increasingly elusive. As a result, there are few widely accepted criteria for measuring quality or effectiveness, either nationally or internationally.

7   System Design – California and Beyond

Few countries have designed effective systems of post-secondary education that provide a coherent strategy to serve the complex academic needs of the 21st Century. In 1960 California developed a plan to re-organize the state's public system of public post-secondary education known as the California Master Plan (Marginson, 2016; Ryan, 2016).

For the purpose of this discussion, there are several salient elements concerning the California Master Plan:
- The Master Plan is part of the state regulations for public higher education – passed by the legislature – and has the force of law.
- It does not affect private higher education – that sector retains full autonomy.
- The Plan created three distinct public higher education systems in California. At the base is the community college system, largely vocational in focus, but also offering academic programmes aimed at preparing students to transfer to the university sector. In the middle is the California State University System

(CSU), consisting of 23 campuses educating 460,000 students, offering baccalaureate and masters degrees. At the top is the University of California system, with 10 campuses and 238,000 students. The UC institutions are all research universities that offer undergraduate and all graduate and professional degrees.
- There is student mobility among the three systems: a student entering a community college may, assuming appropriate grades, easily transfer to a four-year CSU or a University of California campus.

The California Master Plan is an example of how one jurisdiction has managed to organize public post-secondary education with reasonable success and it has served the state for a significant period of time. California, of course, is not alone in attempting to develop policy to address the diversification and massification. A common pattern in continental Europe has been to divide public post-secondary education between traditional universities and a sector focusing more on vocationally-oriented post-secondary education – commonly referred to as universities of applied sciences. In most cases, these universities are authorized to award the same degrees as traditional universities, although in some cases with restrictions. In Germany, this sector is dominated by the highly-regarded Fachhochschulen (Wolter & Kerst, 2015). This distinction between sectors existed in the United Kingdom until 1992, when all vocationally-oriented polytechnics were upgraded to university status, blurring distinctions and creating an ambiguous post-secondary sector. Throughout Europe, it remains a challenge to differentiate among different kinds of universities where missions, programmes and degrees overlap.

8 Classification or Ranking?

How might the different kinds of post-secondary institutions be classified so that this sector can be better understood? Some turn to rankings – global, national and categorical – as a proxy for institutional types, prestige, quality and impact (Yudkevich, Altbach, & Rumbley, 2016; Hazelkorn, 2017). This is a mistake for many reasons. Rankings create a hierarchy of institutions or programmes according to specific and limited criteria. There are a wide variety of rankings, from the three main international sources: Academic Rankings of World University (the Shanghai rankings), QS and the Times Higher Education Rankings. There are also numerous national rankings.

No ranking attempts to incorporate different kinds of post-secondary institutions. Indeed, the most influential ones deal with the small proportion of research-intensive universities and largely measure research output and related themes. It would, in fact, be impossible for any ranking to deal with all categories of post-secondary education, not only because of the variations involved but because of the absence of common measurements.

Much more useful would be a classification system for post-secondary institutions that provides a logical typology of different kinds of institutions based on their missions, profile and principle activities. Such classifications would be most relevant at national levels, but they may be applied to states and provinces, and might be applied globally. A classification is not designed to rank an institution, but simply to provide useful categories, and places an institution in the appropriate group. One such classification, perhaps the only one attempted on a national scale, is the Classification of Institutions of Higher Education, first prepared by the Carnegie Foundation for the Advancement of Teaching in the United States. Developed by Clark Kerr in 1970, the original classification had the advantage of simplicity, placing institutions into a few categories, but more recent versions have added categories and subcategories, trying to capture greater levels of complexity but also making it more complex and perhaps less useful (Carnegie Foundation for the Advancement of Teaching, 1994; Indiana University Center for Postsecondary Research, 2016).

The classification of different kinds of post-secondary institutions that carefully places each institution in an appropriate category relevant to its mission and function would provide governments and the public with information to make sense out of the current and expansive range of post-secondary institutions, and also offer a basis for creating, and appropriately funding, a system of post-secondary education. The challenges of developing such a classification are considerable, and include problems of definitions, obtaining accurate data and coordination. But some system of classification is needed to make sense of the complexity of 21st century post-secondary education.

9 Diversification versus Differentiation

Post-secondary education everywhere is diverse – institutions and schools serve a wide range of purposes and clienteles. The institutions range from world-class research universities offering a wide-range of disciplines, to specialized vocational schools offering certificates in specific trades. All of these institutions constitute contemporary post-secondary education. They have in many cases emerged to meet the needs of mass enrolments and changing economies and societies worldwide. In few cases was careful planning part of the process of expansion. Thus, post-secondary education is diverse with a bewildering range of institutions.

Differentiation is a concept that implies strategy and coordination, with useful distinctions made between institutions based on their purpose. In short, differentiation is necessary and would add logic to the diversification that has taken place. It implies that the elements of a system are linked in some way, or at least coordinated. Creating a map of differentiation is not easy, but is at the same time possible by developing a typology of different types of institutions, and carefully and objectively placing them into the appropriate categories. Once a logical mapping of institutions is accomplished, it will be possible to develop ways of managing the categories of institutions, and eventually creating systems that will allow for better planning, permit linkages among institutions and students, and facilitate more effective relationships between post-secondary institutions and societal actors.

10   Blueprints for the Future

The early 21st century reflects a period of post-secondary education anarchy, at least considering the degree of expansion without effective organization, and the struggle to safeguard quality for the large – and growing – numbers of students who pursue education at this level. Yet post-secondary education is of vital importance for modern economies and societies, and strategies to organize these systems are desperately needed.

The following initiatives may help to ensure that today's academic anarchy becomes the differentiated post-secondary environment of tomorrow to better serve societal needs and support continued innovation and reform. Not all of these recommendations will be practical everywhere as the organization of academic differentiation will vary according to national realities.

- As a first step, a classification of all post-secondary institutions based on their missions and functions.
- The role of the university, as the apex institution in any academic system, must be defined and articulated. At the same time, the key role of research intensive universities as key producers of knowledge and personnel must be protected and enhanced. The research university must recognize its responsibility to the entire academic enterprise.
- The burgeoning and often problematic private post-secondary sector needs to be categorized and regulations put into place to ensure that the private sector can serve the broader public interest.
- Quality assurance is necessary for a differentiated academic environment to ensure that students are adequately served. Quality assurance must, on the

one hand, be simple and practical to implement, and on the other cognizant that the criteria must accommodate all types of institutions.
- Distance education institutions will inevitably be part of a mass post-secondary environment and must be effective integrated.
- These and other arrangements are necessary to manage the new realities of post-secondary massification.

References

Altbach, P. G., Reisberg, L., & Rumbley, L. E. (2010). *Trends in global higher education: Tracking an academic revolution.* Rotterdam, The Netherlands: Sense Publishers.

Altbach, P. G., & Salmi, J. (Eds.). (2011). *The road to academic excellence: The making of world-class research universities.* Washington, DC: The World Bank.

Ben-David, J., & Zloczower, A. (1962). Universities and academic systems in modern societies. *European Journal of Sociology, 3*(1), 45–84.

Carnegie Foundation for the Advancement of Teaching. (1994). *A classification of institutions of higher education* (1994 edition). Princeton, NJ: Carnegie Foundation for the Advancement of Teaching.

Clark, B. R. (1983). *The higher education system: Academic organization in cross-national perspective.* Berkeley, CA: University of California Press.

Douglass, J. A. (2016). *The new flagship university: The paradigm from global ranking to national relevancy.* New York, NY: Palgrave Macmillan.

Hazelkorn, E. (2017). *Global rankings and the geopolitics of higher education: Understanding the influence and impact of rankings on higher education, policy, and society.* London: Routledge.

Indiana University Center for Postsecondary Research. (2016). *Carnegie classifications 2015 public data file.* Retrieved November 30, 2016, from http://carnegieclassifications.iu.edu/downloads/CCIHE2015-PublicDataFile.xlsx

Kerr, C. (2001). *The uses of the university.* Cambridge, MA: Harvard University Press.

Marginson, S. (2016). *The dream is over: The crisis of Clark Kerr's California idea on higher education.* Berkeley, CA: University of California Press.

Ryan, A. (2016). The California dream is still golden. *Times Higher Education, 2246*, 33–37.

Salmi, J. (2016). Excellence strategies and the creation of world-class universities. In N. C. Liu, Y. Cheng, & Q. Wang (Eds.), *Matching visibility and performance: A standing challenge for world-class universities.* Rotterdam, The Netherlands: Sense Publishers.

Shils, E. (1997). Universities since 1900: A historical perspective. In E. Shils (Ed.), *The order of learning: Essays on the contemporary university.* New Brunswick, NJ: Transaction.

Task Force on Higher Education and Society. (2000). *Higher education in developing countries: Peril and promise*. Washington, DC: The World Bank.

Teichler, U. (2002). Diversification of higher education and the profile of the individual institution. *Higher Education Management and Policy, 14*(3), 177–188.

Wang, Q. (2017). A differentiated post-secondary education system in Mainland China. In P. G. Altbach, L. Reisberg, & H. de Wit (Eds.), *Responding to massification: Differentiation in postsecondary education worldwide* (pp. 63–74). Rotterdam, The Netherlands: Sense Publishers.

Wolter, A., & Kerst, C. (2015). The 'academization' of the German qualification system: Recent developments in the relationships between vocation training and higher education in Germany. *Research in Comparative and International Education, 10*(4), 51.

Yudkevich, M., Altbach, P. G., & Rumbley, L. E. (Eds.). (2016). *The global academic rankings game: Changing institutional policy, practice, academic life*. New York, NY: Routledge.

CHAPTER 4

World-Class Universities in a Post-Truth World

Pierre de Maret and Jamil Salmi

Abstract

Under the influence of the international rankings, many universities have made great strides to transform themselves into world-class institutions in the past two decades. A few governments have even set up new universities from scratch, with the avowed objective of achieving world-class status in an accelerated fashion. The strength of these universities is usually measured by the superior qualifications of their graduates and the intensity of their leading-edge research.

However, in a post-truth world where fake news and alternative facts challenge the credibility of scientific expertise, it becomes urgent to scrutinize the ethical and social responsibility of world-class universities. What role must they play in promoting critical thinking and constructing harmonious societies? This chapter explores how world-class universities can impact the tertiary education landscape in a positive way and contribute to the global common good, notwithstanding the growing lack of trust in scientific evidence.

Keywords

World-class universities – post-truth – scientific evidence – Shanghai principles

1 Introduction: A Time of Paradoxes

Post-truth: 'relating to or denoting circumstances in which objective facts are less influential in shaping public opinion than appeals to emotion and personal belief'. (Oxford Dictionary of English)

In today's post-truth world, paradoxes have reached a paroxysm. Inequality increases just as our societies reach unprecedented levels of affluence. Economic wealth is growing but we are facing widening disparities between the rich and the poor. According to Oxfam, 82 per cent of the wealth created in 2017 went to one per cent of the richest people on the planet.

Second, as we become members of knowledge-based societies, a feeling of disempowerment is spreading among large parts of the population, including scientists. This is happening even though knowledge and information are increasing exponentially. Over 6,800 scientific journal articles are published daily – more than 2.5 million a year. We suffer from information overload; data seeking and comparing have become fundamental activities in nearly every aspect of our lives. We can get responses to hundreds of questions: 'what is the best restaurant in town?', or 'what is the best price for a dishwasher?', or 'which country has the highest level of happiness?', or 'what is the extent of inequality in country X?' At the same time, we experience a growing inability to anticipate situations in a rapidly evolving world, to commit to significant change, or simply to make our voice heard.

Government and major companies invest colossal sums to expand higher education and advance knowledge, but public trust in experts has been compromised. Debate among specialists with dissenting views generates more questions than answers. Many experts are aware of the limits of their knowledge, as doubt is part of scientific reasoning. As the cognitive bias known in psychology as the Dunning-Kruger Effect shows, for scientists, 'the more you know, the more likely you are to see how little you know' (Kruger & Dunning, 1999). The opposite is of course also true. The less you know, the less able you are to recognize how little you know, so the less likely you are to recognize your errors and shortcomings. Or, as Bertrand Russell said: 'the whole problem of the world is that fools and fanatics are always so certain of themselves, but wiser people so full of doubts'.

This trend is exacerbated by the fact that previously, knowledge was mostly disseminated through a limited number of channels that were held accountable for their content, while today, in a world of blogging, tweeting and instant messages, everybody's views are assumed to be equally valid and worth considering. Thus, we live in a time of 'information war', with the proliferation of fake news, hoaxes, rumours, conspiracy theories and, last but not least, alternative facts. As we know, the latter expression was originally coined by President Trump's spokesperson after the release of photos comparing the turnout at his inauguration in January 2017 with Obama's in January 2009.

Conspiracy theories have always existed. Conspiracy thinking arises when people faced with complex issues choose to believe a simple – but false – explanation of who to blame. Often, conspiracy theories are more amusing than the honest, but often complicated, truth. Today's social media, with their algorithms based on artificial intelligence, create 'echo chambers' that play an important role in spreading false rumours. In addition, professional fake news writers and disseminators are flourishing and can often be manipulated by foreign interests. Thus, the realization that two-thirds of adults living in the United States are on Facebook and 45 per cent get their main news from it is a matter of deep concern. All the more so as social media are not scrutinized like traditional media as part of regular fact-checking policies and practices in the traditional press.

A related paradox is that, although the proportion of educated people in the population has never been as large as today – the average proportion of adults age 25–34 with a tertiary education qualification having grown from 26 per cent in 2000 to 43 per cent in 2016 in OECD countries, fewer and fewer people are interested in participating in democratic elections, either voting or running for office. Faced with a maelstrom of fake news and contradictory information, voters are unsure of what to believe and make increasingly irrational decisions, following the exhortations of demagogues who appeal to their raw emotions rather than their reason. Misinformation undermines democracy and leads to dramatic policy shifts that may adversely affect the very people who have supported the policy changes. The 2016 referendum vote in the United Kingdom to leave the European Union, the negative vote in the 2016 peace referendum in Colombia and the election of President Trump also in 2016 are the most recent examples in that respect. In the latter case, the attempts by the Republican administration to curtail health care access and benefits are likely to affect, to a large extent, the voter base of the Republican Party.

The academic sphere is not exempt from these negative trends, considering the multiple instances of academic dishonesty reported by the press and the quality assurance agencies. The number of denunciations and retractions due to fraud and plagiarism has never been as high, even in countries reputed for their integrity. In Germany alone, two ministers had to resign because of plagiarism, first the Federal Minister of Defence in 2011 and then, ironically, the Federal Minister of Education in 2013. In 2013, 54 current or former members of the Pakistani Parliament were found to have fake degrees.[1]

The fact that some experts have undisclosed vested interests in the companies that finance their research also contributes to undermining the credibility of scientists and experts in general. Education has failed to instil in political and business leaders a sense of values that would prevent them from erring. As CS Lewis said: 'Education without values, as useful as it is, seems rather to make man a more clever devil'. The worldwide Corruption Perception Index published by Transparency International is telling from that point of view.

Notwithstanding this post-truth context, world-class universities still need to deal with pressing global challenges, such as climate change, migration, global epidemics, a turbulent world economy, financial instability, increased inequality, global trafficking and terrorism, to name a few.

2 Rise of the World-Class University: For Better or for Worse?

Where is the wisdom we have lost in knowledge?
Where is the knowledge we have lost in information? (T.S. Elliot)

As shown in Figure 4.1, the superior results of world-class universities – highly sought graduates, leading-edge research, and dynamic technology transfer – can essentially be attributed to three complementary sets of factors at play in these top universities: concentration of talent, abundant resources and favourable governance (Salmi, 2009). International rankings (such as ARWU, THE, and QS) are commonly relied upon to identify which universities make the cut, on the assumption that world-class universities can be found among the top 100.

Even though the list of top universities has remained fairly stable over the past fifteen years, rankings are published yearly, giving the impression that significant changes happen from one year to the other. In real life, however, it

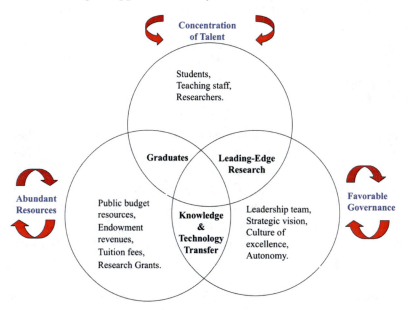

FIGURE 4.1 Characteristics of world-class universities: Alignment of key factors

is unlikely that a relatively bad university will become good within one year; and similarly, a relatively good university will not plummet in a twelve-month span. When the University of Malaya, Malaysia's flagship university, lost almost a hundred positions in the ranking between 2006 and 2007, the collapse was in fact due to a major change in the methodology used by THE. Ironically, the incident almost sparked a national crisis. Parliament called for a commission of inquiry and the vice-chancellor had to resign (Salmi, 2009).

Rankings have become news, often making the headlines and influencing national policies. For some, ranking has become a big business. As yearly rankings tend to be repetitive, some of the rankers are tempted to make the news by producing a never-ending series of new categories of rankings: 'youngest great university', 'university with best employment prospect', 'best university in Asia, in Latin America, etc.'. Rankings are thus in danger of also becoming themselves a new kind of 'fake news'.

The proliferation of rankings does not mean that the methodological flaws that characterize them are disappearing; quite the opposite. Are they measuring all dimensions of performance besides research output, or are they mainly selling international visibility? The reputational surveys used by THE and QS appear to be fraught with subjectivity and, in any case, lack transparency about the methodology applied and the reliability of the respondents (Hazelkorn, 2017).

In addition, rankings fail to measure fundamental dimensions of the role of universities, such as the importance of respecting and instilling ethical principles and operating as socially inclusive and engaged institutions of higher learning. So, one of the missing questions that rankings should raise is whether the graduates are well prepared ethically. After the 2007–2008 financial crisis, many voices challenged the lack of emphasis on corporate responsibility in the programs of business schools.

> American business schools trained many of the people who had their hands on the tiller when the nation's economic ship ran aground. Now, those in leadership positions at top schools are asking themselves what degree of responsibility they bear. The schools had critics before the economic crisis cost millions of Americans their jobs and their retirement savings. Now, the critics are louder, and the questions they raise are being taken more seriously. 'This is a time of great introspection for this institution', says Jay Light, dean of the Harvard Business School.[2]

A recent study undertaken in Colombia, South America, is quite telling in that regard. The think tank that led this investigation looked at the highest degree obtained by 110 famous politicians or business people who had been charged with corruption or other serious crimes in the previous two years and correlated that with the university where they studied in Colombia. Table 4.1 shows the top universities appearing in this kind of 'corruption ranking' from the viewpoint of their graduates, together with the academic excellence ranking prepared by the Colombian Ministry of Education (MIDE ranking).

It is of concern to observe that the top three ranked universities, according to the Government of Colombia's own ranking of academic excellence, are respectively number three, five and seven in the corruption ranking. Table 4.2 shows the professions with the highest concentration of corrupt

TABLE 4.1 Corruption ranking and excellence ranking in Colombia (2017)

University	Corruption ranking	Excellence ranking	Status
Universidad Externado de Colombia	1	15	Private
Universidad Pontificia Javeriana	2	7	Private
Universidad Los Andes	3	1	Private
Universidad Santo Tómas	4	49	Private
Universidad Nacional de Colombia	5	2	Public
Universidad Libre	5	50–100	Private
Universidad del Rosario	7	3	Private
Universidad de Antioquia	8	6	Public
Universidad del Norte	8	11	Private

SOURCE: OBSERVATORIO DE LA UNIVERSIDAD (2017)

TABLE 4.2 Most corrupt professions in Colombia (2017)

Profession	Percentage
Lawyers	43%
Business, Finance, Economics and Accounting	28%
Engineers and Architects	16%
Doctors and Dentists	7%
Humanities	5%
Hard Sciences	1%

SOURCE: OBSERVATORIO DE LA UNIVERSIDAD (2017)

people. This example demonstrates that the search for excellence is not good enough and that universities need to pay more attention to the ethical aspects of education.

Another important aspect is to ascertain the extent to which research in world-class universities remains impartial and unbiased. Are world-class universities able to remain intellectually independent from the political and business world that contributes to their funding? How do they act to prevent or punish academic dishonesty?

A third major issue is the degree to which world-class universities are socially inclusive. By their very nature, most world-class universities tend to be highly selective. The Indian Institutes of Technology are the most competitive institutions in the world, with an admission rate of about 1 out of 100 candidates. Ivy League universities in the United States tend to admit one for every 10 or one for every 15 candidates. Not surprisingly, these selective universities end up having a low proportion of students from disadvantaged groups. Table 4.3, which contrasts the proportion of Pell Grants beneficiaries enrolled in selective and less selective top US universities, offers concrete evidence of the lack of inclusion of many world-class universities.[3] At the same time, these universities run considerable budget surpluses year after year, which would allow them to offer

TABLE 4.3   Proportion of low-income students in top US universities

More inclusive universities	Proportion of Pell Grant recipients	Less inclusive universities	Proportion of Pell Grant recipients
University of California-Los Angeles	35.9%	Stanford University	15.6%
University of California-Berkeley	31.4%	University of Pennsylvania	14.4%
University of Southern California	23.4%	Duke University	14.0%
Ohio State University-Columbus	22.4%	Northwestern University	14.0%
New York University	21.5%	Harvard University	13.0%
Columbia University	21.4%	Yale University	11.9%
University of Missouri-Columbia	21.4%	California Institute of Technology	11.3%
University of North Carolina-Chapel Hill	21.3%	University of Notre Dame	11.2%

SOURCE: CARNEVALE AND VAN DER WERF (2017)

more scholarships and grants to low-income students. Between 2012 and 2015, for example, Harvard's average annual surplus amounted to $1.2 billion, Yale's was $970 million and Stanford's $840 million (Carnevale & van der Werf, 2017).

> At almost one-third of the nation's 500 most selective colleges and universities, less than 20 percent of students receive a Pell Grant. A recent report found that 38 elite colleges had more students from the families in the top 1 percent of incomes than from families in the bottom 60 percent of incomes. (Carnevale & van der Werf, 2017, p. 2)

The rankings should ask a series of key questions about world-class universities that are currently ignored. Do world-class universities foster engaged learning experiences, such as critical thinking, connecting disciplines and applying knowledge to the real world? Are their academic partnerships driven by solidarity? Are the investments made by their endowments socially responsible? Is their campus environmentally sustainable? Is it a 'green campus'?

Over the years, ranking has fuelled a fierce competition for talent. Universities try to lure away top professors, star researchers and the best students from anywhere in the world. More than ever, 'publish or perish' has become the driving force of world-class universities, sometimes encouraging fraud at all levels. A growing number of universities are planning (or sometimes playing) the ranking in order to climb a few positions up, to the point that some universities now have a so-called ranking officer to advise the leadership team and influence the university's strategic plan. But it is unlikely that ranking officers will help improve the ethical and social issues raised here.

3   Universities in a Danger Zone

> Without university there is no science. Without science there is no future.
> (Carlos Andradas, Rector of Complutense University)

In a globalized, complex context, universities are facing increasing risks. Competitive forces driving change in higher education are creating a global marketplace. The risk is indeed that world-class universities are driven by the market and the never-ending search for additional funds, rather than by their own sense of higher purpose. In recent decades, the public image of the university has changed. Seen for a long time as a temple of knowledge where dedicated researchers are serving science, it has become more and more a marketplace with customers and stakeholders, more concerned with funding than with improving knowledge. The university has lost part of its standing and this has generated a decline in people's trust in academic expertise.

Even more worrisome is the wariness that government authorities have shown towards universities. This has had two serious consequences. First, in several countries, top universities have experienced significantly reduced public funding. In the United States, for instance, under the dual influence of the financial crisis and the perception that universities are bastions of liberal thinkers, Republican legislatures in states as diverse as Arizona, Colorado, Oregon and Virginia, have cut annual budgets to state flagship universities to no more than 10 per cent of its annual revenue.

Second, from Hungary to Turkey, to China and Russia, authoritarian rulers are imposing growing restrictions on academic freedom in their public universities. Even academic freedom in Hong Kong universities has been under threat in recent years, as documented by a new report:

> Although academic work in Hong Kong remains considerably freer than in the rest of the People's Republic of China, these trends suggest that elements of academic control in place elsewhere in China are gradually being incorporated into the Hong Kong system, threatening the city's academic freedom and thus its universities' reputations. (Sharma, 2018)

In Russia, the press has reported pressure on public university students to show their support for President Putin (Osipian, 2018). The authorities in St Petersburg have also forced the closure of the independent private European University, renowned for its high teaching and research standards.

The influence of what has been called the 'ranking model' and its questionable effects have also come under scrutiny. A recent article published in Times Higher Education questioned the actual impact of the state's investment in higher education on the development of Singapore (Fong & Lim, 2017). The four research universities in Singapore have steadily climbed in the international rankings, but observers have wondered about the actual benefits for Singapore. The above-mentioned article questions the extent to which the presence of the universities has improved the economic performance of the country. The high proportion of foreign students attracted to these universities does not mean that the foreign graduates remain in the country to contribute to Singapore's development. There are few incentives to do research on locally relevant topics, as in order to publish in the best journals, academics must address research questions of global interest. The model also relies heavily on expensive foreign faculty, to the point that one may wonder if such a model is financially or politically sustainable in the long term. The Singapore example illustrates some of the more pressing challenges that universities are facing. This situation makes it all the more important to reaffirm the contribution of world-class universities to the global public good.

4 World-Class Universities and the Global Public Good

The populist rage identifies the university with the 'establishment'. Indeed, in today's world of growing inequalities, universities stand obviously with the elite, as they remain in the mind of many inaccessible for financial and cultural reasons. A university degree is also generally a prerequisite for better paid jobs and higher responsibilities. In addition, universities not only play a role in the reproduction of the elite, but they even proclaim themselves as 'elite institutions', and this is of course particularly true for world-class universities. Faced with the deep-rooted rejections of the elite and elitism, what can world-class universities do to overcome this new avatar of the Ivory Tower syndrome? Universities often appear to be 'self-serving' and must do a better job of explaining their role and their contribution to society. They ought to do more to answer the concerns of citizens with regards to unemployment and inequality, as the following comments from a Cambridge taxi driver illustrate:

> In May 2017, a taxi driver brought me from Clare College to the Cambridge train station. This was after a meeting with LERU rectors (League of European Research Universities), who had just been discussing the threats and challenges to our research universities as a result of Brexit. However, the taxi driver confronted me with a completely different view. In the 20 minutes of this drive, she talked non-stop and made comments on the city of Cambridge and the landmarks we passed. But unintentionally, she very nicely captured the difference between the academic world and her world, in which she was forced to cope with completely different challenges than our universities.

> At some point, she commented on the booming business in Cambridge. She told me that the university was instrumental therein: many of the staff and faculty were looking for housing, among them many foreigners. That was the reason, she said, that she was forced to live at a one-hour-driving distance from Cambridge, because housing in Cambridge was much too expensive due to the high demand.

'These people', she said, 'complain about housing prices by putting a manifesto in Latin on houses that are being built for a price of £1 million or more, whereas we don't profit at all from the booming business'. She further summarized the world of a Cambridge taxi driver in a few words: local, no access to higher education due to high tuition fees. Her 'facts' were generated on social media. The feeling which spoke out of her words: 'We are not protected in a globalizing world, we are losing out to others, we are not participating in prosperity'. (van der Zwaan, 2018)

In order to address these kinds of concerns, world-class universities should pave the way by showing how to do better with the following key dimensions of their role:
– Inclusion and diversity;
– Preparation of ethical professionals and committed citizens;
– Relevant research;
– Improved communication channels;
– Engagement with society and the world; and
– Environmental responsibility.

With respect to inclusion and diversity, universities should pay more attention to recruiting students from across the socio-economic and cultural spectrum. Many studies have shown that diversity among students and staff improves the teaching and learning experience and fosters tolerance and open-mindedness. To achieve greater inclusion of low-income students, world-class universities should emulate the needs-blind admission process of some Ivy League universities, which enables them to admit a relatively high percentage of low-income students. Such policies are of course easier to implement for those institutions that have a large endowment fund, although wealth is not always synonymous with generosity.

In spelling out their inclusion and diversity policy, world-class universities should not overlook the growing importance of adult learners. Recent studies have shown that, among Ivy League universities, less than one per cent of students are adults returning to study after some professional work experience. In the context of a fast-changing working environment, world-class universities must pay more attention to life-long learning and offer a variety of programs, from career change degrees to short-term training programmes, such as 'micro-degrees'.

World-class universities should do much more to instil ethical principles in students and faculty, and to ensure that socially responsible values are built into the curriculum. Academics must systematically think about the consequences of what they teach, notably in all areas linked to the spread of new technologies. In that context, a number of universities in the United States have taken the initiative to offer new courses on ethics and various aspects of technology, such as computer science and artificial intelligence.

> The medical profession has an ethic: First, do no harm. Silicon Valley has an ethos: build it first and ask for forgiveness later. Now, in the wake of fake news and other troubles at tech companies, universities that helped produce some of Silicon Valley's top technologists are hustling to bring a more medicine-like morality to computer science. This semester, Harvard University and the Massachusetts Institute of Technology are jointly offering a new course on the ethics and regulation of artificial intelligence. The University of Texas at Austin just introduced a course titled 'Ethical Foundations of Computer Science' – with the idea of eventually requiring it for all computer science majors. (Singer, 2018)

In this process, the favourable governance enjoyed by world-class universities is a key factor by offering a framework that is both supportive and regulatory, and that can foster vision, excellence and academic freedom in a responsible way.

World-class universities are very good at conducting excellent 'blue sky' research but should focus more on promoting research that solves real problems and addresses global challenges. When looking at the seventeen Sustainable Development Goals adopted by the General Assembly of the United Nations in September 2015, it is clear that world-class universities can have an impact on almost every one of them (Table 4.4).

A recent 'Climate Change Coalition' initiative, announced by the University of California president, Janet Napolitano, brings together the research efforts of 13 leading Canadian, Mexican and US universities committed to pooling their scientific knowledge and resources in this area.[4] A number of universities have also made efforts to divest from fossil fuels to be consistent with their actions on behalf of a cleaner environment. In the United Kingdom, for example, the University of Edinburgh, the University of Sussex and the School of Oriental and African Studies pledged to sell all their investment in oil, gas and coal companies (Holder, 2008).

Of course, in the post-truth world, or the post-fact world according to Fukuyama (2017), the spread of critical thinking is absolutely essential. Universities have the responsibility to teach how to distinguish real evidence from fabricated information. Truth-seeking skills should be at the core of every curriculum and are the foundation of a true liberal arts education. As populist politicians and demagogues appeal more to emotion than reason in their speech, one should strongly reaffirm the relevance of the traditional rhetoric and teach

TABLE 4.4   Contribution of universities to the sustainable development goals

SDGS	Preparation of skilled professionals	Knowledge generation, adaptation & diffusion	Institutional development & capacity building	Values & citizenship skills
1. Poverty ended	X	X	X	X
2. Sustainable agriculture to end hunger	X	X	X	
3. Healthy lives	X	X	X	X
4. Inclusive & equitable quality education	X	X	X	X
5. Achieve gender equality	X		X	X
6. Water & sanitation for all	X	X	X	X
7. Sustainable energy	X	X	X	
8. Inclusive & sustainable economic growth	X	X	X	
9. Resilient infrastructure	X	X	X	
10. Reduced inequality	X			X
11. Sustainable cities	X	X	X	X
12. Sustainable consumption & production		X		X
13. Managed climate change		X	X	X
14. Sustainable marine resources	X	X	X	X
15. Sustainable use of terrestrial systems	X	X	X	X
16. Peaceful & inclusive societies		X	X	X
17. Global partnership for sustainable development			X	X

SOURCE: SALMI (2017)

it correctly. Epideictic, the branch of rhetoric that deals with praise and blame by playing on emotions, should get more attention, as it explains why emotion and private belief can be manipulated in order to prevail over reason and fact.

> If a government or a company knows the destination and sequence of all of your searches, it is virtually inside your mind. The possibilities are frightening, and the vistas for oppression unbounded. The digital age, originally sold to us as empowering, could yet become the greatest threat to free thought and democracy in history. The very idea of something going viral is an expression of the mob more than of the individual. The fact that Google partially ranks search results in terms of how many other sites have linked to them reinforces groupthink, not individuality. The entire logic of the Web works toward popularity, not quality, and certainly not toward truth. Never before have we had to fight for democracy and individual rights as now in this new and – in some sense – dark age of technology. We must realize that the fight for democracy is synonymous with the fight for objectivity. (Kaplan, 2018)

More generally, research should focus on the perverse effect of social networks, and on their influence in pushing people to vote sometimes against their own interests. Teaching should focus on opening the mind of students to the wider world and other cultures and help them to be comfortable with an ever-changing future.

Inside the university, it is important to reinstate the academic tradition of free and fair debate that has been undermined by relativism and political correctness. World-class universities are well-placed to offer a safe space to assess different views but also to engage outside of the university in public debates on complex issues. To deal with the latter, multi-disciplinary perspectives are often needed and universities are one of the few places that have the means to provide the expertise, to nourish reflection, and to influence policies on the basis of facts and scientific evidence. As van der Zwaan (2017, p. 182) puts it, 'In the future, the university may well derive its most important form of legitimacy from its visibility and leadership in society. Despite the fact that public discourse is showing less and less interest in complexity, tackling complex problems is one of the university's key strengths'.

> ...It is essential that universities clearly establish a position in the societal debate. There will be an increasing need for indisputable facts, and institutions with the authority to provide them. But in order to do this successfully in the 'post-fact' era, universities must be aware of the gap

between the higher- and lower-educated. This gap can only be bridged through adequate outreach: not only by stating the facts, but also putting them in context and interpreting them in a broad range of different ways. This includes directly liaising with the media, but also extends to raising awareness and providing information at various different levels, such as through academic hubs and museums or by organizing debates. The university must look for ways to successfully approach sections of the population which have long stopped reading the paper or watching television, but which predominantly or exclusively get their information from social media.

On the whole, world-class universities should use multiple channels to communicate with the outside world, both locally and globally, to reach a larger audience and demonstrate higher education's contribution to the public good at various levels. A good example of such undertaking is the Lorne-Trottier Public Science Symposium Series, launched by McGill University in 2016, to communicate science responsibly to the public in this 'Age of Anxiety'.[5] In this perspective, world-class universities do not only respond to society's needs but they also help to shape them. It is thus important that they keep their intellectual independence as they are in the front line for 'debunking fake news'. In order to protect their credibility, they must also maintain their intellectual autonomy and be transparent about conflicts of interest.

Finally, it is crucial to recognize that, notwithstanding the competition exacerbated by the rankings, solidarity is a core value of university life. It is the essence of collegiality. Over the centuries, it has fostered the exchange of ideas, the mobility of researchers and joint undertakings. The competition inherent in the rankings phenomenon should not come at the expense of collaboration among responsible universities. World-class universities can equally promote excellence through cooperation and solidarity.

5   Conclusion

A university is not about results in the next quarter, it is not even about who a student has become by graduation. It is about learning that molds a lifetime; learning that transmits the heritage of millennia; learning that shapes the future…. Universities make commitments to the timeless, and these investments have yields we cannot predict and often cannot measure…[that] we pursue…in part 'for their own sake', because they define what has over centuries made us human, not because they can enhance our global competitiveness. (Inaugural speech of Drew Faust, president of Harvard University, 2007)

World-class universities are increasingly under threat in the post-truth world. With global visibility comes global responsibility. World-class universities all over the world should work together as a network for the public good. They must succeed in meeting international standards while being deeply committed to their local environment. As they engage in socially useful learning and relevant knowledge creation, they should also preserve a space where free debate and dissent are welcome. The 'Ivory Tower' could thus morph into a 'Beacon of Hope' and contribute to diminishing the inequalities and the frustration they generate at the local and national level, while contributing to a fairer and more sustainable planet.

From that perspective, we propose a code of conduct for world-class universities in the form of five 'Shanghai Principles', to commemorate the place where this proposal was made for the first time. The Shanghai principles are defined as follows:

- *Inclusiveness.* Academic excellence should become more inclusive rather than continuing to be exclusive because of unnecessary selection mechanisms. Following the example of Arizona State University and the top universities that have a needs-blind admission policy, world-class universities must find ways of welcoming an increasingly diverse student population by removing the financial and monetary barriers that prevent qualified applicants from vulnerable groups from accessing and succeeding in world-class universities.
- *Ethics.* World-class universities should place a strong emphasis on ethical values and behaviours to promote honesty, tolerance and solidarity. For this purpose, it is not sufficient to design one course on ethics that all students should take. Positive values should permeate all academic programmes and become part of the institutional culture of world-class universities. In that spirit, Uzbekistan has just announced plans to set up a new university dedicated to developing scholarly knowledge about Islam and promoting an atmosphere of religious tolerance in the country and beyond in Central Asia. The initiative is worth noting, considering that the five states of Central Asia have provided the largest proportion of foreign fighter recruits for ISIS in recent years (Sawahel, 2018).
- *Objectivity.* An essential responsibility of world-class universities is to promote critical thinking and generate a quasi-obsession for fact-finding among its academics and students. Teaching, learning and research must be conducted in a scientific way, with great emphasis on objective methods of reasoning and inquiry. World-class universities must champion honest communication about what can be legitimately claimed as truthful.
- *Relevance.* Research undertaken by world-class universities must address global challenges, including but not limited to food, health, energy, climate

change, the environment and security. A useful framework to guide research priority setting in that respect is to use the seventeen Sustainable Development Goals agreed upon by the United Nations in September 2015 as a filter.[6]
- *Global Collaboration.* The race to secure a higher position in the international rankings has pushed world-class universities to compete with each other in a compulsive manner. World-class universities should rather act as a community of institutions and scholars cooperating for the global good. In that way, they would be following the positive example of the Talloires Network, an international association of institutions committed to strengthening the civic roles and social responsibilities of universities.[7]

Notes

1 https://www.dawn.com/news/798822
2 https://www.npr.org/templates/story/story.php?storyId=103719186
3 Pell Grants are the main federal financial-assistance program for low-income students in the United States. The recipients can use their Pell Grant for tuition or other college-related costs. About two of every five undergraduate students receive a Pell Grant.
4 http://www.climateactionprogramme.org/news/13-top-universities-form-climate-change-coalition
5 https://www.mcgill.ca/oss/trottier-symposium
6 https://sustainabledevelopment.un.org/?menu=1300
7 http://talloiresnetwork.tufts.edu/

References

Carnevale, A. P., & van der Werf, M. (2017). *The 20% solution: Selective colleges can afford to admit more pell grant recipients.* Washington, DC: Georgetown University Center on Education and the Work Force.

Fong, P. E., & Lim, L. (2017, August 24). Singapore's fling with global stars sidelines local talent. *Times Higher Education.* Retrieved April 5, 2018, from https://www.timeshighereducation.com/opinion/singapores-fling-global-stars-sidelines-local-talent

Fukuyama, F. (2017, January 12). The emergence of a post-fact world. *Project Syndicate.* Retrieved April 5, 2018, from https://www.project-syndicate.org/onpoint/the-emergence-of-a-post-fact-world-by-francis-fukuyama-2017-01

Hazelkorn, E. (2017). *Global rankings and the geopolitics of higher education: Understanding the influence and impact of rankings on higher education, policy, and society.* London: Routledge.

Holder, M. (2018, February 9). Degrees of change: Edinburgh and SOAS universities ditch fossil fuels. *Business Green.* Retrieved April 5, 2018, from https://www.businessgreen.com/bg/news/3026127/degrees-of-change-edinburgh-soas-and-sussex-universities-ditch-fossil-fuels

Kaplan, R. D. (2018, March 2). Everything here is fake. *The Washington Post.* Retrieved April 5, 2018, from https://www.washingtonpost.com/opinions/everything-here-is-fake/2018/03/02/064a3d4a-18c6-11e8-8b08-027a6ccb38eb_story.html?utm_term=.67d2d9799d26

Kruger, J., & Dunning, D. (1999). Unskilled and unaware of it: How difficulties in recognizing one's own incompetence lead to inflated self-assessments. *Journal of Personality and Social Psychology, 77*(6), 1121–1134.

Observatorio de la Universidad. (2017). *Consulted on 17 april 2017.* Retrieved April 5, 2018, from http://www.universidad.edu.co/index.php/noticias/14583-las-universidades-colombianas-en-las-que-estudiaron-los-cuestionados-y-acusados-de-corrupcion

Osipian, A. (2018, February 2). Students under pressure as Putin runs for re-election. *University World News.* Retrieved April 5, 2018, from http://www.universityworldnews.com/article.php?story=20180131095131957

Salmi, J. (2009). *The challenge of establishing world-class universities.* Washington, DC: The World Bank.

Salmi, J. (2017). *The tertiary education imperative: Skills, knowledge and values for development.* Rotterdam, The Netherlands: Sense Publishers.

Sawahel, M. (2018, February 23). Islamic universities have role in fighting extremism. *University World News.* Retrieved April 5, 2018, from http://www.universityworldnews.com/article.php?story=2018022307312293

Sharma, Y. (2018, January 28). Academic freedom is facing 'growing threats'. *University World News.* Retrieved April 5, 2018, from http://www.universityworldnews.com/article.php?story=20180126115034644

Singer, N. (2018, February 12). Tech's ethical 'dark side': Harvard, Stanford and others want to address it. *New York Times.* Retrieved April 5, 2018, from https://www.nytimes.com/2018/02/12/business/computer-science-ethics-courses.html

van der Zwaan, B. (2017). *Higher education in 2040: A global approach.* Amsterdam: Amterdam University Press.

van der Zwaan, B. (2018). The story of the Cambridge taxi driver and the future of the university. In L. E. Weber & H. Newby (Eds.), *The future of the university in a polarizing world* (pp. 205–215). Geneva: Association Glion Colloquium.

CHAPTER 5

Examining Rankings and Strategic Planning: Variations in Local Commitments

Jenny J. Lee, Hillary Vance and Bjørn Stensaker

Abstract

This chapter examines the ways that the third mission is reflected in university strategic plans and compares these strategies between ranked and unranked institutions. Based on over 70 university strategic plans across over 30 countries, the findings identify notable differentiation between ranked and unranked universities. Ranked universities' strategic plans with regard to their third mission are mostly globally and regionally contextualized, while unranked institutions are more frequently mentioned and more locally oriented.

Keywords

Strategic planning – third mission – university rankings

1   Introduction

Those that study global rankings are arguing that this proliferating phenomenon is structuring the field of higher education in unprecedented ways. The argument is that ranked research universities throughout the world are almost trapped by the rankings and that they have ended up in an 'iron cage' where the race for status and prestige is impossible to escape (Hazelkorn, 2015). While there is considerable empirical evidence that rankings do have effects on the strategic choices of universities, the question remains as to whether rankings also have normative effects beyond those being ranked. The question is important and analytical as it is possible to imagine that institutional status may be achieved through various means and ways, and that there might exist several routes to high status (Benneworth, 2013; Jongbloed, Enders, & Salerno, 2008; Marginson, 2016).

However, an unanswered question is whether the search for status implies that institutions have to make strategic choices that also eliminate part of their societal role and responsibility (Marginson, 2016). For example, is it the case that status seeking institutions always have to adhere to dominating global ideas that are transmitted through the global rankings, or are institutions able and willing to prioritize local commitments and local communities as well? This question is important in that there is increasing political interest in the roles and responsibilities institutions of higher education are making to their societies and communities in the areas of regional development, innovation, community service, societal outreach, etc. (Nedeva, 2007; Montesinos, Carot, Martinez, & Mora, 2008).

Thus, we argue that studying 'third missions' – the local and societal contributions of universities to society – are an important task as it is closely related to the changing role of the university, not least due to the status pressure created by global rankings. The current chapter contributes to this debate by investigating the relationship between ranking status and third mission responsibility, and by a close investigation into what sort of third missions current universities are highlighting regardless of their status. The latter issue is derived from the fact that rankings contain many tangible indicators and criteria for third mission activities based on economic contributions to society, and that in search of higher status, institutions may choose to downplay their cultural and societal responsibilities (Slaughter & Rhoades, 2004; Benneworth, 2013).

As to data and methods, the current chapter uses global rankings as a proxy for institutional status (Lee, 2017), but expands the traditional focus of rankings by also including non-ranked institutions in the analysis.

2 Navigating the Strategic Landscape of Higher Education

Our conceptual framework takes as the point of departure that status and reputation have become important objectives for universities, and that ways to strengthen status is a key concern for universities. Still, making strategic choices concerning how to achieve status and boost reputation – due to globalisation – is not an easy task as new global standards have emerged with respect to what leading universities should do, and what profile they should develop (Salmi, 2009). Hence, the race for status has triggered the development of a more strategic university, where external orientation, external analysis and strategic planning have become commonplace (Toma, 2010). Internationally, becoming an entrepreneurial university has become an ideal that many institutions are eager to pursue (Slaughter & Leslie, 1997; Clark, 1998), and numerous universities have strengthened their leadership and management systems in an attempt to boost their capacity to achieve this goal (Fumasoli & Lepori, 2011; Saichaie & Morphew, 2014; Deschamps & Lee, 2015; Morphew et al., 2016). Although strategic planning may not always be as effective as assumed (Birnbaum, 2000; Abdallah & Langley, 2014), such plans have become powerful signals of institutional ambitions, often guiding management decisions and focusing employees on the key values and objectives of the university. In short, strategic plans have become tools to achieve both external and internal legitimacy (Drori & Honig, 2013). Of course, the need for such legitimacy may be different across the globe, and not least, across institutions. While some universities may feel the pressure to adapt to the global scripts and to become entrepreneurial and excellent (Riesman, 1958), others may be allowed to remain loyal to their identity and original institutional mission (Stinchcombe, 1997), illustrating the many ways in which legitimacy may be achieved even in a more globalised higher education sector (Suchman, 1995; Fumasoli et al., 2015; Lee, 2017).

One of the ways to obtain legitimacy is to explore the role universities may take in society, not least when it comes to serving the local populations and the regions in which they are embedded (OECD, 2007). This may be an interesting strategic option, especially for those universities unable to achieve status as part of the ranking game. Focusing on the local student populations and local stakeholders may provide the institutions with local legitimacy. Conversely, a more globally oriented university may not see the benefit to its local status when wanting to pursue improved global status. As such, institutions having lower status may use their local commitment as a way to detect their strategic niches (Pinheiro, Benneworth, & Jones, 2012).

However, serving the 'local needs' may imply very different things, ranking from partnering up with local business and firms to fostering cultural interaction with the local community (Laredo, 2007). Hence, according to Laredo, we should distinguish between third missions that are related to economic concerns such as patents and joint ventures and those that are related to societal and cultural concerns such as public sector collaboration or co-organizing cultural events and activities. Other researchers operate with similar distinctions, especially where the economic dimension is sorted out as something different than more social contributions. Montesinos, Carot, Martinez, and Mora (2008) argue that it is the non-economic contributions of universities that are often ignored by rankings, although they may contribute considerably to the public good. The latter issue is also important for Marginson (2016) who distinguishes the economic and political definitions of public and private goods into four types, divided by market and non-market goods, and state and non-state sector goods. For Marginson, differentiating the economic from the social third mission activities (i.e., market and non-market), is a way to highlight the extent to which the public realm is being served (i.e., state and non-state). Within the broad range of possible public goods, his model allows for the identification of local, or state, versus global, or non-state, benefits. The fact that third mission activities may include both global and local dimensions, as well as economic and social or cultural activities is a characteristic that in general could be imagined to stimulate institutional diversity and develop different institutional profiles (van Vught & Westerheijden, 2012).

To sum up, strategic planning has become a key feature both to demonstrate legitimacy and to signal institutional ambitions. Global rankings are at the same time both confirming existing status hierarchies while they also offer hope for aspirational institutions that want to improve their status and reputation. We have also shown that such status may be achieved in different ways, and that there is a range of third mission options from which institutions may choose. For us, the interesting issue is whether the status offered by rankings contributes to 'locking' institutions into the global scripts mediated by rankings, and whether these rankings are also interesting for 'aspiring' institutions. Three expectations may here be developed. First, those institutions that are ranked will develop strategies that match the excellence/economically focused criteria normally used in global rankings (Hazelkorn, 2015). Second, those institutions that are not ranked will develop strategic plans that are aspirational, imitating the characteristics of those ranked (Drori & Honig, 2013). Third, institutions that are not ranked will have a strong local commitment which makes them immune from the pressures of rankings, and which stimulate them to develop strategies where the social and cultural role of the institutions are more prominent (Altbach, 1981).

3 Methods

This study is part of a larger project examining university strategic plans across the world. The data for this study included six regions: North America, South America, Europe, Africa, Asia, and Oceania. In total, 78 institutions were included in the study from 33 countries across 9 regions (see Table 5.1). Although the dataset included both public and private institutions, the majority (82%) were public universities as some countries do not have well developed or regulated private higher education systems.

Our research considered three major rankings systems: the Academic Ranking of World Universities (ARWU) 2016; the QS World University Rankings (QS) 2016/2017; and the Times Higher Education World University Rankings (THE) 2016/2017. These global rankings largely emphasize research output and global

TABLE 5.1 Study sample by institutional regions and rankings

Region	Ranked	Unranked	Total
East Asia	6	4	10
Europe	16	6	22
Latin America	8	1	9
Middle East/North Africa	7	3	10
North America (excluding Mexico)	5	1	4
Oceania	2		2
South Asia	1	1	2
South East Asia	6	3	9
Sub Saharan Africa	1	7	8
Total	52	26	78

impact, with almost no weight attributed to a university's third mission. One exception is the Times' 'Industry Income' (2.5%), also referred to by the Times as knowledge transfer (Times Higher Education, 2017). None of these ranking systems acknowledge any non-economic contributions to local communities as part of their weighting criteria.

TABLE 5.2 Global rankings criteria in 2017

THE	QS	ARWU
– Teaching (30%) – Research (30%) – Citations (30%) – International outlook (7.5%) – Industry income (2.5%)	– Academic reputation (40%) – Employer reputation (10%) – Faculty/student ratio (20%) – Citations per faculty (20%) – International faculty ratio (5%) – International student ratio (5%)	– Quality of education (10%) – Quality of faculty (40%) – Research output (40%) – Per capita performance (10%)

SOURCE: THE (2017), QS (2017), ARWU (2017).

TABLE 5.3 Third mission economic and social/cultural classifications

Category	Montesinos, Carot, Martinez, and Mora (2008)	Laredo (2007)	Marginson (2016)
Economic	'Enterprising third mission' and 'Innovative third mission'	Spin-offs, patents, industry collaborations	'Market-produced goods'
Social/cultural	'Social third mission'	Cooperation with public bodies, involvements in social and cultural life, and civic participation	'Non-market-produced goods'

The research compared ranked and unranked universities. Those universities that were considered ranked were listed in one of the top 800 in any one of the three major rankings systems under consideration. Unranked universities included those that did not appear in the top 800 of any of these rankings systems. In our analyses, we sought to identify common patterns within the ranked and non-ranked. The initial codes developed into the following categories: Economic Third Mission, and Social or Cultural Third Mission (Laredo, 2007; Marginson, 2016; Montesinos, Carot, Martinez, & Mora, 2008). The Economic Third Mission entailed strategies that would yield direct or indirect financial benefits, unlike the Social or Cultural that would likely not yield such benefits (see Table 5.3).

We also investigated the extent to which these orientations were local (i.e., local city, region, country, region) and/or global. Additional themes referenced various forms of specific locational engagements: 'contributing to the local economy', 'preserving or promoting local culture/scholarship', 'partnering locally (training, community service, etc.)', 'recognition of local challenges/environment', and 'representing the local region/nation/continent'. Within the latter category, additional sub-themes included 'regional (and sometimes continental) representation', 'national representation', and 'nation building'. The findings were analysed by ranked versus unranked.

4 Findings

The study identified notable differentiation between ranked and unranked universities in their strategic planning statements about the third mission. With respect to geographic location, ranked universities' strategic plans were mostly globally and regionally contextualized while unranked institutions were more locally oriented. The unranked expressed clearer plans about contributing to the local economy, while recognizing local challenges and the local environment. Statements referring to the third mission were less frequent among the ranked institutions, and among the fewer occurrences, the plans among these institutions were largely in economic terms towards promoting economic development. The promotion of cultural values was mentioned across the ranks, although ranked institutions' descriptions were mentioned as part of their unique identity and global positioning. While nation building was also featured across the ranked and unranked, the unranked more prominently featured community-scale building.

4.1   Ranked Universities

As one might presume, ranked universities were quite explicit in conveying their ranked status, particularly if they were among the top of any of the major global rankings systems. Along with their identification as ranked institutions, strategies were similarly contextualized based on their relative global, regional, or national reputations. Strategies were often associated with ways to increase or maintain their relative rank.

In many cases, ranked institutions positioned themselves as the best university representative from their countries, and sometimes continents, to the world. Additionally, as in Saudi Arabia, university and national identities were inseparable: 'our vision is built around three themes: A vibrant society, a thriving economy, and an ambitious nation'. As exemplified, the university's role was more than merely educational, but idealistically aimed to serve and benefit the entire country's population and its increased role in the world. In Israel, this was exemplified with the explicit statement of the university's mission 'advancement for the state of Israel'. Similarly, in Malaysia a university's goal was 'to enhance the nation's competitiveness'. Elsewhere in Asia, presence and context were emphasized especially at the national level, as in the case of Indonesia, to promote 'the state ideology and dedicated to the nation's interest'. Other universities situated themselves as global universities that were located in a particular country, with national identity being secondary to a global one (Scotland). As such, ranked universities' geographical orientations tended to be national or geographically broader (i.e., regional, continental or global), and rarely local (i.e., city).

While third mission narratives among the ranked institutions were in general less frequently mentioned compared to the unranked institutions, where present, the appearance of third mission among the ranked was frequently economic: the promotion of technology transfer and related ventures to support industry, increasing knowledge production and producing industry ready graduates, and to enhance university-industry ties. Universities such as those in Mexico, India, China, Germany, and others described the role of their institutions in working with the business sector, producing workers, and attracting foreign investments for the good of the nation. As an example, '[University] will be promoting closer interaction with industry, encouraging growth-oriented technology spin-offs, and working with government to secure a broader scope of action as an entrepreneurial university' (Germany). In Malaysia, a university described its 'Industry Advisory Panel to ensure its educational contents remain relevant to industrial practices'.

Social and cultural third missions among the ranked institutions were particularly less evident compared to the unranked institutions but did exist in particular forms. There were limited examples based on a country's particular colonial history and attempts to rectify the past. Examples included efforts towards decolonization (South Africa) and indigenization (Canada). In the case of the former, a South African university expressed, 'the focus of [our] social action has been the inequalities, prejudices, and structural disadvantages that continue to characterize South African society and our universities'. Student access to higher education was also expressed, particularly in the US with plans to reach underserved students within the state. One institution, for example, discussed a commitment to partner with other regional universities to 'share best practices, policies and programs to provide maximized career readiness particularly among under-represented and limited income students' (US), however even this mission could be seen as economically driven for the benefit of the state. At times, these local foci were in response to past community complaints about a lack of engagement or respect for the local context, as was the case of a ranked urban US university.

Language and culture promotion were also discussed, as in the cases of Spain and Indonesia. One Spanish institution included the goal of 'promotion and dissemination of the Spanish language', another in the same country wanted to 'increase classes offered in Euskara' as well as '[advance] the standardization of Euskara through the master plan'. While some universities, in an effort to become or appear more cosmopolitan and attract students and partners, have started to shift towards English language curriculum, these institutions also recognized that they are in a unique position to promote and preserve the cultural heritage of their communities, regions, or nations. Some also saw themselves as safeguarding their cultural ideologies, as in the case of Indonesia.

4.2 Unranked Institutions

Universities that were not ranked among the top 800 globally showed a different set of patterns in their strategic plans. Unranked institutions appeared less aspirational in terms of progressing within the rankings system, with some exceptions. There were two unranked universities in Turkey espousing international rankings aspirations. Both sought to increase their international rankings, with one explicitly stating in its plans its goal to be 'ranked as one of the top universities in all THE, QS, and ARWU rankings'. More notably, unranked institutions tended to show less attention to traditional rankings measures and more consistently expressed third mission plans. Unlike the ranked universities, these third mission plans had clearer non-economic strategies (as well as some economic strategies) in response to an explicit recognition of their local challenges and their local stakeholders. Additionally, local partnerships were more specifically identified compared to the ranked institutions, which in general tended to use more broad or vague language about partnerships.

Unranked institutions especially exhibited a clearer local orientation in their strategic plans, whereas ranked universities oriented themselves more nationally and internationally. These institutions also most clearly emphasized their country's social and cultural distinctiveness as priorities whereas ranked universities' mentions were less prominent. Across each of the major regions, unranked universities described their social, as well as economic responsibilities to their immediate surrounds. As one example, a Chinese university stated that it 'intends...to increase the support and contribution that [University] could make to [Province]...in terms of economy, culture, and social development', while another in China stated that they were 'basing in [City] and serving [City]'. One Japanese university highlighted that though they had international ambitions, they still recognized their roots with a motto of 'act globally, base locally'.

Similar to ranked universities, economic development goals were featured, although unranked universities were more specific in describing their plans based on local resources. For example, a Norwegian university discussed economic development goals that would capitalize on its local oil and energy production markets while a Moroccan university specified future plans in local entrepreneurship. One Italian institution addressed its partnerships with specific local television and radio stations, publications, spaces, and social networks. The goals of the unranked institutions were found to focus, therefore, more on local industry and less on globalized industries or multinational businesses.

Unranked institutions also prominently discussed their goals in nation building but differed by suggesting a more holistic approach. Particularly among low-income countries, statements such as 'We are committed to developing the nation' and to 'improve the quality of life of Indonesians' (Indonesia) were prevalent. Others were most specific to their historical and post-colonial context as in the case of South Africa, '[University] will strive to be an effective partner in the larger national project of building a sustainable and equitable non-racial, non-sexist, democratic, multilingual society'. Others, as in the case a Moroccan university, made more specific reference to strengthening the religious and cultural identity of their nation.

Most distinctively, the unranked were most explicit about their social and cultural third mission. One examples included a Chinese university's plans to 'preserve and disseminate traditional Chinese culture'. Another distinguishing feature among the unranked were strategies were towards building or supporting community infrastructure. A Turkish university included statements about sharing its facilities with their local community and a Kenyan university had explicit plans to set up local health centres.

Unranked universities also more deeply recognized their role in promoting educational access for their diverse local, and often underserved, populations. Institutions, such as in the cases of Sweden, Singapore and Nigeria, specifically identified the challenges for working students, which make up a large part of those institutions' respective student bodies. In response to those challenges, several universities planned to offer more flexible course hours and degree completion plans. A Hong Kong institution stated plans to 'to meet the actual needs of Hong Kong society by training efficient and well-balanced young people for various services in the community'. Underserved populations were also identified, as in the case of Kenya, as well as the importance of educating locals who had been shut out of other universities in their higher education systems, as in the cases of India and Thailand. At a US university, there was a particular focus on veterans' services, as armed forces veterans were identified as a major source of students. Across these examples, community stakeholders and underserved populations were acknowledged and service to these groups were often prioritized in the strategic plans.

5 Discussion

Strategic plans related to the third mission were notably different based on whether an institution was globally ranked. Ranked institutions tended to contextualize their strategies broadly and globally, and in ways that would reinforce or improve their ranked status, with a greater emphasis on economic development. Unranked institutions, on the other hand, often contextualized their strategies in a more local perspective and included more of a variety of strategies that included economic plans as well, but also cultural and social, with more specificity to serving local stakeholders.

The study sought to broadly capture ways that ranked and unranked universities describe their institutional strategies, although the general differences are not so clearly bifurcated as presented by our examples. Lower ranked institutions sometimes resembled the unranked more than the globally ranked and more commonly featured non-economic, third mission plans. Location also mattered, particular to the extent of a university's commitment to national development. Universities located in lower income countries, especially in the Global South, prioritized national development as a major goal, whether ranked or unranked. Given the relatively fewer number of universities in some countries, as well as levels of resources, some institutions might have a broader set of responsibilities as well as challenges, which might have been reflected in their statements.

When considering the findings of the research, it is also important to recognize that these are plans and may not necessarily be reflective of actual institutional behaviours. However, the statements do provide a comparable way to observe how different universities are strategizing for the future. As the study demonstrated, being ranked or not, differentiates university plans and also shows the extent to which the local context is acknowledged and seemingly included in those plans. What remains uncertain is whether a university must forego its local community needs in the pursuit of global rankings or if a university can ever serve all needs for all stakeholders. More likely, a diverse higher education system, with both ranked and unranked universities, can serve broader society, although the challenges would be greater for smaller countries with less developed systems.

Despite these limitations and areas that require further investigation, this research does make clear that not all institutions are trapped in the rankings game, subjected to a narrow band of legitimacy markers as determined by the global rankings measures. While those who are highly favoured as a globally ranked university explicitly feature their global status and strategize in advancing their global reputation, the unranked do not necessarily follow the same legitimization path. Rather, unranked universities more clearly emphasized their local context and prioritized their underserved local populations as key stakeholders, thereby demonstrating their local legitimacy. The research also suggests that third mission activities can, and perhaps should, extend beyond the market. Unranked universities were more focused on, and perhaps more highly engaged in, non-economic third mission activities, at least as demonstrated by their strategic plans, in comparison to the ranked universities.

Currently, none of the three major global rankings (Academic Ranking of World Universities, the QS World University Rankings, and the Times Higher Education World University Rankings), emphasize the third mission or local engagement. Questions remain as to whether such behaviours should or can be quantitatively measured or whether they will diminish in priority for universities seeking to rise in their global ranks. While there are exceptions, particularly among globally-ranked top national universities in the Global South, an implication might be the extent to which what is valuable about third mission activities must, or can, be measurable or whether third mission and local engagement are of any value in the pursuit of rankings. At the time of this study, some regional and national attempts to measure third mission commitments have been underway. These include the European Indicators and Ranking Methodology for University Third Mission (2017) and Moscow International University Ranking, 'The Three Missions of Universities' (2017), but are currently limited in their adoption across the globe. In the meantime, unranked universities appear to be leading in a broad range of third mission pursuits.

References

Abdallah, C., & Langley, A. (2014). The double edge of ambiguity in strategic planning. *Journal of Management Studies, 51*(2), 235–264.

Academic Ranking of World Universities. (2017). *Methodology*. Retrieved April 5, 2018, from http://www.shanghairanking.com/ARWU-Methodology-2018.html

Altbach, P. G. (1981). The university as center and periphery. *Teachers College Record, 82*, 601–622.

Anderson, N. (2016, December 21). Surge in foreign students may be crowding Americans out of elite colleges. *The Washington Post*. Retrieved April 5, 2018, from https://www.washingtonpost.com/local/education/surge-in-foreign-students-might-be-crowding-americans-out-of-elite-colleges/2016/12/21/78d4b65c-b59d-11e6-a677-b608fbb3aaf6_story.html?utm_term=.86ef79f3b83c

Benneworth, P. (2013). *University engagement with socially excluded communities*. Dordrecht: Springer.

Birnbaum, R. (2000). *Management fads in higher education: Where they come from, what they do, why they fail*. San Francisco, CA: Jossey-Bass.

Clark, B. R. (1998). *Creating entrepreneurial universities: Organizational pathways of transformation*. Oxford: Pergamon Press.

Deschamps, E., & Lee, J. J. (2015). Internationalization as mergers and acquisitions: Senior international officers' entrepreneurial strategies and activities in public universities. *Journal of Studies in International Education, 19*, 122–139.

Drori, I., & Honig, B. (2013). A process model of internal and external legitimacy. *Organizational Studies, 34*(3), 345–376.

European Indicators and Ranking Methodology for University Third Mission. (2017). *Project information.* Retrieved April 5, 2018, from http://www.e3mproject.eu

Fumasoli, T., & Lepori, B. (2011). Patterns of strategies in Swiss higher education institutions. *Higher Education, 61*(2), 157–178.

Fumasoli, T., Pinheiro, R., & Stensaker, B. (2015). Handling uncertainty of strategic ambitions: The use of organizational identity as a risk-reducing device. *International Journal of Public Administration, 38*(13–14), 1030–1040.

Hazelkorn, E. (2015). *Rankings and the re-shaping of higher education: The battle for world-class excellence.* Basingstoke: Palgrave Macmillan.

Jongbloed, B., Enders, J., & Salerno, C. (2008). Higher education and its communities: Interconnections, interdependencies and a research agenda. *Higher Education, 56*(3), 303–324.

Laredo, P. (2007). Revisiting the third mission of universities: Towards a new categorization of university activities? *Higher Education Policy, 20*(4), 441–456.

Lee, J. (2017, April 7). Who is the 'public' in higher education today? *Inside Higher Education.* Retrieved April 5, 2018, from https://www.insidehighered.com/views/2017/04/07/academe-needs-broaden-its-concept-public-good-essay

Marginson, S. (2016). *Higher education and the common good.* Melbourne: Melbourne University Publishing.

McKenna, L. (2015, November 18). The globalization of America's colleges. *The Atlantic.* Retrieved April 5, 2018, from https://www.theatlantic.com/education/archive/2015/11/globalization-american-higher-ed/416502/

Montesinos, P., Carot, J. M., Martinez, J. M., & Mora, F. (2008). Third mission ranking for world class universities: Beyond teaching and research. *Higher education in Europe, 33*(2–3), 259–271.

Morphew, C. C., Fumasoli, T., & Stensaker, B. (2016). Changing missions? How the strategic plans of research-intensive universities in Northern Europe and North America balance competing identities. *Studies in Higher Education, 43*(6), 1074–1088.

Moscow International University Ranking. (2017). *'The three university missions' methodology.* Retrieved April 5, 2018, from https://3missions.ru/files/methodology_17/EN-MosIUR_Methodology_07072017.pdf

Nedeva, M. (2007). New tricks and old dogs? The 'third mission' and the re-production of the university? In D. Epstein, R. Boden, R. Deem, F. Rizvi, & S. Wright (Eds.), *Geographies of knowledge, geometrics of power: Framing the future of higher education* (pp. 85–105). New York, NY: Routledge.

OECD. (2007). *Globally competitive, locally engaged: Higher education and regions.* Paris: OECD.

Pinheiro, R., Benneworth, P., & Jones, G. (Eds.). (2012). *Universities and regional development: A critical analysis of tensions and contradictions*. New York, NY: Routledge.

Pusser, B., & Marginson, S. (2013). University rankings in critical perspective. *Journal of Higher Education, 84*(4), 544–568.

QS World University Rankings. (2017). *Methodology*. Retrieved April 5, 2018, from https://www.topuniversities.com/qs-world-university-rankings/methodology

Riesman, D. (1956). *Constraint and variety in American education*. Lincoln, NE: University of Nebraska Press.

Saichaie, K., & Morphew, C. (2014). What college and university websites reveal about the purposes of higher education. *Journal of Higher Education, 85*(4), 499–530.

Salmi, J. (2009). *The challenge of establishing world-class universities*. Washington, DC: The World Bank.

Slaughter, S., & Leslie, L. L. (1997). *Academic capitalism: Politics, policies, and the entrepreneurial university*. Baltimore, MD: Johns Hopkins University Press.

Slaughter, S., & Rhoades, G. (2004). *Academic capitalism and the new economy: Markets, state, and higher education*. Baltimore, MD: Johns Hopkins University Press.

Stinchcombe, A. L. (1997). On the virtues of the old institutionalism. *Annual Review of Sociology, 23*, 1–18.

Suchman, M. C. (1995). Managing legitimacy: Strategic and institutional approaches. *Academy of Management Review, 20*(3), 571–610.

Times Higher Education. (2017). *World university rankings methodology*. Retrieved April 5, 2018, from https://www.timeshighereducation.com/world-university-rankings/methodology-world-university-rankings-2016–2017

Toma, J. D. (2010). *Building organizational capacity: Strategic management in higher education*. Baltimore, MD: Johns Hopkins University Press.

van Vught, F. A., & Westerheijden, D. F. (2012). Transparency, quality and accountability. In F. A. van Vught & F. Ziegele (Eds.), *Multidimensional ranking: The design and development of U-Multirank*. Dordrecht: Springer.

Watanabe, T. (2016, March 29). UC schools harm local students by admitting so many from out of state, audit finds. *Los Angeles Times*. Retrieved April 5, 2018, from http://www.latimes.com/local/lanow/la-me-ln-uc-audit-admissions-20160328-story.html

CHAPTER 6

World-Class Universities: A Dual Identity Related to Global Common Good(s)

Lin Tian

Abstract

Based on UNESCO's 2015 report (*Rethinking Education towards a Global Common Good*) and various changes in higher education, this chapter explores reasons behind the shift from the public good to the common good in higher education, and world-class universities' special role in relation to global common good(s) through a discourse analysis of four official documents from world-class universities. The findings indicate that world-class universities serve as a global common good due to their international orientation, emphasis on global development and the well-being of global communities. Meanwhile, they produce and shape global common goods such as advanced knowledge and research outputs, and more importantly, help to shape and realize the global common good (i.e. peaceful development) that humans share intrinsically in common.

Keywords

World-class universities – public good(s) – common good(s) – higher education

1   Introduction

Globalization and internationalization, the advancement of science and technology, the enhancement of life-long learning, the trends towards marketization and privatization in higher education – all these contribute to the constant changes in global higher education landscape. Against this backdrop, the term 'public good(s)', which once dominated the field of higher education, is now facing various challenges. In 2015 UNESCO report, *Rethinking Education towards a Global Common Good*, which proposes the 'common good' as a constructive alternative to public good(s) (the latter is traditionally considered to be closely associated with education and its outputs), with a distinct feature of intrinsic value and sharing participation (UNESCO, 2015). However, this informative and inspiring report does not deal much with higher education and world-class universities (WCUs), which are inseparable constituents of a nation's capacity building and an important constituent of the global higher education system. In light of this, with a discourse analysis of four official documents (i.e. president's message, mission statement, vision statement and strategic plan) of WCUs, this chapter investigates the relationship between WCUs and the newly-proposed notion of global common good(s), proposing that WCUs (as a network or group) have a dual identity, that is, as a global common good in themselves, they produce and also contribute to global common good(s), benefiting not only individual students, but also wider global society.

2   Public Good(s) and Higher Education

In many countries, higher education has long been considered as a public good, which is 'a commodity or service provided without profit to all members of a society' as defined by the *New Oxford Dictionary of English*. Economically, public goods feature non-excludability and non-rivalry in their consumption (Samuelson, 1954). First, public goods are non-excludable, which means that once they are in place, they cannot be provided exclusively to some groups of people, and it is impossible to exclude other people from consuming them; second, public goods are non-rivalrous, indicating that some people's consumption of such goods does not diminish others' consumption levels of the same goods (Tilak, 2008). Public goods produce a large quantity of externalities, in the form of public or social benefits (ibid.). In contrast, private goods are altogether different, which are both excludable and rivalrous, and they can be 'produced and distributed as individualized commodities in economic markets' (Marginson, 2014, p. 24).

Market failure, the usual context for the introduction of the concept of public goods, refers to a situation where the allocation of such goods and services is not efficient, because no enterprise can bear the cost for continuing to supply the goods without any beneficiaries' willingness to pay. In other words, who would like to provide the street light (a traditionally-considered public good) via the market when people can enjoy the benefits of the lighting without paying for them? Therefore, the market will not supply such goods, and only a public authority can deliver them and recover payment for such goods and services through general revenues (Menashy, 2009). In this sense, public goods can also be explained politically as goods that depend on government supply (while private goods rely on market supply) (Marmolo, 1999). The decision-making system used in relation to the supply of goods determines the 'publicness' of them. In other words, public and private labels merely indicate different modes of supply, rather than the character of the item itself (Zang & Qu, 2002). According to this, this chapter defines public goods as goods that serve public benefit, which are produced on the basis of public demand and mostly rely on public power, i.e. government. Those goods that cannot be produced without government (or philanthropic) production or funding are characterized by non-excludability and/or non-rivalry in their consumption, for example, national defence, street lighting and first-level schooling.

Higher education has conventionally been regarded as a public good, producing a broad spectrum of externalities (mainly social and public benefits), contributing to the social interest and specific public goods, and benefiting simultaneously individuals and the whole society (Cheng, 2006; Chen, 2008; Tilak, 2008; Marginson, 2018). Many scholars have recognized the public nature of higher education and universities: creating and distributing knowledge, enhancing the life quality of people who are educated, supplying innovations for industry and preparing citizens for democratic decision-making (Yuan, 2009; Su, 2009; Marginson, 2018).

Kant (1979) was perhaps the first person to argue that universities (which are the main providers of higher education) play a crucial role in allying with the national governments, professions and society, generating public goods. Arendt (1993) further expanded upon this concept by stating that universities are full of significance in preserving and transmitting the collective knowledge which is accumulated in the society, and in understanding the world for future generations. Later, Desai (2003) and Tilak (2008), referring to Samuelson's (1954) definition of public goods, suggest that higher education in most countries were state-funded and at the same time, and it produces a large quantum of externalities, known as public and social benefits, accelerating scientific and technological progress in a country, or raising individual employability through improving human capital. However, when being defined in this way (i.e. mainly state-funded), the deduction or removal of state funding from higher education, which results in the growth of marketization and privatization in higher education, explicitly questions the notion of higher education as a public good, which is the usual situation in the higher education system in the US (Lewis & Hearn, 2003). This situation, along with other factors, has posed challenges to the 'public side' of higher education in recent years.

3   Challenges to the Notion of Public Good(s) in Higher Education

Privatization and marketization make the public nature of higher education less obvious (Lambert, 2014; Zemsky, 2003). The trend towards privatization is intensifying in higher education, and more private providers offer educational opportunities (sometimes, even better opportunities) to students; also, as an increasingly marketized higher education sector emerges, and in order to survive, higher education institutions have to behave as for-profit organizations, making revenue generation a priority, which tends to gloss over the long-cherished view of higher education as a public good and to legitimize the sale and purchase of higher education. Undoubtedly, this trend damages the public side of high education to some extent, and also blurs the boundary between public and private.

Apart from this, internationalization in higher education makes the concept of public good(s) based on national interests difficult to apply to higher education, as the public nature of higher education is often closely related to the public interest of a certain country or region, which does not include education activities for citizens of other countries (Huang & Tang, 2017). However, with growing internationalization, this national border has broken down, and is reflected in the increasingly frequent cooperation among universities in various countries, the continuous expansion of cooperation areas, the increase of students and faculty mobility, and the rising number of overseas branch campuses and joint educational projects. As a result, the internationalization of higher education brings benefits to countries and universities participating in the cooperation and interaction. This underlines a more dynamic and interactive relationship among different countries and regions in the field of higher education.

Moreover, the changing global landscape emphasizes common more than public. At present, the ever-changing knowledge and technology in our world makes it impossible for learners to acquire all the knowledge needed for their whole life through the formal learning in school (this kind of education is public in most cases, which is provided by the government, with less emphasis on the correlation of individuals' pay and use) and means life-long learning and learning through various channels as an indispensable part of the education system. According to UNESCO's report, a common good has a distinct feature of intrinsic value and sharing participation (UNESCO, 2015), which encourages people to be proactive in the learning process with shared efforts through various channels, thereby bringing benefits to all participants and changing the process from educating to learning, but a public good may not stimulate people to share participation in the learning process, since it often generates free-riding, which may render obtaining education as a passive process in some cases.

It can be seen that the notion of public good(s) in higher education has been challenged in various aspects. The social contract linking higher education with society, that is, the idea that higher education serves the national and public interest with national funding, has been challenged (due to the intensifying trend of privatization, marketization and internationalization); also, the idea of life-long active learning attaches more importance to common participation in learning rather than being educated with public support, which is a trend of the times. Thus, we urgently need to update our understanding of higher education.

3.1   *A Shift from Public to Common in Higher Education*

Common goods can be defined as goods that are 'characterized by a binding destination and necessary for the realization of the fundamental rights of all people, irrespective of any public or private origin' (UNESCO, 2015, p. 77). 'The good realized in the mutual relationships in and through which human beings achieve their well-being' (Hollenbach, 2002, p. 81), which is 'inherent to the relationships that exist among the members of a society tied together in a collective endeavour' (UNESCO, 2015, p. 78). Deneulin and Townsend (2007) argue that a celebratory dinner, an orchestral, or a team sport can be thought as common goods. They then take the orchestra as an example to illustrate how a common good is produced and how its benefits can be enjoyed. The good itself, an orchestra, cannot exist without each musician playing their respective parts and performing collectively for the whole audience. In other words, the good exists in the shared action which generates it. Also, benefiting from such good is by participating in it, whether in the orchestra or audience. Hence, the shared action is both intrinsic (unless various musicians' participation and performance, the orchestra cannot exist at all), and instrumental (it is necessary, efficient and convenient to perform as an orchestra) to the good itself; and its benefits (an orchestra; beautiful music; excellent performance) are generated from the course of that shared action. Such kind of goods are intrinsically common in their production and their benefits, reflecting the distinct characteristics of intrinsic value and sharing participation, which is different from a public good (Deneulin & Townsend, 2007, p. 25; UNESCO, 2015).

It is necessary to distinguish 'common goods' from 'the common good'. Common goods are a micro concept, including various one-off common goods, such as the above-mentioned examples, a celebratory dinner, an orchestral and a team game (Deneulin & Townsend, 2007, p. 26). *The* common good is a more overarching, macro concept. Specifically, the common good is the 'benefit or interests of all', as defined by the New Oxford Dictionary of English. However, the 'all' here has a boundary, only including a group of people who share the same physical living space and whose lives interact and are intertwined in multiple ways. The common good could be a village, a town or a city. For a city, residents participate in the life of the city, and they 'generate a good that could not exist otherwise and which is partly constitutive of the wellbeing of each of them' (Deneulin & Townsend, 2007, p. 26).

In this sense, a city that is the common good resembles a concert as a common good, but endures through time. The end of a concert means the nonexistence of the concert as a common good, but the city continues in the residents' participation and they create benefits which only exist in their participation and interaction (a city could also be regarded as such benefit), and these benefits also contribute to the well-being of everyone (Deneulin & Townsend, 2007). Accordingly, the goodwill that human beings share and communicate with each other, such as values, civic virtues and a sense of justice, all belong to the common good (Deneulin & Townsend, 2007).

Thus, higher education itself can be regarded as both a common good and the common good, because receiving higher education can be regarded as a specific activity. Educators, students/learners and other stakeholders would all benefit from participation; however, higher education is not a transient activity, and it has been maintained over time, benefiting generation after generation, and will continue to promote social and national development. Given that some scholars emphasize the common good as more related to an abstract value, with its essence as 'the common good things' that maintain a social relationship model rather than achieving a specific purpose (Hayek, 1973; Huang & Tang, 2017), this chapter sees higher education as a common good that serves the common good.

Based on the above analysis, shifting from the idea of public good(s) to common good(s) in higher education would be better for the following three reasons:

First, higher education would step out of the long-disputed topic of whether it is a public good or a private good, and as a common good, the nature of higher education is no longer defined by how it is supplied (public or private supply), but more related to its results (for the realization of the fundamental rights of all people). Then, to a certain extent, the idea of higher education as a common good could justify a diversity of providers of higher education. In this sense, government (which sponsors most public universities) is not the only provider of higher education, which could include private universities and for-profit organisations. The sources of funding for public universities are also diverse, integrating resources and power from various stake-holders and thereby promoting the efficiency of higher education in some respects.

Second, the concept of higher education as a common good which serves the common good helps build a more inclusive world and promotes the construction of a community and sense of shared future for humanity. As the internationalization of higher education continues to grow, globalization around the world is increasingly challenged (e.g., by the election of Donald Trump in the United States and the United Kingdom's referendum vote to leave the European Union). Against this backdrop, a common higher education will help ease the tide of reversed globalization by virtue of its common good, because the concept of the common good refuses to be closed and conservative, encouraging global universities and educators to collaborate jointly and participate actively; in addition, the common good of higher education highlights the humanistic values of education and development, respects life and human dignity, the equality of rights and social justice, values cultural pluralism, international solidarity and the sharing of responsibilities (UNESCO, 2015). Therefore, the common higher education will surely cultivate global citizens who respect, embrace and understand other people and different cultures. They will become be instrumental in solving conflicts in human civilization and building an inclusive world of harmony.

Third, confronting the demand for active learning, life-long learning and learning through various channels, the notion of the common good may complement the concept of the public good, which lacks a correlation between pay (a person's involvement in the provision of a public good) and their use of it, because a public good is open to free-riding, whereas a common good highlights the collective endeavour of all participants, and its benefits are generated from the course of that shared action (Deneulin & Townsend, 2007). Adopting this concept, higher education is constructive, since it encourages people to be proactive and cooperative in the learning process so that all participants can share the benefits.

3.2　*WCUs' Dual Identity Related to Global Common Good(s)*

In practice, higher education serves the common good by cultivating talents, advancing research and providing social service, which are delivered by higher education institutions. This new era, which is marked by globalisation and internationalization, new information and communication technologies, extensive environmental concerns and climate change, the widespread introduction of neo-liberal economic policies and dramatic policy changes (e.g. Britain's decision to leave the European Union), brings both opportunities and challenges for higher education institutions around the world.

Universities, as relatively independent organisations in society, are obliged to take these opportunities to develop themselves and promote the whole society, and meanwhile respond to the challenges, thereby enhancing human well-being in both the national and global society. In this sense, it is argued that WCUs, as leading or elite universities internationally, apart from seizing opportunities for self-development, need to position themselves in the forefront of seeking conceptual and practical solutions to the pressing challenges for the benefit of all humanity.

WCUs consist of both leading public and private universities worldwide, have the most qualified faculty, attract the best and brightest students all around the world, regardless of their background, conduct world-class education and build international reputations; WCUs are dedicated to constructing an active academic environment with free discussions and open dialogues of ideas and values so as to strengthen the liberal development of individuals; WCUs focus on the international landscape and constantly adjust themselves according to the outside world; WCUs are committed to solving global challenges and actively cooperate with other organizations. In this regard, WCUs have already transcended the ideas of public and private, with an emphasis on human development, world interconnectedness and the well-being of the global communities, playing a role as a global common good.

In the past decades, the building and development of WCUs have been high on the policy agenda of various stakeholders across the globe. An increasing number of countries, in both developed and developing, recognise WCUs' indispensable roles in societal, political, cultural and individual development at both the national and global levels. In this regard, WCUs serve not only social interests or contribute to the public good, in which 'human well-being is framed by individualistic socio-economic theory' (UNESCO, 2015, p. 78), they are concerned more with international perspectives, underlining the interconnectedness of the world and highlighting the good life (well-being) of global communities that humanity forms, thereby contributing to the global common good, which is common to all people as benefits or interests.

Therefore, WCUs (as a network or group) are a high-level global common good since they also shape, develop and generate other global common goods (e.g. knowledge and research outputs) while at the same time contribute to the global common good.

4   The Special Role of WCUs

In order for a better understanding of WCUs' special role in contributing to the global common good, four official documents (i.e. president's message, mission statement, vision statement and strategic plan (the latest version)) on the university websites are collected, classified and analysed in relation to their three major functions: talent cultivation, scientific research and social service.

The reasons for choosing these four types of formal documents are as follows: First, the president's message is a university leader's summary of the university's history, current situation and future development. Second, a university's mission statement contains the functions of a university, representing not only the traditional concept of university operation, but also the strategic outlook of the university. Third, a university's vision statement is future-oriented, which is beyond reality and internalized as a common language in the consciousness of all university members, guiding the development of a university (Zhao & Zhou, 2006). Fourth, strategic planning is an overall and systematic design of a university, which is based on the existing conditions of a university and is intended for a university's future development (Bie & Zhang, 2010). Therefore, an in-depth analysis of these four types of documents will help people to better understand the university's self-declared functional orientation and its direction for future development.

The top 100 universities (which are widely acknowledged as WCUs) in the Academic Ranking of World Universities (2016), QS World University Rankings (2016) and THE World University Ranking (2016) were chosen as samples, and a total of 61 WCUs' four official documents were collected and analysed (see Table 6.1 for university list and Table 6.2 for the available documents of WCUs).

After analysing the above-listed documents from 61 universities, the main keywords (those which appear the most frequently) relating to their three functions were classified into a framework adapted from Parsons's (1960,

TABLE 6.1   WCUs in three major university rankings

Universities	Rankings[a]		
	ARWU	THE[b]	QS
Harvard University	1	6	3
Stanford University	2	3	2
University of California–Berkeley	3	10	28
University of Cambridge	4	4	4
Massachusetts Institute of Technology	5	5	1
Princeton University	6	7	11
University of Oxford	7	1	6
California Institute of Technology	8	2	5
Columbia University	9	16	20
University of Chicago	10	10	10
Yale University	11	12	15

(Cont.)

TABLE 6.1 WCUs in three major university rankings (*cont.*)

Universities	Rankings[a]		
	ARWU	THE[b]	QS
University of California–Los Angeles	12	14	31
Cornell University	13	19	16
University of Washington	15	25	59
Johns Hopkins University	16	17	17
University College London	17	15	7
University of Pennsylvania	18	13	18
Swiss Federal Institute of Technology Zurich	19	9	8
The University of Tokyo	20	39	34
Imperial College London	22	8	9
University of Michigan–Ann Arbor	23	21	23
Duke University	25	18	24
Northwestern University (US)	26	20	26
University of Toronto	27	22	32
University of Wisconsin–Madison	28	45	53
New York University	29	32	46
University of Illinois at Urbana–Champaign	30	36	66
Kyoto University	32	91	37
University of British Columbia	34	36	45
University of Manchester	35	55	29
University of North Carolina–Chapel Hill	35	56	78
University of Melbourne	40	33	42
University of Edinburgh	41	27	19
University of Texas at Austin	44	50	67
Heidelberg University	47	43	72
Technical University Munich	47	46	60
King's College London	50	36	21
University of Munich	51	30	68
The University of Queensland	55	60	52
University of Helsinki	56	91	91
University of Bristol	57	71	41
Tsinghua University	58	35	24
Uppsala University	60	94	98
McGill University	63	42	30
Purdue University–West Lafayette	63	70	92

(*Cont.*)

TABLE 6.1 WCUs in three major university rankings (*cont.*)

Universities	Rankings[a]		
	ARWU	THE[b]	QS
Carnegie Mellon University	68	23	58
Beijing University	71	29	39
Rice University	72	87	90
Boston University	75	64	89
University of California–Davis	75	51	85
Pennsylvania State University–University Park	77	68	95
The Australian National University	77	47	22
Monash University	79	74	65
The Ohio State University–Columbus	79	72	88
University of Sydney	82	60	46
National University of Singapore	83	24	12
Ecole Normale Superieure–Paris	87	66	33
Brown University	90	51	49
Swiss Federal Institute of Technology Lausanne	92	30	14
KU Leuven	93	40	79

a. The same position in the same ranking in the table indicates the parallel position of two universities.
b. The website of THE World University Ranking is marked as ranking of 2017 or 2016–2017, but it is actually the ranking of 2016, which is consistent with the other two rankings of 2016.

SOURCE: ARWU (http://www.shanghairanking.com/ARWU2016.html); THE (https://www.timeshighereducation.com/world-university-rankings/2017/worldranking); QS (http://www.topuniversities.com/university-rankings/world-universityrankings/2016)

1970) AGIL analysis scheme (see Figure 6.1), which conforms to structural functionalism. According to structural functionalism, the higher education system and universities can be regarded as a subsystem of the society, and they are connected with the surrounding environment. Universities form a relatively stable and small-scale social structure whose positioning in the society hinges on their functions. In this sense, structural functionalism not only focuses on a specific function of universities, but also the combination of universities' different functions, so as to define and understand universities rationally (Parsons & Smelser, 1956; Ren, 2012; Zhuang, 2013; Wang & Xia, 2016).

A DUAL IDENTITY RELATED TO GLOBAL COMMON GOOD(S)   113

TABLE 6.2 Available documents of WCUs (N = 61)[a, b]

Types of documents	Available number	Contents (number)
President's message	37	Talent cultivation (33)
		Scientific research (24)
		Social service (27)
Mission & Vision	52	Talent cultivation (47)
		Scientific research (41)
		Social service (50)
Strategic plan	41	Talent cultivation (37)
		Scientific research (37)
		Social service (33)

a. Since the mission and vision statements often appear on the same page of the website, so this chapter counts them together in Table 6.2.
b. The absence of some universities' information is due to the unavailability of relevant documents on the university's website.

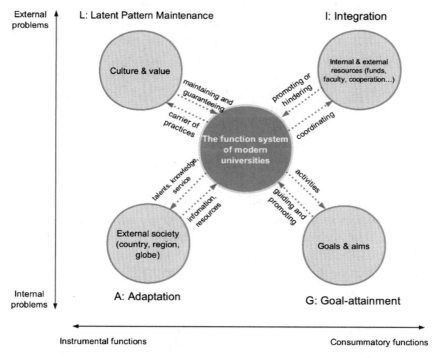

FIGURE 6.1 The adapted AGIL scheme for the function system of modern universities

Therefore, on the basis of structural functionalism, an analysis of WCUs' function may help people comprehensively understand WCUs' role.

For the purpose of this chapter, the following paragraph only presents part of the keywords in relation to each function under the AGIL model and gives a description with contextualization.

4.1 Talent Cultivation

Talent cultivation means building an individual's character and morals through the formal process of teaching and learning (Tilak, 2008, p. 453; Conceição & Heitor, 1999), which indicates that university education combines the transmission of knowledge from teachers to students' individual characteristics, in a process where the interpretation of ideas leads to the accumulation of knowledge, specifically of skills (Conceição & Heitor, 1999, p. 48). After analysing the documents of WCUs, the main keywords about talent cultivation can be classified as shown in Table 6.3.

In general, WCUs focus on the demand for talent in the global labour market and attach great importance to the impact of globalization and internationalization on talent cultivation. They aim to provide students with high-quality courses and exceptional learning experiences, and offer students an inspirational learning environment with creativity, free inquiry and academic freedom; to impart the knowledge, wisdom and skills needed by students to thrive as global citizens who are equipped with a global vision and international competitiveness; to develop future generations of leaders; to educate globally responsible citizens with critical thinking and professional skills, who will actively participate in the civic, political, economic and cultural activities of society. These educated students will also become members in a world of cultural diversity, who understand, preserve and promote national, regional, international cultures.

WCUs have world-class faculty and teaching facilities, advocate internationalized, innovative teaching methods and use information technology to improve these methods, encourage participatory, interactive and cooperative learning, and foster practical and innovative skills. In addition, WCUs are also actively developing various policies and programmes associated with talent cultivation, for example, the 'Melbourne model' at the University of Melbourne, Australia, and the 'Teaching Excellence Initiative' at the Technical University Munich, Germany.

4.2 Scientific Research

Scientific research contributes to the creation, advancement and dissemination of knowledge (of course, talent cultivation also contributes to this aspect), which embodies the well-established idea that universities are the nurseries of

TABLE 6.3 Keywords related to talent cultivation (simplified version)

Elements	Keywords[a]	Context (for example)
A: Adaption[b]	world/international/global... society/social community	...contribute to the needs of a changing society... ...ensure they are fit for purpose in the national and international marketplace...
G: Goal attainment	world/international/global... excellence/excellent experience creativity/creative leaders/leadership leading/world-class/first-class/best/top... society/social/community future/life	We will be renowned for the excellence of our undergraduate and graduate education: excellence in student cohort, excellence in teaching, excellence in student experience... ...aims to nurture global leaders... possessing both deep specialism and broad knowledge...
I: integration[c]	– educator: (high/best/top) quality World/international/global...innovative/creative/critical diversity/diverse – learners/students: best/outstanding/distinct/top... talented/talent opportunities undergraduate attract (most talented...) – content: knowledge scholarship/intellectual world/international/global... diverse (discipline) inter-discipline/multidiscipline open/creative/free	...have a world-class faculty in every field that it offers, and sustaining this rare and consistent quality is one of our highest priorities... ...we thrive on...the pursuit of new knowledge, and the search for creative ways to put our discoveries to good use, we continuously strengthen our investments in innovation... ...we will attract the very best students in terms of ability and potential...those students will be provided with a world-class learning experience...

(Cont.)

TABLE 6.3 Keywords related to talent cultivation (simplified version) (Cont.)

Elements	Keywords[a]	Context (for example)
	– method: supportive/inspiring/ inclusive/creative/new (pedagogy/method) diversity/diverse (discipline) technology... interactive/interaction/ cooperative	
L: Latent pattern maintenance[d]	support environment supportive/new (policy/ model)	We support intellectual freedom, courage and creativity. We encourage the pursuit of innovation and opportunities...we create a vibrant, inclusive environment in which ideas flourish and future generations, regardless of background are empowered...

a. Keywords here contains only part of all words of high frequency due to the space limitation.
b. Adaption here mainly refers to external demands.
c. Integration here may include resources for use, methods, content, rules and regulation for coordination, etc.
d. Latent pattern maintenance means Internal culture and value, supporting policy, etc.

new ideas, creation and innovations and that they gradually become 'reservoirs of knowledge' (Mintrom, 2008, p. 232). Also, knowledge itself is a pure public good, which is non-excludable and non-rivalrous. After analysing the documents of WCUs, the main keywords about scientific research can be classified as shown in Table 6.4.

Overall, driven by the information technology and knowledge-based economy, WCUs are committed to solving global issues of common concern for humanity, while at the same time meeting the social development needs of countries and regions. WCUs aim to become the world's most important scientific research centres, carrying out scientific research projects of the highest quality, discovering and disseminating cutting-edge knowledge and putting knowledge to work on a large scale and with excellence; providing timely solutions to the most complex international problems; and promoting

TABLE 6.4 Keywords related to scientific research (simplified version)

Elements	Keywords[a]	Context (for example)
A: Adaption	(societal/social) needs nation/state/national	...pursue discoveries that will lead to improved quality of life and competitiveness for the state and our nation. ...evolve structures and processes to identify trends for investment, and foster innovation, risk-taking, and collaboration.
G: Goal attainment	excellent/top/outstanding/world-class/best... international/global/world knowledge/scholarship innovation/creativity... new/cutting edge/original education impacts	...to be a top quality international center of scholarship...and research. ...is committed to developing new knowledge that improves people's lives...contributes to a better understanding of the world. ...investigate the most challenging, fundamental problems in science and technology...
I: Integration	– conditions: excellent/top/best/world-class student/staff/faculty/researcher support/supportive... freedom funding – content: top/best/world-class/... international/global/world... knowledge/scholarship innovation/creativity... new/cutting edge/original interdisciplinary... society/society/societal challenging/complex/difficult environment/environmental community/communities culture/cultural life/lives	...new federal funding has permitted considerable expansion of the University's research enterprise we must sustain the remarkable community of researchers, teachers, and learners, enhance new cross-University collaborations and new connections among the University, the surrounding community, and new partners in industry and research ...address the world's most challenging problems through an interdisciplinary approach

(Cont.)

TABLE 6.4 Keywords related to scientific research (simplified version) (*Cont.*)

Elements	Keywords[a]	Context (for example)
	– forms: collaboration/cooperation/ partnership... interdisciplinary... postgraduate/master... community/communities	we will build on our global reputation in key areas of national and international significance, such as energy, sustainability, water, health, food security and social equity, through an emphasis on high-quality, interdisciplinary global collaboration
		we develop a global reputation for excellence in postgraduate education. Addressing global challenges through our disciplinary excellence and distinctive cross-disciplinary approach...
L: Latent pattern maintenance	support/supportive... funding	...always stood for freedom of spirit, thought and speech, together with freedom of research and teaching...

a. Keywords here contains only part of all words of high frequency due to the space limitation.

social, cultural, economic, medical development at national, regional and global levels through scientific research activities. In terms of scientific research funding, these universities usually receive a large amount of state funding and have multiple funding sources. At the same time, WCUs also invest much on scientific research.

These universities have the most advanced scientific research teams, facilities and powerful scientific research cooperation networks. WCUs focus on graduate education, and encourage students, faculty and full-time researchers to participate in research activities, conducting research through an interdisciplinary approach, with local, regional, national, international and multi-party cooperation (with government, universities, companies, industry, NGOs, etc.). WCUs often have a long tradition of independent scholarship and academic freedom while fostering a culture in which innovation plays an important role. Some universities have developed a series of specialized scientific strategic plans (such as the 'Strategic Research Plan' in McGill University, Canada) and others also have special financial policies that support scientific research activities.

4.3 Social Service

The function of social service has many synonyms, including service, community service, public service, social engagement and community engagement, and these terms share similarities while maintaining some differences (Pinheiro, Langa, & Pausits, 2015; Watermeyer, 2015; Chantler, 2016). The function of social service goes beyond business and economic aspects. Universities have a wider vision of service and engagement which incorporates social, economic, cultural, political and environmental aspects of capacity building. The social service function is manifested by universities making contributions to civil society, government and the private sector, enhancing not only the economic performance but also assisting to improve life quality and the effectiveness of public engagement (Howard & Sharma, 2006). After analysing the documents of WCUs, the main keywords about social service can be classified as shown in Table 6.5.

The teaching and research activities of WCUs serve the needs of society which can be seen as the basic service universities provide to wider society. During this process, WCUs develop a strong and constructive relationship with the wider communities by contributing to the cultural, social and economic wellbeing.

At the national level, WCUs promote national economic development, provide alumni with opportunities for work, internships and training, and they

TABLE 6.5 Keywords related to social service (simplified version)

Elements	Keywords[a]	Context (for example)
A: Adaption	society/social/societal/socially community/communities all/human/human-beings life/lives/well-being/welfare	...research and teaching should serve the needs of society... ...contributing to the cultural, health, social, and economic wellbeing of the local and regional community...
G: Goal attainment	service (s)/serve... all/human/human-beings world/international/global... excellent/best/top/distinctive... life/well-being/welfare contribute(s)/contribution(s) benefit(s)/beneficial (positive) impact/influence	...to impact society in a transformative way – regionally, nationally, and globally – by engaging with partners outside the traditional borders of the university campus...to address critical issues facing society regionally, nationally, and globally...

(*Cont.*)

TABLE 6.5 Keywords related to social service (simplified version) (*Cont.*)

Elements	Keywords[a]	Context (for example)
I: Integration	– participator: university; student; staff/faculty; alumni – content: world/international/global... community state/nation/ national/nationally knowledge/ scholarship... public/publicly excellent/distinctive/best... economic/economy/income industry/industrial/business local/locally cultural/culture challenge(s)/problem(s) – method: knowledge/scholarship/ intellectual connection/cooperation/dialogue engage/engagement/engaging innovation/innovative/creative alumni government(s) research teaching	...benefit society on a national and a global scale; ensuring significant contributions to public policy-making and economic growth... ...contribute effectively to the cultural, social, and economic life of the city of and the region... ...serve society by promoting and contributing to economic, cultural, and social advances ...delivering global impact through a network of innovative international activities, collaborations and partnerships grow our international profile through working in partnership and using our Grand Challenge expertise in global health, sustainable cities, human wellbeing and intercultural interaction to help solve problems and deliver global impact... ...establish the strategic partnerships – both here and abroad...to confront some of the most pressing global challenges...
L: Latent pattern maintenance	partnership/connection(s)/ connect/link(s)/cooperation(s) support policy(policies)	...stands for inclusiveness and diversity...anyone who wishes to contribute to its ambitions... can feel welcome and enjoy equal opportunities. Create a comprehensive public engagement strategy...

a. Keywords here contains only part of all words of high frequency due to the space limitation.

also obtain donations from alumni. WCUs are devoted to maintain and pass on their countries' cultural characteristics, benefiting the world on the basis of serving their own countries. Internationally, WCUs aims to influence the development and development of the world in a transformative way, benefiting all mankind in the fields of economy, culture, politics and environmental protection, contributing to the sustainable, stable and peaceful development of the whole world, and serving the global common good. They participate extensively in international public affairs (including social, political and cultural aspects), cooperate with universities at home and abroad, and actively engage beyond the campus.

At the same time, both faculty and students are encouraged to participate in various forms of volunteer projects and overseas exchange activities in WCUs. WCUs often have long-cherished social service tradition and some specific strategic plans for promoting such service, for instance, the Social Engagement Plan at the University of Melbourne in Australia and the Community Engagement Statement at Warwick University in the United Kingdom. Some universities also provide special funds and policies to support social service activities.

In summary, these three functions underpin the WCUs' special role related to global common good(s). In terms of talent cultivation, WCUs are making efforts in constructing a human capital pool consisting of the most distinguished and outstanding talents which becomes the most important national and global resource. As for scientific research, WCUs intend to conduct the most advanced research and develop state-of-the-art knowledge, and tackle challenging international problems so as to improve humanity's wellbeing. Regarding social service, WCUs aim to cope with the most complex and difficult global challenges for the benefit of human society, influencing the development and progress of the world in a transformative way, contributing to sustainable and peaceful development for all mankind and the whole world. This reflects the fact that, WCUs, as leading research universities functioning globally, will develop global common goods such as advanced knowledge and excellent research, and contribute to the common good (inclusive culture, peaceful development, etc.) that humans share intrinsically in common.

5 A Balanced Role of WCUs

Just as Nicholas Dirks, chancellor of University of California, Berkeley, said: 'Now, more than ever, the progress we make in confronting salient global challenges and opportunities will depend on the ability of universities around the world to collaborate, coordinate and share knowledge'. Therefore, among all universities, WCUs, at any one time, should take the initiative to nurture world-class education, research and provide extensive social service, thereby embracing opportunities, coping with challenges and enhancing sustainable development of the whole world.

Apart from this, WCUs also need to balance their roles in developing global common goods, making national contributions and conducting local engagement to achieve global sustainability. At a global level, the educational and research work of WCUs contribute to the stock of knowledge in academic fields as well as tackling pressing challenges so as to improve the wellbeing of humanity; Massive Open Online Courses (MOOCs) offered by most WCUs disseminate knowledge to every corner in the world and give equal opportunities for people worldwide to high-quality teaching. At the national level, high-level education from WCUs nurtures national leaders and democratic/responsible citizenship; cooperation between WCUs and government, organizations, industry and business boosts national economic and social development. At the local level, engagement with the local community contributes to the building of social capital and the resolution of local issues, provides continuing education opportunities for the locals and also improves community social and economic infrastructure.

Overall, WCUs, as a special and higher level global common good, are full of significance in accelerating the development of the nation, the region and the world. Their role in generating global common goods while at the same time serving the global common good should be cherished and enhanced in the future.

References

Arendt, H. (1993). *Between past and future: Eight exercises in political thought*. London: Penguin.

Bie, D. R., & Zhang, Z. (2010). Jiao yu li nian yu shi jie yi liu da xue de xing cheng [Educational concept and the formation of world-class universities]. *Gao Deng Jiao Yu Yan Jiu* [Higher Education Research], (7), 7–14.

Chantler, A. (2016). The ivory tower revisited. *Discourse: Studies in the Cultural Politics of Education, 37*(2), 215–229.

Chen, Y. C. (2008). Gao deng jiao yu gong yi xing de xian shi li xing [The Practical Reasons for the Higher Education as a Public Good]. *Fudan Jiao Yu Lun Tan* [Fudan Education Forum], 6(1), 10–13.

Cheng, H. Q. (2006). Shi lun zheng fu zai gao deng jiao yu zhong de ze ren: gong gong wu pin li lun de shi jiao [A discussion on the responsibility of the government: a perspective of public good]. *Jiangsu Gao Jiao* [Jiang Su Higher Education], 3, 47–49.

Conceição, P., & Heitor, M. V. (1999). On the role of the university in the knowledge economy. *Science and Public Policy, 26*(1), 37–51.

Deneulin, S., & Townsend, N. (2007). Public goods, global public goods and the common good. *International Journal of Social Economics, 34*(1–2), 19–36.

Desai, M. (2003). Public goods: A historical perspective. In I. Kaul (Ed.), *Providing global public goods: Managing globalization*. Oxford: Oxford University Press.

Hayek, F. A. (1973). *Law, legislation and liberty, volume 1: Rules and order*. Chicago, IL: University of Chicago Press.

Hollenbach, D. (2002). *The common good and Christian ethics*. Cambridge: Cambridge University Press.

Howard, J., & Sharma, A. (2006). *Universities' third mission: Communities engagement* (BHERT Position Paper No. 11). Retrieved January 28, 2017, from https://www.bhert.com/publications/position-papers/B-HERTPositionPaper11.pdf

Huang, J. X., & Tang, X. M. (2017). Cong gong yi shi ye dao gong tong li yi – cong lian he guo jiao ke wen zu zhi jiao yu li nian de zhuan bian tan qi [From the public good to the common good – A discussion based on the change of UNESCO's educational concept]. *Jiao Yu Fa Zhan Yan Jiu* [Research in Educational Development], (9), 78–84.

Kant, I. (1979). *The conflict of the faculties* (M. J. Gregor, Trans.). New York, NY: Abaris Books.

Lambert, M. T. (2014). *Privatization and the public good: Public universities in the balance*. Cambridge, MA: Harvard Education Press.

Lewis, D. R., & Hearn, J. (2003). *The public research university: Serving the public good in new times*. Lanham, MD: University Press of America.

Marginson, S. (2014). Higher education as a public good in a marketized East Asian environment. In A. Yonezawa, Y. Kitamura, A. Meerman, & K. Kuroda (Eds.), *Emerging international dimensions in East Asian higher education*. Dordrecht: Springer.

Marginson, S. (2018). Public/private in higher education: A synthesis of economic and political approaches. *Studies in Higher Education, 43*(2), 322–337.

Marmolo, E. (1999). A constitutional theory of public goods. *Journal of Economic Behavior and Organization, 38*(1), 27–42.

Menashy, F. (2009). Education as a global public good: The applicability and implications of a framework. *Globalisation, Societies and Education, 7*(3), 307–320.

Mintrom, M. (2008). Managing the research function of the university: Pressures and dilemmas. *Journal of Higher Education Policy and Management, 30*(3), 231–244.

Parsons, T. (1960). *Structure and process in modern societies*. Giencoe, IL: Free Press.

Parsons, T. (1970). *The social system*. London: Routledge & Kegan Paul Ltd.

Parsons, T., & Smelser, N. (1956). *Economy and society: A study in the integration of economic and social theory*. London: Routledge.

Pinheiro, R., Langa, P. V., & Pausits, A. (2015). One and two equals three? The third mission of higher education institutions. *European Journal of Higher Education, 5*(3), 233–249.

Ren, Y. H. (2012). *Da Xue Gong Neng de Zheng Ti Xing Ji Qi Chong Jian* [The integrity of university function and its reconstruction] (Doctorate thesis). Southwest University, Chongqing, China.

Samuelson, P. A. (1954). The pure theory of public expenditure. *The Review of Economics and Statistics, 36*(4), 387–389.

Su, L. Q. (2009). Gong gong xing: gao deng jiao yu de ji ben shu xing [Public goods: The basic attribute of higher education]. *Xian Dai Jiao Yu Ke Xue* [Modern Education Science], *3*, 71–72.

Tilak, J. (2008). Higher education: A public good or a commodity for trade? *Prospects, 38*(4), 449–466.

United Nations Educational, Social and Cultural Organization, UNESCO. (2015). *Rethinking education: Towards a global common good.* Paris: United Nations Educational, Social and Cultural Organization (UNESCO). Retrieved January 28, 2017, from http://unesdoc.unesco.org/images/0023/002325/232555e.pdf

Wang, Y., & Xia, J. G. (2016). Lun ying yong ji shu da xue zai she hui xi tong zhong de ding wei – ji yu AGIL mo xing de fen xi [On the positioning of university of applied technology in social system – An analysis based on AGIL model]. *Zhong Guo Gao Jiao Yan Jiu* [China Higher Education Research], *5*, 77–80.

Watermeyer, R. (2011). Challenges for university engagement in the UK: Towards a public academe? *Higher Education Quarterly, 65*(4), 386–410.

Yuan, Q. L. (2009). Lun gao deng jiao yu de gong yi xing yu si yi xing [On the public welfare and private good of higher education]. *Gao Deng Jiao Yu Yan Jiu* [Higher Education Research], *30*(8), 43–48.

Zang, X. H., & Qu, C. (2002). Cong ke guan shu xing dao xie zheng jue ce – lun 'gong gong wu pin' gai nian de fa zhan yu yan bian [From objective attributes to constitutional choice – The development and evolution of the concept of 'public goods']. *Shan Dong Da Xue Xue Bao: Ren Wen She Hui Ke Xue Ban* [Journal of Shan Dong University: Humanities and Social Sciences], *2*, 37–44.

Zemsky, R. (2003). Have we lost the 'public' in higher education? *The Chronicle of Higher Education, 49*(38), B7.

Zhao, W. H., & Zhou, Q. L. (2006). Da xue zhan lue gui hua zhong shi ming yu yuan jing de nei han yu jia zhi [The connotation and value of the mission and vision statements in university strategic plans]. *Jiao Yu Fa Zhan Yan Jiu* [Research in Educational Development], *13*, 61–64.

Zhuang, Q. H. (2013). Cong jie gou gong neng zhu yi shi jiao kan xian dai da xue zhi du gou jian [An analysis of the construction of modern university system from the perspective of structural functionalism]. *Jiang Su Gao Jiao* [Jiangsu Higher Education], *5*, 50–52.

CHAPTER 7

The Art of Starting a New University: Lessons of Experience

Jamil Salmi

Abstract

In the past three decades, several highly resourced research universities have been established from scratch around the world to pursue the goals of academic and research excellence in an accelerated fashion. These institutions have benefited from unusually large infusions of initial capital that facilitated rapid development. They also grew from careful planning to ensure innovation in their design and function from the beginning. These universities have received significant international attention, but, to date, have been little studied. Many have already made significant contributions to the international, as well as national, higher education environment. While this category of accelerated universities is likely to remain limited to a small number of institutions globally, other ventures with similar goals will undoubtedly be considered in coming years and thus lessons learned from this experience will be both important and useful. This chapter outlines the main characteristics of recent case studies and analyses the opportunities and challenges that influence the pursuit of innovation and excellence in the contemporary academic world.

Keywords

Accelerated universities – research-intensive universities – academic excellence

> The opportunity to start from a blank page and create an entire institution from concept to reality is a rare and precious gift. It enables many possibilities that would be unthinkable at established universities…But it requires vision, passion, and courage to attempt to innovate and to deliberately create a new and improved learning culture.
> RICHARD MILLER, Founding President of Olin College

∙ ∙ ∙

Mistake is the best teacher.
ANONYMOUS

∴

1 Introduction

The past sixty years have witnessed an unprecedented expansion of higher education in most parts of the world. Countries have taken care of the impressive rise in the social demand for postsecondary education by creating new public universities and/or allowing private institutions to start. What happened in South Korea is perhaps the most emblematic example of mass expansion. With a tertiary education enrolment of barely two per cent at the time of independence in 1945, the system has grown so rapidly and vastly that Korea can boast today the highest participation rate among OECD nations.

Confined initially to the industrial world, the mass expansion of higher education has progressively reached the developing world. Even the poorest countries of the planet have experienced fast university expansion in the past twenty years. But in most cases, the main focus of national authorities has been on quantitative increase rather than qualitative transformation. That is, until the arrival of the Academic Ranking of World Universities, also called the Shanghai ranking, in 2003.

With the publication of the first Academic Ranking of World Universities and the emergence of other international rankings in its wake (THE, QS, HEEACT, etc.), institutional leaders, researchers and politicians have turned their attention to the top universities in the league tables. Growing interest in the so-called world-class universities has translated into endeavours to assess the importance of this phenomenon, analyse the characteristics of world-class universities, and understand the paths followed by the most successful universities in the world (Altbach, 2004; Salmi, 2009; Altbach & Salmi, 2011).

As a result, often for reasons of national prestige, governments in a growing number of countries have launched 'excellence initiatives', consisting of large injections of additional funding, to induce substantial and rapid progress in the performance of their top universities. Most interested economies have adopted a strategy of competitive funding to encourage existing universities to transform themselves as they seek to achieve excellence in research. A few countries have also supported mergers by providing financial incentives (Denmark, Finland and France for instance) or political directives (China and Russia for example).

A few nations, however, have opted for establishing new universities from scratch, on the assumption that improving existing institutions is more arduous, especially from a governance viewpoint, and requires more time. Thus, in the past decade, Abu Dhabi, Kazakhstan, Luxembourg, Saudi Arabia and Singapore, for example, have all adopted this new university strategy, following the earlier examples of the Hong Kong University of Science and Technology and similar initiatives in South Korea (Korea Advanced Institute of Science [KAIST] and Technology, and Pohang University of Science and Technology [POSTECH]).

These universities have received significant international attention and, in some cases, have already made major contributions to their countries and to global higher education. However, they have been little studied to date. To remedy this gap, the author and a few colleagues organized a summit of presidents of what could be called 'start-up universities'. At the end of the summit, which took place at the Massachusetts Institute of Technology (MIT) in February 2016, the participating presidents agreed to document the experience of their start-up universities through case studies based on a common template. This chapter analyses the main findings of these case studies, which include the following institutions:

- Ecole Polytechnique Fédérale de Lausanne in Switzerland (EPFL);
- Hong Kong University of Science and Technology (HKUST);
- Masdar Institute of Technology in Abu Dhabi (Masdar);
- Olin College of Engineering in Massachusetts, US (Olin);
- Nazarbayev University in Kazakhstan
- Singapore University of Technology and Design (SUTD);
- Skolkovo Institute of Science and Technology in Russia (Skoltech); and
- The University of Luxembourg (Luxembourg).

The case studies reviewed in this chapter are all examples of what could be called start-up universities, with the exception of EPFL, whose radical transformation is a tale of a small, local school of engineering that managed to evolve rapidly into a new institution of world standing, widely considered today as the top institute of technology in the francophone world.

A special feature of the start-ups discussed in this chapter is that all have had significant financial resources devoted to them. While it is unusual to have this level of funding made available, it is not unprecedented. At the end of the 19th century and the beginning of the 20th, for example, several of America's top universities were established with major funds from philanthropists (and thus free of pressures from government) – examples include the University of Chicago, Rockefeller University and Stanford University. All of these institutions proved to be highly successful in a relatively short period of time, and were founded by visionary leaders with innovative ideas about higher education. It should be added that these three universities had a significant influence on broader higher education developments in the United States and worldwide, particularly in developing new ways of organizing research, but also, especially in the case of Chicago, of new approaches to the curriculum. It remains to be seen whether the cases in this chapter will have a similar impact, either in their national context, the greater region, or the international sphere.

Against this background, this chapter attempts to draw the common threads coming out of the experience of start-up universities in various parts of the world. It starts by assessing the extent to which the path followed by these institutions corroborates the findings of previous work on the establishment of world-class universities. It then identifies new lessons that can be derived from their trajectory as they set about to achieve academic excellence in an accelerated fashion.

2 Characteristics of World-Class Institutions

With no exception, all of the start-up universities analysed in this chapter confirm that, in order to achieve the superior results of well-performing universities – highly sought graduates, leading-edge research and dynamic technology transfer – academic institutions seek to align the fundamental drivers of excellence that are the concentration of talent (academics and students); abundant resources to offer a rich learning environment and support an advanced research; and favourable governance features that encourage strategic vision, innovation and flexibility (Salmi, 2009). This is true as much for the universities and institutes of technology pursuing leading-edge research as for Olin College of Engineering, which is geared to preparing outstanding graduates.

2.1 Talent Development

The main priority of the newly established institutions has been to recruit exceptional faculty and talented students, using a variety of strategies. As far as staff recruitment is concerned, in many cases the institutions went after foreign academics to begin their activities, as illustrated by Nazarbayev University, Masdar, SUTD, Skoltech and Luxembourg. For SUTD, Masdar and Skolktech, close collaboration with MIT was instrumental in providing access to top academics for the launch period. HKUST relied almost exclusively on the Chinese diaspora during its first years of operation, hiring a combination of experienced professors and promising young researchers. Nazarbayev University received assistance initially from its several foreign partners. In the case of EPFL, the Polytechnic went after North American and European star researchers as part of its strategy to upgrade its performance. Olin, which as an undergraduate college is not focused on research but on the production of sought-after graduates, faced at the beginning the big challenge of attracting highly-qualified academics away from prestigious existing institutions. This was achieved by the lure of a revolutionary teaching and learning methodology.

Similarly, when it came to getting talented students to apply, the institutions adopted several complementary strategies. On the educational side, students valued the opportunity of studying in English (at Nazarbayev University for example) or having access to a different kind of programme (innovative engineering at Olin College, or a US-style curriculum at HKUST for instance). On the financial side, incoming students could study free of charge or get generous scholarships covering the tuition fees and living expenses. In Kazakhstan, Luxembourg and Abu Dhabi, having the promise of a high-quality university established locally for the first time was a big pull factor. Having very innovative features was especially important in areas with strong local competition, as noted in the HKUST, SUTD and Olin cases.

Being a niche institution or having niche programmes as the start-up institutions seek to build excellence is an important factor of success. With the exception of the University of Luxembourg, all institutions under review are specialized institutions in science and engineering, or in design, architecture and engineering in the case of SUTD. Even the University of Luxembourg has endeavoured to become a world leader in a small number of carefully selected areas such as finance, cyber security and medical research.

2.2 Sustainable Funding

All the institutions analysed benefited from high levels of resources at the time of inception. In most cases, it came in the form of strong financial backing by the State as these institutions received special treatment compared to the existing public universities in their country. Olin College of Engineering, the only private institution among the case studies, is no exception, although its resources did not come from government but from a generous endowment set up by the former Franklin Olin Foundation.

Reliance on a single source of funding, whether from the public purse or private backers, is always an element of vulnerability. Nazarbayev University has been hard hit by the fall in oil prices in the past few years, which had led to severe cuts in the national budget. Olin College's endowment lost almost half of its value as a result of the 2007 financial crisis, forcing the institution to revisit its business model and give up on the no-tuition fee policy adopted at the beginning as a powerful incentive to attract high quality students.

An important consideration in ascertaining the long-term financial sustainability of start-up universities is to secure alternative income sources that can complement government funding. None of the institutions in the case studies, with the exception of Olin College since the financial crisis, have relied heavily on tuition fees. Notwithstanding Olin's experience, setting up a large endowment that will provide resources for special projects and a cushion for difficult times is perhaps one of the safest strategies in the long run. In the longer term, the other key source of income is research funding. The availability of competitive grants for research can also be an important source of funding, as illustrated by EPFL's success in accessing European Research Council (ERC) funding. This has also be a favourable factor for HKUST and STUD.

2.3 Favourable Governance

In almost all cases, the newly established universities have benefited from favourable governance arrangements allowing them to operate with more flexibility than regular universities. In the few countries where the existing public institutions already had appropriate setups, such as Hong Kong and Singapore, the new university enjoyed a similar governance and management system. SUTD adopted, in addition, a shared leadership model to support its multidisciplinary nature.

In the other cases, government had to make special provisions to give the start-up university a more advantageous regime than the prevailing conditions in the country. This was the case in Kazakhstan, for example, where Nazarbayev University was created by a new Act setting it apart from the other public universities. The Abu Dhabi and Russian authorities followed a similar approach for Masdar and Skolktech, respectively. The new EPFL president was fully empowered by the Board as the institution embarked on a transformative path. When it was established in 2003, the new University of Luxembourg was put under the authority of a very nimble Board, with only seven members, all of whom come from outside the University (four of them with academic experience) and three non-voting representatives of the University (the president, one professor and one student). As the only private institution among the institutions under review in the book, Olin College has benefited from a very flexible governance structure from the beginning.

It is also interesting to note that, in the majority of cases, the first president of the institution was a foreigner – sometimes the entire leadership team was made of non-nationals – reflecting the view that having leaders with extensive international experience would be vital to launch the new institution successfully. In the case of HKUST, the first president came from the Chinese diaspora, having been the president of a US university. Even though the president of EPFL who led the upgrading of the institution was not a foreigner, he had extensive experience as a professor in top US universities, which helped shape the transformative path followed by EPFL. The only exception is Olin College of Engineering, but here again much of the success of this innovative venture can be attributed to the personality and leadership qualities of Richard Miller, the founding president.

3   New Lessons

3.1   *Breaking Traditional Academic Barriers*

A common thread among all the case studies analysed is the emphasis on multidisciplinarity and the emphasis on collaborative arrangements that bring traditional scientific disciplines together. Most institutions under review have put in place new structures that encourage more cross-disciplinary teaching, learning and research activities. SUTD was designed from the outset as an interdisciplinary institution organized around pillars rather than schools and departments, where active learning was the norm throughout the curriculum. A large chunk of EPFL's research expansion has been in biomedical engineering, at the crossroads of engineering and the life sciences. An interesting development at HUKST has been the integration of research and teaching in a much stronger way than any other university in Hong Kong. The University of Luxembourg has established two interdisciplinary centers linked to its main areas of excellence (finance and cyber security, and biomedicine).

Olin College is perhaps the institution that has been most innovative in terms of moving away from traditional curricular and pedagogical practices. Its curriculum combines engineering, entrepreneurship and humanities in a unique way. Olin students cross-enroll at Babson College (a business focused institution) and Wellesley College (a liberal arts undergraduate college) for entrepreneurships and humanities courses, respectively. Olin College organizes learning primarily around project-based and design-based activities performed by students working in teams. It has no academic departments and does not offer tenure to its faculty members. A typical programme involves several teachers from different disciplines providing integrated courses with interdisciplinary material. As a result, Olin College has succeeded in creating an academic culture emphasizing interdisciplinary learning and educational innovation. Rick Miller, the founding president of Olin College, spoke eloquently about the unique educational experiment that the establishment of the new school of engineering represented:

Olin had this unique opportunity to rethink education for two years before we taught any classes – this is during the construction of the campus. So one of those years, we dedicated to experimentation with students. We called it the Olin Partner year, because the kids that came that year were not taking courses, but they were actually partners with us in experimentation.

We learned two things from this. The first thing [is] you don't need to have two years of calculus and physics before you can make stuff. Kids are actually capable of learning on their own, particularly when they're motivated. Secondly, and more importantly, the impact of this experience on the students was absolutely transformational. It was now as if they were two feet taller. The kids basically said, 'Yes, this is what I want to do for the rest of my life. I know now if I have a few kids around me like this, and a couple of old guys to ask questions of once in a while, I can change the world. I can design anything I can imagine'.

Here's basically what happens. If you sat down in the cockpit of a 747 and you don't have a pilot's license, and the challenge is to figure out how to fly this thing and to do it in two days, you probably would get stuck a lot. But what if you had five of you in the room, and what if one of you had had some flight instruction somewhere else, another one had in a played in a flight simulator for a while, some people recognized what a horizon indicator looked like, what the altimeter was. What I'm calling the mean time between failure – the mean time between getting frustrated and stuck, to making progress and then getting frustrated and stuck again – that time distance goes way down if you have a group rather than one person. And kids do this almost intuitively.

And we realized if we could make that happen in everything that happens educationally at this school, these kids will teach themselves and you won't be able to stop them – and when they're finished they'll be ready to take on challenges that change the world.

So, here's one of the realizations: if you look at a catalogue of courses and you read the one-paragraph description for what we're going to learn in this class, that is analogous to a recipe for a soufflé in a restaurant. But how the soufflé actually tastes depends on the chef. It depends on how you put those ingredients together and what the interaction is like with the student. So this whole business of separating things into courses and having this one teach the math, and that one teach the physics, and that one teach the engineering, and assuming that the students are watching how the whole forest is going together just doesn't work.

So now we have courses that have titles that people don't normally see in engineering schools. Principles of Engineering is one. Another is called Design Nature. And what happens is that those subjects are inherently integrated. So the subject itself you can't get through by just learning physics. Physics is embedded in the projects that you do, and every one of those courses is project-oriented. So students actually are formed in teams immediately and the faculty are formed in teams that are teaching them.

One of the [other] things that we discovered, very simple, [is] how do people learn? It turns out people primarily learn from stories – that storytelling is the fundamental skill that all excellent teachers are good at. Furthermore, the stories that work in terms of contributing to education are stories about people. So, Olin is deliberately working to inject people back into the narrative of what engineering is about. Rather than having the role of the teacher the omnipotent source of all information – where you're intended to sit there in rows and take notes – they now see essentially a play going on in front of them while these two guys are debating what really happened. And then there's this constant interaction with the students, so it's more like a graduate seminar.

Our approach is essential to deal with our planet's big challenges. At some point the feasibility of having every generation have a better life than the previous one is going to come in to conflict. I have rarely talked to a high school kid who isn't concerned about these issues. Now, those problems are not easily solvable. They're all coupled, they are connected, they are interdisciplinary. They transcend time zones. They transcend political boundaries. To attack problems like that, it takes a completely different kind of mindset – a different kind of education. Young people are like wet cement. Thinking in a systems way, thinking across disciplines and across political boundaries, is something that will be easier to teach if we start with undergraduates and we do this across the globe. (Buderi, 2014)

3.2 *Partnerships and Collaboration*
The case studies show that most institutions relied heavily on institutional partnerships to jumpstart their activities, especially in recruiting academic

staff, developing their curriculum, preparing for programme accreditation and initiating collaborative research projects. EPFL, HKUST, Nazarbayev University and the University of Luxembourg worked with several partners, while Masdar, Skolktech and SUTD privileged a single main institutional partner, MIT. As mentioned earlier, Olin College delivers its curriculum in partnership with Babson College and Wellesley College, with students from the three institutions cross-enrolling.

3.3   Mergers

Several countries that launched excellence initiatives to accelerate the transformation of their universities into world-class institutions actively promoted mergers. As documented elsewhere, these mergers were not always successful because it is generally difficult to mesh two different institutional cultures (Salmi, 2016). One interesting finding coming out of the EPFL story is that mini-mergers, involving one or several faculties, appear to be more effective than full mergers between two or more institutions. By absorbing the mathematics, physics and chemistry departments of the University of Lausanne, EPFL was able to strengthen the science base of its programmes in a very effective manner.

3.4   Location

While having ample resources is indispensable to attract talented administrators, academics and students, money is not enough. It is equally important to offer uniquely attractive learning and research conditions, an animated and stimulating campus life, together with an auspicious living environment where the families of those directly associated with the new university can feel happy. Location is a key factor in that respect. Situated less than 20 miles south of Boston, Olin College of Engineering can take full advantage of everything Massachusetts has to offer. The proximity of Babson College and Wellesley College is also a great advantage. Similarly, Hong Kong, Lausanne and Luxembourg are vibrant cities – Lausanne and Luxembourg in fully democratic countries – and all three offering many opportunities for employment and a rich cultural life.

3.5   Maintaining the Momentum

During the first years after beginning to implement their vision, the leaders of start-up universities face the daunting challenge of keeping the momentum in the absence of tangible ways of measuring and demonstrating actual progress in the early stages of the institution. Having in place the right inputs and creating a favourable institutional culture are certainly priority endeavours, but they are not enough. Success is not guaranteed until the institution is able to show in a concrete way that it has reached excellence in teaching, learning and research.

This means getting evidence that employers recognize the first graduates as 'best in class' and that the international research community scientific takes notice of the outstanding scientific output of the institution. Tracer studies and employer surveys are the right instruments in the first case. As for research results, which take longer to demonstrate, the ARWU and Leiden rankings, especially in the key areas of academic excellence chosen to define the niche of the institution, can be useful proxies. In Europe, the results of ERC research grants competitions, which have a success rate of less than 10 per cent, give a good sense of research potential. The number of highly-cited scholars that the new institution has managed to recruit is a meaningful indicator, as well.

One way of maintaining the momentum is to develop, from the very beginning, a strong culture of evaluation that allows for the early detection of problems and identification of areas for improvement. Only by having the right mindset of self-criticism, helped by appropriate monitoring instruments and flexible mechanisms to make corrections, can start-up institutions avoid going on the wrong track, or becoming rapidly complacent if they allow themselves to be blindsided by the abundance of resources they can draw on during the start-up phase to achieve relatively rapid results. Among the founding precepts defined to guide the creation of Olin College, the 'expiry principle' states that the College will be constantly evaluating what it does and seeking to improve its programmes and operations. In addition to the internal quality assurance mechanisms, which apply not only to academic aspects but also to all other dimensions of institutional operations, Olin College relies on several channels to receive regular feedback and advice from the outside world (alumni network, employers, biannual meeting of the President's Council, etc.).

To obtain constructive feedback and guidance, most institutions have included highly experienced foreigners as members of their board, and some have established an international advisory council that meets once or twice a year. In addition to its regular Board, Olin College set up a President's Council that meets twice a year to provide advice to the leadership team.

4 Conclusion: Drivers, Challenges and Risks

The case studies on well-funded new universities analysed in this chapter have revealed a number of valuable lessons about the core elements of the strategies adopted, the types of issues arising during the start-up phase, and the measures that can help resolve them. In the first instance, the experience of these university start-ups confirms that it is indispensable to have in place, from the very beginning, the right form of governance and high levels of funding needed to build an appealing learning and research environment and attract talented academics and students.

In the second place, one of the new findings is the prominence of leadership as a critical if not the main driver of success. While previous works on world-class universities has emphasized the importance of appropriate governance and analysed key elements, such as institutional autonomy, agile management and academic freedom, the case studies in this book reveal the catalytic role of an inspirational president/rector/vice chancellor capable of articulating a captivating vision that motivates the entire academic community and convinces external stakeholders in a sustained manner.

Furthermore, in most cases the visionary leader stayed on for a long time, which helped consolidate and sustain the exceptional efforts made during the design and launch periods. At the same time, the long tenure of a strong president/vice-chancellor/rector can evolve from being a favourable element of continuity to becoming a risk factor when succession plans are not carefully put in place. Start-up universities need to consider this issue earnestly as they transit from the initial build-up years to the steady fast phase.

A third finding is that reliance on foreign partners during the launch phase, while extremely useful for putting in place the right ingredients to foster a favourable academic environment, can make it more difficult for the start-up university to create an original institutional and academic culture. The temptation is great to imitate or replicate the model of the main institutional partner(s). The challenge of creating a shared academic culture and a coherent transformation vision among all constituting units should never be underestimated.

A fourth finding is the challenge of long-term financial sustainability, no matter how well-endowed an institution is at the beginning. Being well-resourced during the initial investment phase and for the first few years after the start-up university has been launched are not sufficient. Financial stability and sustainability in the long run are a fundamental condition of success. Strategies must be in place to protect these institutions from political upheavals and financial crises. A related question worth investigating in this context is whether those universities that benefitted from wealthy and politically influential backers at the beginning will be better protected, or face bigger sustainability challenges in the long run, than institutions in more democratic societies.

A fifth finding is the difficulty that start-up universities sometimes face in finding the right balance between their global and local roles. On the one hand, their aspiration to become world-class institutions pushes them to benchmark themselves against the characteristics and trajectory of global universities. On the other hand, making a meaningful contribution to the development of the national economy requires focusing on local research and training needs. This tension can also be seen in the choice of the publication language to disseminate the results of scientific research. International visibility requires publishing in English in the most prestigious scientific journals. But the country in which the start-up university is located could be better served by publications in the national language. This issue has been debated recently in countries as dissimilar as China, Saudi Arabia and South Korea.

The last finding relates to the importance of the ecosystem into which start-up universities are born and start to operate. While the argument could be made that a new university helps build a favourable environment, the truth is that, in many cases, institutions that are established in a difficult environment – politically, socially or culturally – struggle to attract and retain the most talented academics, students and administrators, and experience management rigidities when institutional autonomy continues to be restricted. Conversely, in countries with open borders, the rule of law, multicultural communities, ample professional opportunities, and full academic freedom, universities have a greater appeal for international scholars and students and can make faster progress on the road to academic excellence.

These conclusions can of course be only tentative, considering that most institutions analysed are still very young. But they provide, hopefully, useful pointers for anyone planning to start a new university or institute, as is the case today in countries as diverse as China, India, Nepal, Nigeria or the Philippines. The 'edu-entrepreneurs' keen on starting new ventures, whether in the public or the private sector, should keep these lessons in mind.

Launching a new institution with the aspiration of attaining the highest possible academic standards is a noble but extremely difficult enterprise. The road to academic excellence is full of pitfalls. One of them is to assume that abundant resources are sufficient to accelerate the pace. It is important to always remember that achieving excellence in teaching, learning and research remains a long-term endeavour, requiring thoughtful and measured approaches for sustainability. As Daniel Lincoln wrote, '...excellence, like all things of abiding value, is a marathon, not a sprint'.

Acknowledgement

This chapter draws on the findings of case studies included in a book co-edited by Philip Altbach, Isak Froumin, Liz Reizberg, and Jamil Salmi (2018). *Accelerated Universities: Ideas and Money Combine to Build Academic Excellence*. Leiden: Brill Sense.

References

Altbach, P. G. (2004). The costs and benefits of world-class universities. *Academe*, *90*(1), 20. Retrieved April 5, 2018, from http://www.aaup.org/AAUP/pubsres/academe/2004/JF/Feat/altb.htm

Altbach, P. G., & Salmi, J. (Eds.). (2011). *The road to academic excellence: The making of world-class research universities*. Washington, DC: World Bank.

Buderi, R. (2014). *Olin college president Rick Miller on reengineering engineering*. Retrieved April 5, 2018, from http://www.xconomy.com/boston/2014/09/24/olin-college-president-rick-miller-on-reengineering-engineering/?single_page=tru

Salmi, J. (2009). *The challenge of establishing world-class universities*. Washington, DC: World Bank.

Salmi, J. (2016). Excellence strategies and the creation of world-class universities. In E. Hazelkorn (Ed.), *Global rankings and the geopolitics of higher education: Understanding the influence and impact of rankings on higher education, policy and society*. London: Routledge.

PART 2

National and Regional Responses

∴

CHAPTER 8

The Role of American World-Class Universities in Serving the Global Common Good

Genevieve G. Shaker and William M. Plater

Abstract

Most American world-class universities originated with civic purposes: to educate students as participants and leaders of a democracy, and to generate knowledge for community improvement. In modern times, some fear they have strayed from this purpose and believe they need to renew their commitment to the public. We argue that a commitment to the global common good is at the very heart of being 'world-class' and that these institutions are and must be in service to society. Institutional leaders may issue this call, but individual faculty will carry out the responsibility and are the key to effectively contributing to society. Among faculty everywhere, those privileged to work at world-class universities are expected to provide leadership and be role models for the personal – and professional – duty to serve the global common good. Faculty (and their institutions) will likely rise to the challenge because of their shared historic foundation, record of perseverance, and ability to contribute in alignment with their differentiated missions.

Keywords

Public good – common good – world-class universities – faculty – academic professionalism – civic-mindedness – community engagement

1   Introduction

America's world-class universities are found among its research universities. They are the institutions that rise above their peers as engines for knowledge production and places where intellectual pursuits and academic freedom are paramount (Altbach, 2004). These successes are fuelled by ample human, fiscal and capital resources. These universities are international in their character and global in their focus ('The Formula for a World-Class University Revealed', n.d.). The best students seek them out and their faculty are top achievers. Most are private universities, and some are hundreds of years old – among the nation's first post-secondary institutions (Thelin, 2011).

Many American world-class universities (and research universities) originated with civic purposes: to educate students as participants and leaders of the democracy and to generate knowledge for community improvement (Checkoway, 2001). But some fear they have strayed from this purpose and need to renew their commitment to the public (Boyte, 1998; Checkoway, 2001; Mathews, 1997). American universities find themselves at a crossroad: to the right lies increased attention to economic development and personal advancement; to the left lies increased attention to the needs of society and the collective welfare of all; straight ahead lies a contested and uncertain future subject to forces and pressures external to institutions.

Different institutions may take different paths forward. There may well be a need for some institutions to follow each of the open paths. World-class universities, however, may have only one collective, shared choice.

We argue that a commitment to the global common good is at the very heart of being 'world-class' and that these institutions are and must be in service to society. Institutional leaders may issue this call, but individual faculty will carry out the responsibility. 'The best professors see their work as a "calling"' (Altbach, 2004, p. 6) and, if so, the promise and potential of world-class universities to do the most good should be secure. The focus on world-class universities as the unit of analysis often misses the point that the effectiveness of institutions depends largely on the independent, discretionary, and often separate acts of individual faculty.

Colleges and universities in their combined work do, indeed, perform as institutional citizens whose mission and purpose direct them more or less to acts on behalf of the public good. Still, 'it is essential for us to recognize that the prospect of colleges and universities performing a collective role as citizens depends...on the work of individual faculty' (Plater, 1999, p. 143).

A variety of forces are constraining America's universities and making faculty work in service to the common good increasingly tenuous and difficult. While of uncertain duration, current social conditions in the US have politicized and polarized higher education to a degree not seen in decades (Cohen, 2016; Klebnikov, 2015). Not only have traditional conditions such as academic freedom, tenure and free speech been questioned and eroded, but the longstanding American value that has assured education as a basic right and a public good has been undercut by governments' withdrawal of public funds over many years (Priest & St. John, 2006; Webber, 2017).

The slow transformation of institutions over the decades has made them more vulnerable to political as well as economic forces, especially following the election of President Trump and the rise of a movement by conservatives to label liberal education as *politically* liberal and therefore suspect. Current legislation pending Congressional approval for the reauthorization of the Higher Education Act, for example, reflects the economic and political perspective on education as a private benefit in reshaping federal financial aid policies and plans (American Council on Education, 2018). Some state legislatures have begun to take direct action to address what elected officials perceive as overly liberal institutional orientations: 'Around the country, Republican legislatures have been taking a greater interest in the affairs of their state universities to counteract what they see as excessive liberalism on campus' (Saul, 2018). The Arizona legislature, for example, has cut higher education budgets in the state by 54 per cent since 2008 (Sullivan & Jordan, 2018) while it 'has taken a direct role, fostering academic programs directly from the state budget and sidestepping the usual arrangement in which universities decide how to spend the money' by funding specific programmes to address perceived liberal bias (Saul, 2018).

While vocational and professionally-oriented programmes are often exempted from such criticism, the overall impact of suspicion and distrust falls on all faculty. With increased dependency on non-public funding coupled with the political critique of academic purpose, leadership, and learning outcomes, many research universities have opted for a passive, if not silent, role as institutional citizens. As a result, the 'calling' of faculty and their willingness to act individually in advancing the common good has grown in importance.

Despite the institutions' weakened position, a large number of individual faculty (and non-academic staff) have maintained (and in many instances even increased) the focus and intensity of their work to advance the common good (Shaker, 2015). Those faculty who either work at a university with an international mission or who have a personal commitment to the global common good are not only sustaining the collective work of institutions through their acts but in many instances are forming new networks and modes of transnational collaboration. Faculty continue to work collaboratively with colleagues around the world on issues such as climate change, religious tolerance, women's rights and human rights and migration, despite government policy positions and media pressures (e.g. Pinker, 2018). It is faculty from America's world-class universities that often lead in these actions both because of institutional commitment and the protection afforded by prestige, shared by faculty and their institutions alike.

This is a tumultuous and uncertain time. It is a time that reflects a slow decades-long decline in public support of higher education, principally through funding, and that now has reached a more explicit and openly political critique of the social role of higher education. Despite its antecedents, this new climate of accelerating politicization of higher education – and its role in advancing a common good – has caught many educators by surprise. Political forces as well as the more pervasive disruptive forces of technology, instantaneous global communication and global challenges affecting climate, health, human rights and personal security are converging to impact the role of colleges and universities worldwide. Within the American education sector, the commitment to advance the global common good depends on the sustaining efforts of individual faculty while institutions struggle to regain their footing and reclaim their historic commitment to the common good. Faculty (and their institutions) will likely rise to the challenge because of their shared historic foundation, record of perseverance in the face of earlier challenges, and ability to contribute in alignment with their differentiated missions.

2   Education and the Global Common Good

> There is no more powerful transformative force than education – to promote human rights and dignity, to eradicate poverty and deepen sustainability, to build a better future for all, founded on equal rights and social justice, respect for cultural diversity, and international solidarity and shared responsibility, all of which are fundamental aspects of our common humanity. (Irina Bokova, UNESCO Director General, UNESCO, 2015, p. 4)

In 1948, the United Nations (UN) Universal Declaration of human rights asserted that education is a human right and as such it is a public good. Yet the term 'public good' is laden with an economic meaning and suggests that there is an alternative, a 'private good'. The tension between education as a private good and a public benefit has grown steadily in the US since the time of the UN resolution and the US's post-World War II reaffirmation of a general commitment to advancing the public good (Daviet, 2016). The US showed this core commitment through education (notably, through the transformative GI Bill that opened higher education to much larger public participation), domestic policy (including major public works designed to increase transportation and community development), and foreign policy (based in large part on accepting a responsibility for nation-(re)building) (Mumper, Gladieux, King, & Corrigan, 2016).

Of these, the tension of public versus private benefit and the societal shift towards the latter philosophy has been most apparent in education at all levels, but especially among post-secondary institutions. The shift has many causes, but the Vietnam era war protests and the activism of students and faculty in response to the war, the civil rights movement and economic disparities likely played a role as the public became aware of social and political roles taken by institutions, or their members. Growing political attention to economic development in an increasingly globally competitive marketplace placed a premium on post-secondary education as the pathway to social mobility and better jobs. It is this history that has made the current retreat from a widely-shared public view of higher education as a public benefit and a recognition of the importance of academic research as the means to advance the common good so jarring. It is important, therefore, to understand the past as prologue to the current disruptive period of pain and promise – a period which may hold the seeds of new energy for reclaiming the public purpose of higher education and the collective work of individual faculty whose sense of purpose and professional duty recognizes the global common good.

While still considered a public good if not a human right, post-secondary education accumulated baggage that led many to see the value of degrees – and education – in economic terms. As a result, responsibility for educational costs has gradually shifted from public support for affordable and accessible education to the individuals who would benefit from their degrees and their higher earning capacity. While the debate is not over, momentum has favoured the private benefit perspective. Growing awareness of the cost of higher education to individuals with the consequences of limiting access and increasing personal debt draws attention to the tensions, public policy considerations, and longer-term effects on society. There is a renewed concern for the role of higher education as both a right and a necessary condition for sustaining America's democratic society. As it happens, concern about the role of education as the means to ensure the public good has become global. In the United Kingdom, for example, there is a debate about the role of England's elite – world-class – universities and whether they are principally the vehicle for attaining privilege and status or for enabling the greater, common good. Simon Marginson of University College London argues forcefully that 'if higher education sells itself as a pass-card into the elite – even while failing to deliver on this for most graduates – no wonder the pushback against elites readily translates into pushback against higher education (Marginson, 2018). Although the debate is framed differently elsewhere and perhaps with less intensity, he sums up the growing global dilemma succinctly: 'The great democratic question of the value and purpose of higher education has been hijacked to service a Treasury-driven argument about limited public financing' (Marginson, 2018).

In 2015, UNESCO called for a re-contextualizing of education as a global common good, as the Director General indicated in the afore-mentioned quotation from the report, Re-Thinking Education. The organization was suggesting not only that basic education be treated this way, but that post-secondary education and knowledge-development 'are common to all people as part of a collective societal endeavour' (UNESCO, 2015, p. 9). As such, the organization argued, the primacy of education goes beyond the individualistic socio-economic theory suggested by the phrase, 'public good'.

From this perspective, the value of higher education is better understood from a humanistic perspective, characterized by a holistic view of human development, rather than an economic one, which hinges on matching costs to beneficiaries (Blessinger & Makhanya, 2018; Daviet, 2016). The humanistic view is characterized by equity, inclusion and diversification of the higher education system. Institutional variety is desirable and indeed necessary to serve the many and different needs of societies and their members.

In the United States, higher education is typically understood as serving the common (or public) good in at least the following ways: by educating for citizenship, educating for employment, generating knowledge to benefit all, and engaging with communities to improve quality of life (Shaker & Plater, 2016b). The US post-secondary system is complex, diverse and differentiated by institutional mission. Institutions are public or private; large, small, or in-between; focused on research or teaching; selective or more open in their admissions; and everything in between and by degree. Each type of school (e.g. community college, comprehensive university, liberal arts college) contributes to the common good in a way that aligns with its mission, and many of these missions attend to that community-based responsibility (Shaker & Plater, 2016b).

3   Differentiating US Institutions in Service to the Global Common Good: Diversity with a Common Purpose

The earliest US institutions of higher learning were private, non-governmental institutions that typically included in their statements of purpose a responsibility for preparing future leaders of society – all for the betterment of humanity (Thelin, 2011). Harvard, the nation's first college, was established in the spirit of serving all of humanity through education, as one of the founding documents of 1640states: '[…] one of the next things we longed for and looked after was to advance learning and perpetuate it to posterity' (New Englands First Fruits, 1643). In a recent book on the history of higher education, Charles

Dorn has documented that 'during the early national period, a social ethos of civic-mindedness informed higher education's dedication to the common good' (Dorn, 2017, p. 10). The purposeful spirit of America's first colleges became more definite over time as they accepted a societal role, such that Woodrow Wilson, former Princeton University president and later President of the US, was fond of reminding everyone that Princeton was founded in service to the nation (Wilson, 1902).

Wilson, personalizing that commitment, played a major role as president in deepening national values around democracy and a global common good, as he 'developed a program of progressive reform and asserted international leadership in building a new world order' that anticipated the formation of the UN and its predecessor, the League of Nations, nudging the US from a nationalistic focus on its own public good towards a greater engagement with the global common good (The White House, n.d.). This is what leaders educated in America's private colleges were expected to do.

Private colleges, some 4,000 of all types and sizes with over 2,000 offering baccalaureate and higher levels of education, still dominate American higher education in the number of institutions. Collectively they enrol over 30 per cent of all students studying at the baccalaureate level (Chingos, 2017). The most elite private research universities dominate rankings of America's world-class universities based on their longer histories and distinctive purposes. They also play a critical leadership role for public institutions, the first of which emerged nearly two centuries after Harvard's founding (Thelin, 2011).

The tone for all of American higher education was more firmly – and broadly – set in 1862 with the passage of the Morrill Act and the creation of public institutions funded by the public to serve the public (Thelin, 2011). It established what came to be known as land-grant colleges and universities funded with public resources to advance the public good: '...in order to promote the liberal and practical education of the industrial classes in the several pursuits and professions in life' (7 US Code § 304, n.d.).

From its early start, these public-serving institutions formed an association, now known as the Association of Public and Land-grant Universities (APLU), to reaffirm and provide mutual support in serving the public good. With over 230 members in the US, Canada, and Mexico, APLU plays a dominant role in reminding research universities of their founding purpose through periodic reports and action agendas that ensure its members are committed to championing ideas that drive the discovery and dissemination of new knowledge to solve the most vexing challenges of their country and region. They are committed to free peoples who have access to the education and opportunity necessary to shape their own destinies (APLU, n.d.).

If there is a distinction to be made between the public and the common 'good', these public universities and colleges were clearly attuned to the public good. They have evolved to embrace the more holistic and humanistic common good.

The land-grant universities, over time, have been augmented with over 400 comprehensive public colleges and universities that share a kindred spirit of advancing the common good along with the earlier, research-oriented universities. The Association of American State Colleges and Universities (AASCU) reflects this social responsibility with its mission: 'Strengthening the role of state colleges and universities as 'Stewards of Place' through support of their teaching-learning, research and service missions' (AASCU, n.d.). Supported in part through public funds at the federal (national), state, and local levels, public institutions of all kinds acknowledge a fundamental commitment to supporting and advancing the common good in both economic and social dimensions.

Community colleges were established in the US in the early 20th century to provide educational opportunities for local communities – as a means to advance the public good through education and workforce development (Thelin, 2011). By 1920, an association was formed to support the mission of community colleges as an intermediate step towards baccalaureate education while also serving as the terminal degree for many workforce needs in local communities. Community colleges serve the common good through broad accessibility; affordability; foundational liberal arts education, developmental education and vocational programmes; and responsiveness to communities' workforce and societal needs.

As noted, world-class American universities include many private, non-profit institutions – a phenomenon that is largely unique in the world – that are well-represented in most world rankings based on research or innovation (Altbach, 2004). One association inclusive of the most elite and self-proclaimed world-class universities, both public and private, is the Association of American Universities (AAU), whose 60 US member universities 'earn the majority of competitively awarded federal funding for academic research, are improving human life and wellbeing through research, and are educating tomorrow's visionary leaders and global citizens' (AAU, n.d.). Of the 60, 34 are public and 26 are private. The AAU specifically embraces its special duty to go beyond the inherent obligation of all public institutions to advance the public good. It does this by accepting a leadership role across the entire post-secondary sector: 'AAU members collectively help shape policy for higher education, science, and innovation; promote best practices in undergraduate and graduate education; and strengthen the contributions of research universities to society' (AAU, n.d.).

The AAU's statement of purpose demonstrates the ways in which modern research universities are 'citizens' of society. They serve the common good through the fulfilment of their institution-specific and mission-driven teaching, research and service activities, and also are innovators, exemplars, and leaders for the whole education sector. Beginning with World War II, for example, the federal government entrusted Americans' security, health and scientific/technological innovation to research universities above all others (Mumper et al., 2016; Thelin, 2011), and the greater portion of this charge was given to America's world-class universities, the most elite of the research universities.

America's world-class universities possess the human, financial, intellectual, cultural and physical resources beyond other institutions and necessary for grappling with society's greatest challenges (Altbach, 2004). These resources coupled with public trust instilled by the government mean that world-class universities have a duty to address world-class issues, issues that are beyond the missions and capacity of regional, local and specialized institutions. Be it crises in health, in poverty, in the environment, or transnational security, world-class universities can bring to bear not only their resources but can convene and lead consortiums of other universities to seek solutions. These universities can work across government lines, partner with the business sector, draw on philanthropic and government resources, and incubate social change. Many research-intensive US universities have embraced the terminology of 'grand challenges' to focus attention and resources on a select number of globally-important issues affecting local communities (Popowitz & Dorgelo, 2018). Our own institution, Indiana University, for example defines its Grand Challenges programme as addressing 'major, focused and large-scale problems facing humanity that can only be solved by the application of dedicated research findings across disciplines in collaboration with community partners' ('Grand Challenges IU', n.d.).

The expectation of Americans that world-class universities and all post-secondary institutions contribute to the common good is reflected in several accountability measures (Shaker & Plater, 2016b). One, accreditation, addresses the investment of public funds in post-secondary institutions of all types. Several of the accrediting bodies have made it a requirement for recognition – and hence eligibility for federal funds of all kinds, from research to student aid – that the candidate for accreditation or renewal be able to account for how it serves society. As one example, the Western Association of Senior Colleges and Universities has as its first requirement that 'the institution's formally approved statements of purpose are appropriate for an institution of higher education and clearly define its essential values and character and ways in which it contributes to the public good' ('WSCUC/WASC Senior College and University Commission', n.d.).

Another example of broad public accountability comes from the National Science Foundation, which essentially has two criteria for reviewing proposals: what is the intellectual merit of the proposal and what are its broader impacts? (US NSF, n.d.). By the latter, the NSF expects the research that it funds to have benefits for society and requires proposals to identify the likely impact of the research. Philanthropic foundations and other government funders utilize similar language, but the investment of public funds in education – whether for educating students or conducting research – requires results that advance at least the national public good.

4 World-Class Universities, Contested Purpose, and a Renewed Commitment to the Global Common Good

The current contested political and economic environment for defining the purposes of higher education in the US did not occur overnight. Universities, especially the research-intensive universities, began their own re-examination of purpose in response to reduced public support and the emerging political critique, setting in motion competing narratives about the role of higher education in society. In the process of their own self-reflections and telling their own stories, institutions have become actors differentiated from other social institutions. While there are many voices and differing narratives, the effect has been to make institutions their own advocates for their respective purposes and roles in society.

In the mid-1980s, a few university leaders – notably leaders of world-class universities – detected an appreciable decline in the public purposes of their institutions and wondered about the commitment of other institutions. The leaders of Brown, Georgetown, and Stanford Universities formed Campus Compact in 1985 because they 'believed that higher education could be a more effective contributor to the sustainability of a democracy with more robust support structures for community engagement' (Campus Compact, n.d.). With over 1,000 institutional members, Campus Compact now has as one of its fundamental purposes to prepare 'students for lives of engaged citizenship, with the motivation and capacity to deliberate, act, and lead in pursuit of the public good' (Campus Compact, n.d.-b). In many ways, the creation of this organization awakened a national movement towards a renewed commitment to advancing the common good.

'Even the best universities are not the best in everything', Altbach wrote in 2004 (p. 7), issuing a timely reminder that even world-class universities had made choices about what to prioritize among the usual three missions of teaching, research and service. It was in this time period that some faculty noticed that research universities had drifted from their core and historic missions of educating leaders and incubating community improvement through new knowledge applied to local, national and global problems, and doing so in the way that only they could (Checkoway, 2001). Instead, they had transformed 'from civic institutions into some of the world's most powerful research engines, and in so doing, have undergone major changes in their objectives and operations' (Checkoway, 2001, p. 128). Universities, critics noted, had turned away from viewing academic knowledge as a 'public good to which citizenry has claims' (Slaughter & Rhoades, 2009) and towards an academic capitalist model in which knowledge products were developed, marketed, and sold in the private market.

At least one source of the need to seek external avenues for funding was likely the multi-year decline in state-level support for public institutions, which has only recently recovered to some degree (McGuinness, 2016; Seltzer, 2017). This support varies widely among states, and many are continuing to reduce funding. Self-reflection and self-assessment have become one of the distinguishing features of the reawakening of interest in the public mission of higher education, along with the critique that institutions have lost their public purpose in the pursuit of knowledge for commercialization, or the education of students more for jobs than citizenship. At the same time, many – even a majority – of public policy leaders and elected officials have taken an alternative view and fault institutions for not having a more aggressive commitment to economic development and the private benefits of both education and research (Harris, 2017; Ravitch, 2016; Weingarten, 2017).

Writing in the late 1990s and early 2000s, scholars contended that research universities (and their leaders and faculty) needed to renew their commitment to the public (Boyte, 1998; Checkoway, 2001; Mathews, 1997). Checkoway (2001) suggested that research universities could accomplish this by strengthening student learning to prepare them for citizenship, encouraging and supporting faculty to conduct research that improves community, increasing institutional capacity for this work, and fostering understanding of the connection between diversity and democracy.

Enough momentum had developed among faculty and institutions nationwide to lead the US Department of Education to appoint a National Taskforce on Civic Learning and Democratic Engagement. The taskforce reported its findings in January 2012 in a report titled A Crucible Moment, reflecting the growing sense of urgency among institutions. The report 'documents the nation's anemic civic health and includes recommendations for action that address campus culture, general education, and civic inquiry as part of major and career fields as well as hands-on civic problem solving across differences' and it 'calls on higher education and many partners in education, government, and public life to advance a 21st century conception of civic learning and democratic engagement as an expected part of every student's college education' (AAC&U, 2012, p. 1) In essence a strong call to action, the report has stimulated a large number of collaborative programmes and projects as well as actions by individual institutions to re-examine and renew their own commitments to the common good. The actions of faculty acting out of a strong personal commitment to the common good has been the bedrock of institutional revitalization of public purpose.

One important characteristic of this renewal has been an intentional commitment to extend public purpose to encompass global responsibilities, growing out of a parallel consideration of internationalization of higher education and the reality that most of the most urgent issues for the US are global in nature – climate change, health, immigration, food security, human rights and so on. A Crucible Moment, for example, contains a specific recommendation that institutions 'advance a contemporary, comprehensive framework for civic learning – embracing US and global interdependence – that includes historic and modern understandings of democratic values, capacities to engage diverse perspectives and people, and commitment to collective civic problem-solving' worldwide (AAC&U, 2012). There is a growing appreciation among American academic leaders, following the lead of educators in other nations, for the distinction made by the UNESCO report, Re-Thinking Education, between the public good and the global common good. Increasingly, institutions appear to be accepting their public responsibilities in a global context, appreciating how global interdependence now requires advancing a shared, global common good. As Simon Marginson suggested in 2011, 'we must break our imagined dependence on states as the source of the collective, of global public good(s). Because knowledge lends itself to global flows, in a knowledge-intensive age research universities are important creators of global goods' (p. 430).

Despite the growing institutional self-awareness and a willingness to speak out on their own behalf, the headwinds against change are strong. Few political leaders at state or national levels have listened to narratives such as A Crucible Moment. Today, universities face additional challenges affecting their ability to redirect their course towards the common good. American sentiments about the role of higher education in society are at an all-time low. A 2017 Gallup poll of Americans found that 56 per cent had only 'some' or 'very little' confidence in colleges and universities; more alarming, 67 per cent of Republicans expressed low confidence and 32 per cent said institutions are 'too liberal' (Lederman, 2017). Liberal arts education, the hallmark of institutions like Harvard and Yale, is embattled, ridiculed and thought of as without worth in many quarters, although the liberal arts are vigorously defended by proponents (Cohen, 2016; Klebnikov, 2015). A populist, anti-intellectual mood has swept the country, as evidenced by the 2016 Presidential election in which the focus on educational policy has been economic development and an explicit advocacy for education as a private benefit (Harris, 2017; Ravitch, 2016; Weingarten, 2017).

University philanthropic endowments are under scrutiny by the public and Congress, as their spending philosophies and organizing purposes are being questioned (Satija, 2018). Some of the largest donors have been criticized for choosing to give to institutions that already hold generous assets and for supporting purposes that are not need-based (Foster, 2016). Moreover, a new national tax code for 2018 includes a provision to tax endowments of private universities, based on their valuation per student, that may affect about 30 institutions – including a number that are considered to be world-class (e.g. Yale, Harvard, Princeton, Stanford, MIT, California Institute of Technology, University of Chicago) (Kreighbaum, 2017).

Despite the headwinds, some world-class universities are taking concrete steps to advance the global common good. In 2006, for example, 11 world-class universities (including UC Berkeley and Yale) from nine nations formed the International Alliance of Research Universities with the purpose of collaboration in research and advancing world leadership through education. As one of its founding principles, the Alliance 'will be strategic, drawing together a select group of research-intensive universities that share similar values, a global vision and a commitment to educating future world leaders. Central to these values is the importance of academic diversity and international collaboration' (IARU, n.d.). A number of other transnational associations are forming with similar civic purpose and a shared commitment to enhancing the global common good, such as the Talloires Network, 'an international association of institutions committed to strengthening the civic roles and social responsibilities of higher education [...] and build a global movement of engaged universities' (The Talloires Network, n.d.). Member institutions and their leaders will depend on the faculty to carry out the aims of the Alliance, The Talloires Network, and other like enterprises.

In brief, political and economic forces may be challenging the historic dual and integrated purpose of US colleges and universities to provide public benefit as well as economic advancement in favour of only economic, but institutions are holding steady in their commitment to advancing the common good. One major reason for the resurgent institutional voice and narrative is the self-conceptualization of faculty work as a profession with a duty to the public good. It is faculty on whom the eventual resolution of the contested purposes depends.

5. World-Class Faculty at Work for the Global Common Good

Faculty in all institutions anywhere in the world are the irreducible element that defines quality and accomplishment. Faculty – as an academic workforce – vary enormously both within nations and among nations (Altbach, Reisberg, & Rumbley, 2010). In the US, the development of an academic occupation as a profession hinges on a commitment to the common good (Rice, Saltmarsh, & Plater, 2015). There is evidence that faculties of institutions from the early colonies until the emergence of public universities in the 19th century shared a sense of public purpose and a commitment to the role of education in advancing humanity. The formal professionalization of faculty, however, occurred very late in the history of American higher education and was the direct result of the creation of the American Association of University Professors in 1915 (Rice et al., 2015).

The organization articulated a principle based on the 'nature of the academic calling' that the 'conception of a university as an ordinary business venture, and of academic teaching as a purely private employment, manifests also a radical failure to apprehend the nature of the social function discharged by the professional scholar' because 'the responsibility of the university teacher is primarily to the public itself' (AAUP, 1915, pp. 294–295). The traditional faculty ethos hinged on the quest for truth and the good inherent in the ethical pursuit of knowledge (Shaker, 2015). The US academic workforce has certainly not been immune to the changes wrought by societal forces – for example, more faculty than ever before work part-time or without the promise of tenure – and world-class universities are not immune to this trend, which lessens the ability of faculty to attend to long-term and civically-centred goals. The notion of universities as largely profit-making enterprises not only led universities to adapt by becoming more capitalistic, it put the core values of faculty – as knowledge creators and disseminators – into jeopardy during the last several decades (Slaughter & Rhoades, 2009).

In near tandem to academia's neoliberal shift, US institutions and their faculties have engaged in a serious and public discussion of the purpose of faculty work and its ends. With his important 1990 book, Scholarship Reconsidered, Ernest Boyer served as the catalyst for this ongoing debate growing from his oft-cited statement, quoting Oscar Handlin, '[Our] troubled universe can no longer afford pursuits confined to an ivory tower. [...] Scholarship has to prove its worth not on its own terms but by service to the nation and the world' (Boyer, Moser, Ream, & Braxton, 2016, p. 85). Boyer's work has refocused attention on individual faculty as the source of scholarship's intent and purpose of scholarship. All faculty, according to Boyer, regardless of the institution they may serve, share in this duty to serve the nation and world through their work. Though treated as new and groundbreaking at the time, Boyer was reaffirming the conceptual underpinning of academic work as a profession, first articulated as such by John Dewey and his contemporaries who formed the AAUP, for the modern era. The AAUP itself has continued to evolve and now claims as one of its central purposes 'to ensure higher education's contribution to the common good' (AAUP, n.d.).

As we have argued elsewhere, individual faculty are inclined to advance the common good based in large part on a personal belief about higher education's importance in society (Shaker & Plater, 2016a). These faculty see education as the key mechanism for improving society and providing opportunity for all people. In this view, universities are in and of the community, not guarded from it within the 'ivory tower' (Tierney & Perkins, 2015). While largely unknown and invisible to a sceptical public, individual faculty make daily choices to advance the common good, in small but incrementally significant ways. They do this by eschewing financial rewards for public access to intellectual property, for example, or choosing to spend time and effort on projects for the benefit of society while deferring or foregoing activities that might bring greater reward, recognition or advancement (Shaker, 2015). As a recent work in progress proclaims, 'The faculty, in fact, is the beneficiary of and has been entrusted with the non-market social benefits that higher education can provide; as such, our primary loyalty must be to those for whom we hold those benefits in trust. We have to take the lead in transforming our institutions – and in demonstrating, in arguing, as broadly and as publicly as possible the common good that those institutions serve – in order to ensure that such a common good continues to exist' (Fitzpatrick, 2018, p. 26).

Faculty make discretionary choices about how to use their time, talent and resources. They can make these decisions out of a sense of greater purpose (Altbach, 2004; Shaker, 2015; Shaker & Plater, 2016a). Academic work, as a vocation, is a calling to serve the greater good of humanity though teaching, research and service – applying the knowledge and insights of research to the solution of societal problems. The cumulative, collective work of faculty for the common good is in part a function of how individuals opt to use their time as they integrate paid work and their extra, voluntary contributions of effort beyond their position descriptions. Such work most often is not fully counted, even as the results of that work are claimed by institutions and relied on by trustees, policy makers and the public. One study estimates that as much as 30 per cent of faculty time on average is spent on the kinds of teaching activities that might be considered discretionary and oriented towards the common good (Nelson Laird, 2015).

One of the underlying principles of tenure is that it represents a bond between the individual faculty member and the institution as accepting reciprocal responsibilities: the institution to provide protection from political or external interference, while faculty exercise discretion in how they pursue their work under the duty to advance the common, shared public good, including a duty to remain current in their areas of expertise, both for research and for teaching (Plater, 1998). The tenure system, a bedrock of American world-class and research-intensive universities, is based on trust without detailed record keeping or individual accountability. Instead, there is a more general form of accountability based on results – what faculty accomplish by the choices they make. This is most evident in research where products in the form of books, articles, policy briefs and commercially viable intellectual property are more easily noted and counted. But it is also present in teaching: the work of faculty to prepare better educated and effective citizens and employees. As a spokesperson for a leading foundation supporting US higher education has attested, 'A "quiet revolution" in college teaching appears to be growing dramatically thanks to a genuine desire to serve today's students better and greater calls for accountability in higher education, but now we must ensure the benefits of these more effective approaches are shared equally by all students' (Humphreys, 2018). The impact on society as a whole through the individual acts of teachers committed to effective teaching – and learning – for all has results well beyond those implied by job descriptions.

Even if much of the work faculty contribute to the common good is not counted and rewarded, nonetheless the overall commitment of the profession and individuals' adherence to the call of professionalism ensure a strong, sustained engagement of the institutions they serve to the public good, even when institutional purpose flags or is challenged by political leaders:

We agree that nothing could be more important than a shared, deep understanding of the cultural variables centred on the public purpose of higher education and the full extent of faculty work, even when it is so transparent that it is not seen, so essential that it is not counted (Shaker & Plater, 2016a, p. 19).

As noted throughout this essay, world-class universities have a specific responsibility for leadership among all American institutions of higher education. Nowhere is that more apparent than in their role in educating the future academic workforce. AAU institutions, for example, award over 40 per cent of all doctorates earned in the US and educate a disproportionate share of graduates who move into faculty positions ('Association of American Universities', n.d.-b). World-class universities have an exceptional opportunity to shape future academic professionalism at a time of fundamental changes in the composition, preparation, and sustainability of a new, more diverse, contingent academic workforce. One of the major projects underway to help imagine and prepare the best models for the future professoriate has given thought to the role of the public good in faculty work. The Delphi Project based at the University of Southern California has noted that:

> Higher education is intended to benefit the public good, not just the students who pay to enroll in courses. The collective work of colleges and

universities – of their faculties – supports the public's welfare and vitality in many ways, such as by fostering democratic engagement, by ensuring college access through partnership with K-12, through research that benefits society, by offering public critique of social policies, or through capably filling positions of leadership on community boards. (Kezar, Maxey, & Holcombe, 2015, p. 27)

In light of this, a fundamental characteristic of a future faculty model is to ensure the continued commitment to providing services or benefits to the greater public.

Research universities, as noted, are diverse and differentially motivated but they all share a sense of responsibility for their capacity to influence and impact higher education generally through their leadership and example. In one significant example of this self-recognition, a number of research universities convened to develop a series of recommendations for how they and their peers could impact the overall public purpose of US research intensive universities. Their statement 'argues that research universities' top-tier faculty, outstanding students, considerable financial resources, and state-of-the-art research facilities, position them to contribute to community change relatively quickly and in ways that will ensure deeper and longer-lasting commitment to civic engagement across higher education' (Stanton, 2008, p. 20). There are many such instances of faculty at leadership institutions seeking to reaffirm their responsibility to use their resources, position and prestige to encourage, support and lead all levels and types of post-secondary institutions to fulfil their public purpose. The inspiration for such convening stem from a 1999 Wingspread meeting that issued a 'Declaration on Renewing the Civic Mission of the American Research University', which in turn served as the basis for the broader, more inclusive 'Presidents' Declaration on the Civic Responsibility of Higher Education' that begins 'As presidents of colleges and universities, both private and public, large and small, two-year and four-year, we challenge higher education to re-examine its public purposes and its commitments to the democratic ideal' (Campus Compact, 2012).

Through an explicit, intentional commitment to prepare future academics for their roles as the arbiters of the public good leadership institutions can sustain the transformative power of education articulated by the UNESCO (2015) report. Without a conscious and deliberate intent to honour the public mission envisioned by Dewey and his successors in establishing the professoriate as a profession, highly trained, bright and competent graduates may well become the agents of education for private benefit to the detriment of humanity. World-class universities will do more than any other identifiable educational structure to develop the faculty whose research, professional service, leadership and teaching will serve the global common good and to ensure that educational transformation is positive and actually creates a better future for our posterity, as the founders of Harvard so hoped might happen. As the Campus Compact Presidents' Declaration states, 'We will know [success] by the civic engagement of our faculty' (Campus Compact, 2012).

6   Conclusion

In the US, institutions that seek recognition as world-class base their claims on their impact on advancing the global common good, but they acknowledge that their effectiveness is dependent on a broad base of contributing institutions and their diverse faculties. We argue that the shared denominator of US educational contribution to the global common good rests on the intent of faculty – as professionals – to advance the common good personally and collectively. As such, faculty are the key to effectively contributing to the global common good regardless of the institution that employs them, although those institutions whose mission explicitly embraces a duty to advancing the common good aligns both individual and institutional intent.

Faculty are the core of the academic enterprise and as such carry out the universities' work. They are knowledge generators, research engines, master teachers, involved community members, contributors to institutions and disciplines, administrators and leaders – admittedly each to varying degrees of engagement and levels of quality. Among faculty everywhere, those faculty privileged to work at world-class universities are responsible for providing leadership and acting as role models in their service to the global common good. As we noted at the outset, the current political, social and economic conditions in the US may profoundly effect higher education's role in the future of American society. The stakes are significant and the outcomes uncertain. The case for the will, perseverance and sense of duty of faculty to advance the global common good offers considerable promise that the institutional as well as personal commitment to this ideal will prevail. Now, as throughout American history, we will indeed know success through the civic engagement of our faculty.

References

7 US Code § 304 – Investment of Proceeds of Sale of Land or Scrip. (n.d.). Retrieved February 23, 2018, from https://www.law.cornell.edu/uscode/text/7/304

AAC&U. (2012). *A crucible moment: College learning and democracy's future*. Retrieved February 23, 2018, from https://www.aacu.org/crucible

AASCU. (n.d.). *Vision and mission.* Retrieved February 23, 2018, from http://www.aascu.org/strategic-plan/VisionandMission/

AAUP. (1915). *Appendix I: 1915 Declaration of principles on academic freedom and academic tenure.* Retrieved June 8, 2018, from https://www.aaup.org/NR/rdonlyres/A6520A9D-0A9A-47B3-B550-C006B5B224E7/0/1915Declaration.pdf

AAUP. (n.d.). *About.* Retrieved February 25, 2018, from https://www.aaup.org/about-aaup

Altbach, P. G. (2004). The costs and benefits of world-class universities. *Academe, 90*(1), 20–23.

Altbach, P. G., Reisberg, L., & Rumbley, L. E. (2010). *Trends in global higher education: Tracking an academic revolution.* Rotterdam, The Netherlands: Sense Publishers.

APLU. (n.d.). *Zone of knowledge.* Retrieved February 23, 2018, from http://www.aplu.org/about-us/zone-of-knowledge.html

Association of American Universities. (n.d.-a). *Who we are.* Retrieved February 23, 2018, from https://www.aau.edu/who-we-are

Association of American Universities. (n.d.-b). *AAU by the numbers.* Retrieved February 26, 2018, from https://www.aau.edu/who-we-are/aau-numbers

Blessinger, P., & Makhanya, M. (2018, February 2). Towards higher education in service of humanity. *University World News.* Retrieved February 23, 2018, from http://www.universityworldnews.com/article.php?story=20180130100345559

Boyer, E. L., Moser, D., Ream, T. C., & Braxton, J. M. (2016). *Scholarship reconsidered: Priorities of the professoriate.* San Francisco, CA: Jossey-Bass. Retrieved from http://BZ6FJ9FL8E.search.serialssolutions.com/?V=1.0&L=BZ6FJ9FL8E&S=JCs&C=TC0001556107&T=marc

Boyte, H. C. (1998, October 23). Off the playground of civil society: Freeing democracy's powers for the 21st century. *Civic Engagement.* Retrieved February 26, 2018, from https://digitalcommons.unomaha.edu/slceciviceng/20

Campus Compact. (n.d.). *Who we are.* Retrieved February 23, 2018, from https://compact.org/who-we-are/history/

Checkoway, B. (2001). Renewing the civic mission of the American research university. *The Journal of Higher Education, 72*(2), 125–147. Retrieved from https://doi.org/10.2307/2649319

Chingos, M. M. (2017, February 16). Don't forget private, non-profit colleges. *Brookings.* Retrieved February 23, 2018, from https://www.brookings.edu/research/dont-forget-private-non-profit-colleges/

Cohen, P. (2016, February 21). *A rising call to promote STEM education and cut liberal arts funding.* Retrieved February 23, 2018, from https://search.proquest.com/docview/1766935883/abstract/A2B15012CBB243D2PQ/1

Daviet, B. (2016). *Revisiting the principle of education as a public good* (Working Papers No. 17). Retrieved February 24, 2018, from http://repositorio.minedu.gob.pe/handle/123456789/4645

Dorn, C. (2017). *For the common good: A new history of higher education in America.* Ithaca, NY: Cornell University Press.

Fitzpatrick, K. (2018). *Thinking generously: The university and the public good.* Retrieved March 13, 2018, from https://generousthinking.hcommons.org/5-the-university/possibilities/

Foster, W. (2016, April 27). Why big donors are under fire for big gifts. *Forbes.* Retrieved February 24, 2018, from https://www.forbes.com/sites/bridgespan/2016/04/27/why-big-donors-are-under-fire-for-big-gifts/

Grand Challenges IU. (n.d.). *About.* Retrieved February 23, 2018, from https://grandchallenges.iu.edu/about/index.html

Harris, A. (2017, May 23). What Trump's proposed 2018 budget would mean for higher ed. *The Chronicle of Higher Education.* Retrieved February 24, 2018, from https://www.chronicle.com/blogs/ticker/what-trumps-proposed-2018-budget-would-mean-for-higher-ed/118577

International Alliance of Research Universities (IARU). (n.d.). *About IARU.* Retrieved February 24, 2018, from http://www.iaruni.org/about/about-iaru

Kezar, A., Maxey, D., & Holcombe, E. (2015). *The professorate reconsidered: A study of new faculty models.* Los Angeles, CA: University of Southern California.

Klebnikov, S. (2015, June 19). Liberal arts vs. STEM: The right degrees, the wrong debate. *Forbes.* Retrieved February 23, 2018, from https://www.forbes.com/sites/sergeiklebnikov/2015/06/19/liberal-arts-vs-stem-the-right-degrees-the-wrong-debate/

Kreighbaum, A. (2017, December 18). Large endowments would be taxed under final GOP tax plan. *Inside Higher Education.* Retrieved February 24, 2018, from https://www.insidehighered.com/news/2017/12/18/large-endowments-would-be-taxed-under-final-gop-tax-plan

Lederman, D. (2017, December 15). Is the public really losing faith in higher education? *Inside Higher Education.* Retrieved February 23, 2018, from https://www.insidehighered.com/news/2017/12/15/public-really-losing-faith-higher-education

Marginson, S. (2011). Higher education and the public good. *Higher Education Quarterly, 65*(4), 411–433. Retrieved June 7, 2018, from https://doi.org/10.1111/j.1468-2273.2011.00496.x

Marginson, S. (2018, March 19). Higher education should be funded as a public good. *Inside Higher Education.* Retrieved March 19, 2019, from http://www.universityworldnews.com/article.php?story=20180313102919183

Mathews, D. (1997). Character for what? Higher education and public life. *Educational Record, 78*(3–4), 10–17.

McGuinness, A. C. (2016). The states and higher education. In M. N. P. Bastedo, P. G. Altbach, & P. J. Gumport (Eds.), *American higher education in the twenty-first century: Social, political, and economic challenges* (4th ed.). Baltimore, MD: Johns Hopkins University Press.

Mumper, M., Gladieux, L. E., King, J. E., & Corrigan, M. E. (2016). The federal government and higher education. In M. N. P. Bastedo, P. G. Altbach, & P. J. Gumport (Eds.), *American higher education in the twenty-first century: Social, political, and economic challenges* (4th ed.). Baltimore, MD: Johns Hopkins University Press.

Nelson Laird, T. F. (2015). Gifting time: Faculty activities with a philanthropic orientation. In G. G. Shaker (Ed.), *Faculty work and the public good: Philanthropy, engagement, and academic professionalism*. New York, NY: Teachers College Press.

New Englands First Fruits. (1643). *London: Printed by R.O. and G.D. for Henry Overton*. Retrieved from http://archive.org/details/NewEnglandsFirstFruitsInRespectFirst-OfTheCounversionOfSome

Pinker, S. (2018, February 13). The intellectual war on science. *The Chronicle of Higher Education*. Retrieved February 23, 2018, from https://www.chronicle.com/article/The-Intellectual-War-on/242538

Plater, W. M. (1998). Using tenure: Citizenship within the new academic workforce. *American Behavioral Scientist, 41*(5), 680–715. Retrieved from https://doi.org/10.1177/0002764298041005007

Plater, W. M. (1999). Habits of living: Engaging the campus as citizen one scholar at a time. In R. G. Bringle, R. Games, & E. A. Malloy (Eds.), *Colleges and universities as citizens*. Needham Heights, MA: Allyn & Bacon.

Popowitz, M., & Dorgelo, C. (2018). *Report on university-led grand challenges*. Retrieved February 23, 2018, from https://escholarship.org/uc/item/46f121cr

Priest, D. M., & St. John, E. P. (Eds.). (2006). *Privatization and public universities*. Bloomington, IN: Indiana University Press.

Ravitch, D. (2016, December 8). When public goes private, as Trump wants: What happens? *The New York Review of Books*. Retrieved from http://www.nybooks.com/articles/2016/12/08/when-public-goes-private-as-trump-wants-what-happens/

Rice, R. E., Saltmarsh, J., & Plater, W. M. (2015). The public good and the future of academic work: Reflections on the public good and academic professionalism. In G. G. Shaker (Ed.), *Faculty work and the public good: Philanthropy, engagement, and academic professionalism*. New York, NY: Teachers College Press.

Satija, N. (2018, January 7). How rich universities waste their endowments. *Washington Monthly*. Retrieved February 23, 2018, from https://washingtonmonthly.com/magazine/january-february-march-2018/well-endowed/

Seltzer, R. (2017, February 6). States report 3.4 percent increase in higher education appropriations. *Inside Higher Education*. Retrieved February 23, 2018, from https://www.insidehighered.com/news/2017/02/06/states-report-34-percent-increase-higher-education-appropriations

Shaker, G. G. (Ed.). (2015). *Faculty work and the public good: Philanthropy, engagement, and academic professionalism*. New York, NY: Teachers College Press.

Shaker, G. G. (2015). Seeing philanthropy in faculty work: An introduction. In G. G. Shaker (Ed.), *Faculty work and the public good: Philanthropy, engagement, and academic professionalism.* New York, NY: Teachers College Press.

Shaker, G. G., & Plater, W. M. (2016a, July). *The public good, productivity and faculty work: Individual effort and social value.* Retrieved February 23, 2018, from https://www.tiaainstitute.org/publication/public-good-productivity-and-purpose

Shaker, G. G., & Plater, W. M. (2016b, July). *The public good, productivity and purpose: New economic models for higher education.* Retrieved February 23, 2018, from https://www.tiaainstitute.org/publication/public-good-productivity-and-purpose

Slaughter, S., & Rhoades, G. (2009). *Academic capitalism and the new economy: Markets, state, and higher education.* Baltimore, MD: Johns Hopkins University Press. Retrieved February 23, 2018, from https://jhupbooks.press.jhu.edu/content/academic-capitalism-and-new-economy

The Formula for a World-Class University Revealed. (n.d.). *Times higher education.* Retrieved February 22, 2018, from https://www.timeshighereducation.com/world-university-rankings/news/the-formula-for-a-world-class-university-revealed#survey-answer

Thelin, J. R. (2011). *A history of American higher education.* Baltimore, MD: Johns Hopkins University Press.

The Talloires Network. (n.d.). *Who we are.* Retrieved February 24, 2018, from http://talloiresnetwork.tufts.edu/who-we-are/

The White House. (n.d.). *Woodrow Wilson.* Retrieved February 23, 2018, from https://www.whitehouse.gov/about-the-white-house/presidents/woodrow-wilson/

Tierney, W. G., & Perkins, J. F. (2015). Beyond the ivory tower: Academic work in the 21st century. In G. G. Shaker (Ed.), *Faculty work and the public good: Philanthropy, engagement, and academic professionalism.* New York, NY: Teachers College Press.

UNESCO. (2015). *Rethinking education: Towards a global common good?* Paris: UNESCO.

US NSF. (n.d.). *Broader impacts, review criterion.* Retrieved February 23, 2018, from https://www.nsf.gov/pubs/2007/nsf07046/nsf07046.jsp

Webber, D. A. (2017). State divestment and tuition at public institutions. *Economics of Education Review, 60,* 1–4. Retrieved from https://doi.org/10.1016/j.econedurev.2017.07.007

Weingarten, R. (2017, May 3). AFT president: DeVos and Trump are dismantling public education. *Time.* Retrieved February 24, 2018, from http://time.com/4765410/donald-trump-betsy-devos-atf-public-education/

Wilson, W. (1902). Princeton for the nation's service. *Science, 16*(410), 721–731.

WSCUC/WASC Senior College and University Commission. (n.d.). *Standard 1: Defining institutional purposes and ensuring educational objectives.* Retrieved February 23, 2018, from https://www.wscuc.org/resources/handbook-accreditation-2013/part-ii-core-commitments-and-standards-accreditation/wasc-standards-accreditation-2013/standard-1-defining-institutional-purposes-and-ensuring-educational-objectives

CHAPTER 9

Pursuing Excellence in Graduate Education and Research While Serving Regional Development

Rita Karam, Charles A. Goldman, Daniel Basco and Diana Gehlhaus Carew

Abstract

To be competitive as a state, Texas needs to compare favourably with other states and countries. The number of research universities in Texas is increasing rapidly, but too few of these institutions are ranked at the highest levels internationally. Texas's institutions also do not attract the same share of federal research and development funding as other states, especially California. To further increase the competitiveness of its universities, Texas will likely need to make additional public investments in research capacity for institutions at several stages of development. This chapter examines policies that Texas can use to encourage institutions to pursue excellence in graduate education and research, while meeting state labour market needs.

Keywords

Higher education – economic development – workforce development – labour markets – university rankings – research funding – graduate education

1 Introduction

Graduate education and research are crucial factors in meeting national, state and local workforce needs, but states and regions must balance several factors in formulating their strategies.

In this chapter, we consider developments in Texas, a large and growing US state. Texas has a total population of 28 million and 1.5 million students enrolled in higher education (as of 2017). It is served by 48 public universities and 38 private universities, as well as numerous community colleges and career training institutes.

In Texas, the number of master's, doctoral, and professional degrees has been growing – increasing by 40 percent over the past ten years. In 2014, Texas institutions awarded about 44,000 of these degrees.

The Texas Higher Education Coordinating Board's (THECB) adoption of the 2015 60x30TX strategic plan is also likely to affect the number of graduate degrees. The strategic plan calls for at least 60 per cent of Texans aged 25–34 to hold a quality higher education certificate or degree by 2030 (THECB, 2015), which will require higher education institutions in Texas to increase their annual degrees and certificate awards by about 80 per cent over a 15-year period. Growth in annual degrees is also likely to lead to an increase in graduate education that at a minimum matches its growth rate over the last decade. Graduate education expansion needs to be well managed and directed towards the fields that need advanced skills the most; otherwise graduate programmes could become misaligned with state needs and resources.

Both public institutions and private colleges offer higher education in Texas. However, Texas's higher education relies much more heavily on its public institutions to produce graduates compared to some states such as California, Florida and New York. Texas also has an unusually complex ecosystem of public higher education compared to many states. The higher education system includes 48 public universities, of which 38 are general academic and 10 are health-related institutions. These institutions offer undergraduate programmes and master's, doctoral, and professional degrees. Almost all of the universities belong to one of six different state university systems; only four institutions are not part of a system.

THECB, a state agency that oversees all public postsecondary education in Texas, is tasked with reviewing new degree programmes. Programmes that require more than $2 million in new investment during the first five years, as well as all new engineering degree and doctoral programme proposals, require an in-depth review. Other programmes can be approved without an in-depth review.

2 Study Goals and Objectives

While the 60x30 plan calls for a general expansion of higher education in Texas, this study looks at evidence from labour market data, comparisons with other states, and discussions with institution and system leaders to assess Texas's need to expand graduate degree production in particular. THECB expects to develop a strategic plan to align graduate education in the state with the goals of the 60x30 plan. Findings from this study may be useful in framing issues that THECB should address in that strategic plan.

Specifically, this study had three objectives:
- Assess the need to expand graduate programmes in Texas public higher education institutions.
- Provide guidance to THECB and higher education institutions on how to prepare and evaluate graduate programme proposals.
- Recommend policies to manage any needed expansion of graduate programmes in Texas.

3 Approach

We chose a mixed-method approach for this project. We used quantitative methods to assess (1) Texas's position in graduate education and research, and (2) Texas's labour market demand and need for graduate education. In addition, we conducted in-depth qualitative case studies at 12 Texas public institutions to understand what motivates institutions to expand graduate programmes. In our analyses, we compared Texas to the three other largest states in the country: California, New York and Florida. Each of these states has a significant number of universities with graduate education and research missions.

To guide the examination of the factors that influence graduate education, we first created a logic model depicted in Figure 9.1. The logic model shows the inputs, outputs, outcomes and impacts of graduate education. While the logic model presents the factors sequentially, the reality is more complex. However, the logic model highlights critical factors for which information is available to examine the relationship from initial inputs into higher education institutions to the ultimate impacts of interest.

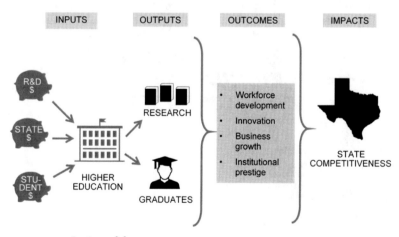

FIGURE 9.1   Logic model

In this study, we focus on state competitiveness as the ultimate impact of interest for THECB and state policymakers. Inputs for public higher education institutions include research and development (R&D) obligations, state appropriations and student tuition, which lead to high-quality research and well-prepared graduates. These outcomes help create a strong workforce, fuel innovation, promote business growth and improve institutional prestige, ultimately strengthening the state's overall competitiveness. Students who earn graduate degrees are also likely to benefit from expanded career opportunities and higher incomes.

4   Labour Market Demand for Graduate Degrees

Labour market demand provides a critical signal about the level of education and type of skills employers are looking for, which informs the type of education universities should provide. But it is challenging for higher education institutions to measure and interpret labour market demand. They have difficulty because some graduate degrees, like undergraduate degrees, are a close match for particular occupations and others are much more generally applicable.

In this study, we examined labour market demand by estimating which occupations in Texas will likely see the largest increase in new jobs requiring a graduate degree over the next few years. Figure 9.2 summarizes our projections. Across the top occupations for graduate demand, we estimate more than 120,000 new jobs requiring graduate education will be created in Texas between 2012 and 2022. As the chart shows, business, healthcare and teachers are the groups with greatest demand.

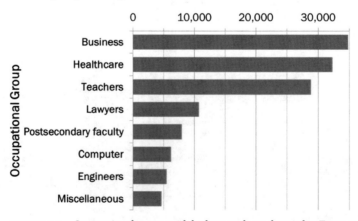

FIGURE 9.2   Occupational groups with highest graduate demand in Texas, 2012–2022

The Texas Workforce Commission data that we used to estimate labour market projections are based on economic forecasts and historical trends in employment. Thus projections for lawyers and perhaps other occupations may not reflect trends that have changed in these occupations since the forecasts were made.

5   Growth of Texas Degree Production

We also examined graduate degree production by broad field to understand if Texas's recent growth in graduate degree production signals a potential for the state to match future demand. Figure 9.3 indicates the number of graduate degrees for Texas in 2005 and 2014 for broad fields. These fields do not map directly to the labour market data above but in some cases can be compared directly to the occupational groups shown in Figure 9.2.

The chart in Figure 9.3 highlights that Texas's increased graduate degree production since 2005 has mainly been in business and health fields. Graduate degree production in business fields grew by about 48 per cent and in health fields by about 75 per cent. The strong projected demand shown earlier for the related occupational groups in Figure 9.2 may indicate a continued need for growth in business and health graduate degrees.

Given the projected increase in graduate demand, Texas appears to be better positioned to produce enough graduates in education. The situation is different

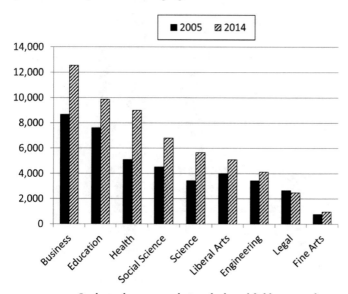

FIGURE 9.3   Graduate degree completions by broad field, 2005 and 2014

in engineering, however. Over the ten-year period we examined, growth in graduate engineering degrees in New York (67 per cent), Florida (62 per cent), and California (40 per cent) outpaced growth in Texas (21 per cent). But even as engineering degree production in Texas has been slow to grow, engineering jobs in the state have increased an estimated 30 per cent in ten years and are projected to grow two to three times as fast as these other three states, potentially leading to unmet demand. Of course, the high production in other states may allow employers to recruit engineers from these states to meet some of their demand.

6   Racial/Ethnic Composition of Graduate Degree Recipients

Texas has a large, diverse population, and its Hispanic population is growing particularly rapidly. However, Figure 9.4 shows that Texas's graduate degree production does not fully reflect this reality. When looking at the racial/ethnic distribution of 2014 public institution graduate degree recipients (as a fraction of those who are citizens or permanent residents) compared to the general Texas population of 18- to 64-year-olds that year, whites and Asian-Americans are over-represented, and Hispanics are significantly under-represented. Public higher education institutions seeking to increase the representation of minorities in graduate education face a significant

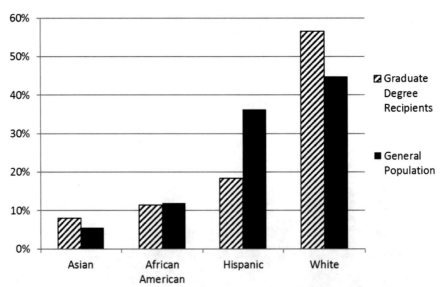

FIGURE 9.4   Percentage race/ethnicity distribution of public university graduate degree recipients and general population (18- to 64-years-old) in Texas, 2014

challenge, especially as Texas's population continues to grow and become more diverse.

7 Texas's Position in Graduate Education and Research

To this point, we have focused on historical trends to estimate how Texas's higher education ecosystem might meet a relatively straightforward concept of labour market demand, but other factors also play a key role in bolstering Texas's competitiveness and ability to attract employers. Employers which are making location decisions, especially in innovative industries that demand a base of R&D, consider a number of issues, including the broader and longer-term outcomes highlighted in the logic model in Figure 9.1: workforce development, research performance and institutional prestige. To understand Texas's standing in these areas relative to other large states, we compared Texas to California, Florida, and New York.

7.1 *Growth of Graduate Degrees*
Initially, we analysed graduation data to understand the relative growth in graduate and professional degree production across Texas and the comparison states. Figure 9.5 indicates that Texas has grown its graduate degree production by more than 41 per cent over the ten-year period from 2005 to 2014. This increase represents the largest percentage growth of any of the states analysed. However, Texas still remains behind California and New York in total graduate degree production.

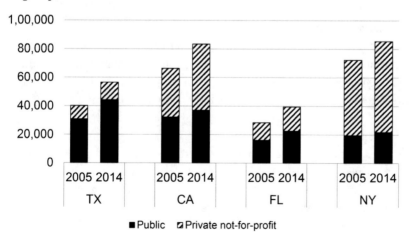

FIGURE 9.5   Graduate and professional degree production, 2005 and 2014

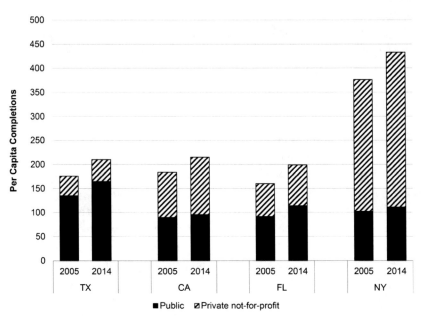

FIGURE 9.6   Per capita graduate and professional degree production, 2005 and 2014

While Texas, California, Florida and New York represent the four most populous states, their populations vary significantly. To contextualize graduate degree production by state, we examined the per-capita degree production. Figure 9.6 indicates that when controlling for population size, Texas's production is comparable to California's production. Unlike the comparison states, the vast majority of Texas's graduate degree production is supplied by public institutions.

7.2   *Graduate Attainment*

We also examined the overall graduate attainment rates for each state's population of 25- to 64-year-olds to understand how degree production is influencing the overall workforce. Figure 9.7 indicates that while Texas's graduate attainment is growing, it remains behind comparison states.

7.3   *Research*

As the logic model in Figure 9.1 indicates, research is another primary output of higher education institutions. However, to conduct high-quality research, universities first need to secure funding. We examined the overall funding the federal government – the top funder of research to universities – has obligated to universities from 2004 to 2013 (latest data available) to better understand how Texas has performed in this area.

PURSUING EXCELLENCE IN GRADUATE EDUCATION AND RESEARCH 171

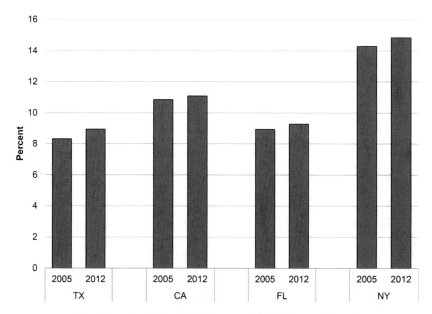

FIGURE 9.7 Percentage of residents, 25- to 64-years-old, holding a graduate degree, 2005 and 2012

Figure 9.8 shows the obligation trends over the ten-year period. It is important to note that overall federal funding for research was relatively flat over this time span, except for the 2009 stimulus funding. However, despite relatively stable overall funding, Texas's share of obligations has declined in recent years. In 2013, Texas received only 34 per cent of the total level of funding provided to California. Adjusting for population differences, Texas reached about 49 per

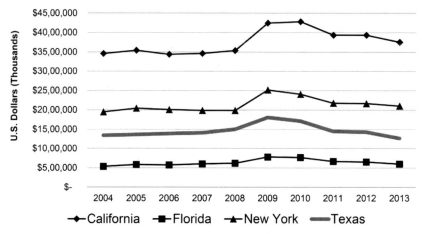

FIGURE 9.8 Federal obligations to higher education for R&D, 2013

cent of California's funding level, 44 per cent of New York's, and 156 per cent of Florida's.

To further understand research differences across states, we examined expenditures at the institutional level. Figures 9.5–9.8 illustrate the 2013 expenditures for all institutions in each state that spent at least $50 million on research. For each state, we classified institutions as public, private, or health related. Health-related institutions are privately or publicly controlled organizations that focus solely on health-related education and research (e.g., independent medical schools). Institutions that currently include medical schools are indicated with an asterisk.

Figure 9.9 indicates that in 2013, Texas had 17 institutions with research expenditures of more than $50 million and six with expenditures of more than $200 million a year. Of these six institutions, only two are general public universities – Texas A&M University and the University of Texas at Austin. The others are health-related institutions that have different funding resources and constraints than general universities. It is also important to note the significant difference in funding between the top two general public institutions and the next set of public institutions. Texas Tech University spent only $83 million on research in 2013 while the University of Texas at Austin, the next highest general public institution, spent $643 million on research.

By comparison, California had 15 institutions with research expenditures of more than $50 million in 2013; 11 had expenditures of more than $200 million on research. Of these 11 institutions, six are publicly controlled. Figure 9.10

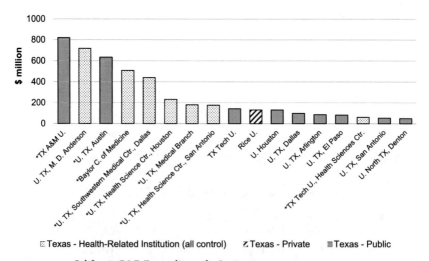

FIGURE 9.9 California R&D Expenditures by Institution, 2013

PURSUING EXCELLENCE IN GRADUATE EDUCATION AND RESEARCH 173

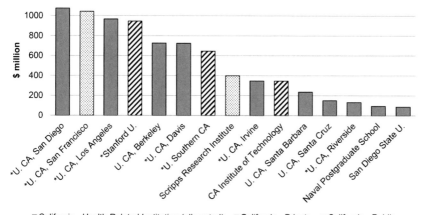

FIGURE 9.10   California R&D expenditures by institution, 2013

also highlights the differences in institutional organization between the two states. While Texas has several health related-only institutions, until recently it has had no academic medical centre integrated with general academic campuses. By contrast, this integrated medical-general model is responsible for the majority of California's top research spending institutions.

Figure 9.11 illustrates the seven institutions in Florida that spent more than $50 million on research in 2013. While the graph indicates that Florida had a much smaller set of institutions that dedicate resources to research, it only had two fewer institutions than Texas with expenditures of more than $200 million on R&D.

Finally, Figure 9.12 indicates that New York had 16 institutions that spent more than $50 million on R&D in 2013 and 10 institutions that spent more

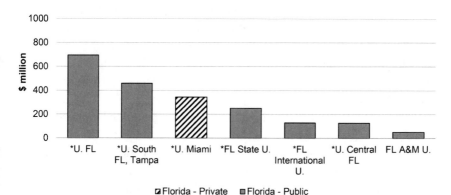

FIGURE 9.11   Florida R&D expenditures by institution, 2013

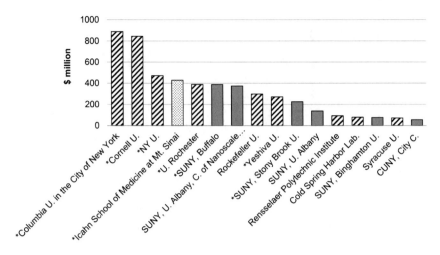

FIGURE 9.12   New York R&D expenditures by institution, 2013

than $200 million. The majority of these 10 institutions are privately controlled universities.

In comparing research expenditures across states, Texas's health-related institutions clearly are a unique set of resources responsible for the majority of research in the state. However, Texas did not spend nearly the amount on research that California's top institutions did in 2013. This finding indicates that Texas has a long way to go if it wants to be on par with California in terms of research output. In addition, the declining share of research obligations from the federal government signals a potential concern for Texas.

7.4   Ranking

Institutional prestige is an outcome of higher education institutions' efforts to admit the brightest students and produce the greatest research. While graduate degree production and research funding are good signals of this ultimate outcome, directly measuring institutional prestige, where possible, is useful. Therefore, we analysed two indicators of institutional prestige that universities commonly use in promoting their own organizations.

The Carnegie Classification of Institutions of Higher Education categorizes all US universities on their research intensity if they award at least 20 research-focused doctoral degrees each year. This classification is conducted every five years and is based on the number of PhD degrees awarded and sponsored research funding (assessed both in absolute terms and relative to the number of faculty at the institution). Carnegie classifies research-intensive institutions into three groups: Research 1 (R1) – highest research activity, Research 2 (R2) – higher research activity, and Research 3 (R3) – moderate research activity. R1 status is seen as a prestigious achievement that many universities aim to attain as it indicates a strong emphasis on research on par with the top universities in the United States.

Figure 9.13 indicates the number of institutions within each state that were classified as R1, R2, or R3 in 2005 and 2015. Texas significantly increased the number of its recognized research universities, growing from 16 to 25 in a ten-year period. This growth is the largest among the states we analysed. The number of R1-recognized institutions grew from three to eight in Texas while California and New York saw no growth in R1 institutions over the same time period. This finding indicates that while federal research obligations are not growing for Texas overall, individual institutions have grown their research portfolios.

We also used the Academic Rankings of World Universities (ARWU) to compare institutional prestige across states. ARWU use six objective metrics that focus on measuring research and graduate outputs to rank the top 500 institutions in the world. These metrics include 'number of alumni and staff winning Nobel Prizes and Fields Medals, number of highly cited researchers selected by Thomson Reuters, number of articles published in journals of nature and science, number of articles indexed in Science Citation Index – Expanded and Social Sciences Citation Index, and per capita performance of a university'.

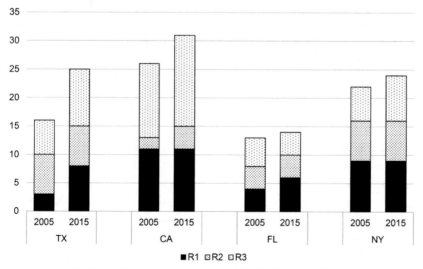

FIGURE 9.13 Number of Carnegie research universities (R1, R2, and R3) by state, 2005 and 2015

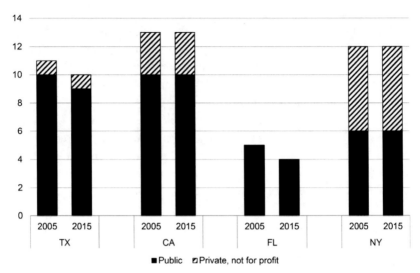

FIGURE 9.14 Number of institutions ranking in top 500 of ARWU by state, 2005 and 2015

Figure 9.14 indicates the number of universities in each state that were listed in the top 500 universities according to ARWU in 2005 and 2015. Given the lack of growth in top universities across all the states, we also looked at the trend for the United States as a whole. Overall, the number of ranked US universities dropped 13 per cent over the ten-year period. This drop indicates escalating international competition. However, Texas and Florida each lost only one institution.

Of the 10 Texas universities in the top 500 in 2015, only four institutions were ranked in the top 100. By contrast, 11 of California's 13 ranked universities were in the top 100. New York had four in the top 100, and Florida had one. This result indicates that while Texas is broadly competitive internationally, competition is increasing, and Texas has less representation at the most-competitive levels compared to California.

7.5 *Strategies for Raising Competitiveness*

Texas's position compared to other states and countries is important to its state competitiveness. The ranking indicators we presented above show that Texas is increasing its number of Carnegie-recognized research universities at a fast rate but, especially compared to California, is not represented at the highest levels of international competition and does not attract the same share of federal research funding. If Texas desires to further increase the competitiveness of its universities, it will likely need additional investments in research capacity.

Research universities benefit from a concentration of resources and deliberate strategies to invest in research activity (see Brewer, Gates, & Goldman, 2002; Salmi, 2009). Since California separates public universities into two systems based on mission, it can direct higher levels of funding to the research-intensive University of California campuses compared to the California State University campuses. Texas, on the other hand, allocates funding for education based on semester credit hours, broad field, and level of education but with no higher funding rates based on the research mission of certain campuses. Instead, Texas provides some state funding specifically based on research activity, recognizing that public universities need investments in research programmes to promote excellence.

We found that the basic design of these funding programmes is sound in aiming to increase the research capacity of Texas public institutions. The programmes generally concentrate additional state resources on institutions that have already developed a measure of success in building research programmes. Furthermore, they allocate funding based on measured performance in attracting research funding or, in the case of the Governor's University Research Initiative (GRUI), to campuses that can attract world-class researchers from out of state.

7.5.1   Recommendations

To enhance the competitiveness of Texas public higher education institutions, continue, and consider increasing, state research programme funding. To continue to build the competitiveness of Texas public institutions, the state should continue its research funding programmes and it may wish to consider increasing funding. Such increased funding could provide a greater match rate to campuses, further accelerating the development of research infrastructure on campuses that have shown some success in building nationally competitive research programmes.

To enhance institutions' ability to recruit key researchers from other states, consider more flexibility in GRUI. Specifically with regard to the GRUI, representatives of some emerging research universities with low endowments stated that while they might be able to attract notable out-of-state researchers who would qualify for this funding, they did not have sufficient flexible funds (like endowment income) to meet the local matching requirement with non-state funds. The state may wish to consider a more flexible approach to matching requirements that allows a broader selection of universities the opportunity to attract these researchers to Texas.

FIGURE 9.15   Institutional motivators for new graduate degree programmes

8   Graduate Program Decision-Making Process

The case studies focused on analysing the decision-making process at the institution level, emphasizing factors both internal and external to the institutions. From our case study interviews, we identified a number of motivators that lead institutions to propose new graduate programmes. Some motivators are concerned with institutional prestige – or how an institution is positioned (as a whole or within specific fields) relative to other institutions and how it views and understands its mission. Other motivators are closer to the departmental level because they focus more on expanding specific graduate programmes as a result of student or labour market demand, increased competition among graduate programmes within the field, or new requirements from professional organizations. Therefore, in Figure 9.15, we classified these motivators across a continuum, representing different levels at the institution.

8.1   Seeking Research-Intensive Status or Concentrating in a Specific Field

Texas may wish to increase the number of public research universities that are nationally and internationally competitive. However, there are challenges associated with institutional movement. One challenge is that such a movement might lead to changes in the mission of the institution and affect student access, especially since institutional ranking takes into account undergraduate admission and selectivity. Another challenge is that the pressure to become a research-intensive institution may lead to the expansion of graduate programmes that are not essential in meeting student or labour market demand, such as academic PhD programmes. This is because to become research intensive, an institution would need to have a large number of PhD programmes covering multiple disciplines. Institutions might establish such programmes even if there is not a clear need for them in Texas's labour market.

We provide two recommendations pertaining to institutional positioning and expanding research agendas. The first relates to proposal review, and the second addresses a broader issue related to changes in institutional mission and student access.

8.1.1 Recommendations

To place more emphasis on institutional support and policies in reviewing doctoral programme proposals. Although THECB currently considers the institution's strategic plan in its review of doctoral programme proposals, it could place more emphasis on links between proposed doctoral research programmes and the availability of institutional support for research as well as institutional policies conducive to research.

If the doctoral programme changes the institution's strategic plan or direction, THECB could require the institution to make changes to its strategic plan first to embody and support the proposed doctoral programme. However, it is important that THECB not systematically exclude institutions from expanding into doctoral education, or expanding their doctoral offerings, provided the institutions have supportive missions, strategies, resources, and policies.

To review student access regularly and consider alternative pathways when needed. Although institutions should be able to expand their research or PhD programmes, they and the state should also be sensitive to how such expansion could affect student admission to undergraduate programmes. The institution or its system could periodically review any changes in student access. If changes in admission occur, we recommend that the institution or system explore alternatives for how to serve students who would no longer be admitted, for instance through expanding articulation with community colleges or even expanding their own student population to ensure access to less academically prepared students. THECB could provide general guidelines on how institutions could deal with student access issues if missions change.

8.2 *Engaging in Positive Margin Activities*

A critical objective for expanding master's programmes is to generate revenue that could be used for strengthening and supporting doctoral programmes.

This objective is not a concern as long as the master's programmes are meeting workforce and student demand and their quality has not been compromised. Although some departments have master's programme accreditation review, many do not.

8.2.1 Recommendations

To ensure the quality of master's programmes through accreditation or an alternative process. While all graduate programmes must be externally evaluated at least once every seven years, institutions may opt for a specific external review if the programme is not accredited by a recognized body in the academic field. One option to ensure the quality of master's programmes is for them to be accredited, if accreditation for the subject matter is offered by accrediting agencies. Another option is for institutions to implement a rigorous quality assurance process that uses independent experts to assess the quality of the programmes on a set of criteria that are already established in the field. Obtaining accreditation or evidence of some review by external experts is likely to improve how employers and prospective students view the legitimacy of the programme, which in turn would increase an institution's competitive edge.

To develop THECB criteria for evaluating online master's program quality. THECB could also provide guidance to institutions on how to evaluate the quality of their online master's programmes. Many online programmes are approved as simple changes of delivery mode from existing face-to-face programmes rather than undergoing a full proposal review. The Learning Technology Advisory Committee (LTAC) and THECB could develop criteria for reviewing online master's programmes, including those changing their delivery mode. Institutions could be involved in this process or asked to provide input regarding the criteria.

8.3 *Competition*

Competition can be healthy and lead to innovative and high-quality programmes, but it can also have a downside. Competition may generate programme duplication if similar graduate programmes are vying for students within the same geographic area. To keep competing programmes from closing down, institutions might change their standards to attract less academically prepared students, and the quality of the programmes might be affected. Furthermore, online programmes, especially in education and some of the health sciences, tend to be similar and have no geographic boundaries, resulting in both increased competition for student enrolment and duplication. However, engineering online programmes often do not face the same issues since these graduate programmes attract international students and the supply of international students is greater compared to domestic students.

8.3.1 Recommendations
To avoid program duplication by promoting collaboration rather than competition at the system level. University systems could use their periodic meetings of provosts to discuss how to best manage competition among their campuses, reduce redundancy, and encourage healthy competition and collaboration. This recommendation does not mean that there should not be similar graduate programmes within the same system or across systems. As long as there is student and workforce demand and the programmes are of high quality and are serving various regions in Texas, duplication is not a problem. However, in instances where the student and workforce demand are insufficient and not all institutions are equally equipped to implement high-quality research graduate programmes, collaboration among institutions to provide graduate education benefits the institutions, system, and state. University systems could explore ways to incentivize collaboration. They also could provide resources and technical assistance to help institutions develop joint graduate programmes that emphasize institutional strengths and build on their capacities.

8.4 *Labour Market Demand*
Reliable employment forecasting is very challenging. Demand for new skills depends on a number of factors, including technological progress, government policies and global conditions. For some disciplines, such as the humanities, assessing demand is even more difficult because there is no clear link to one occupation, but such disciplines could prepare students in general skills that apply to many occupations.

However, institutions could improve their mechanisms for matching their graduate programmes with workforce needs by engaging in ongoing research activities and surveying employers and graduates to assess demand for skills and the quality of graduates.

8.4.1 Recommendations
Support institutional access to labour market analysis tools. THECB currently encourages institutions to use national and state data to determine workforce needs when proposing new graduate programmes. THECB could acquire licences or facilitate joint licences for commercial products that simplify the use of these government data and add real-time analysis of job postings.

To provide THECB guidance on acceptable sources beyond BLS and TWC. THECB currently encourages institutions to use BLS and TWC data to determine workforce needs when proposing new graduate programmes. But there is a shortcoming to such databases. The datasets do not map specific degrees to workforce data.

To capture labour market needs, institutions should follow traditional methods for data collection and analysis, including primary and secondary quantitative and qualitative data. THECB could support institutions by identifying some of the acceptable approaches for continually obtaining data from employers and increasing institutional engagement with industry.

To provide education and training to ensure that data and tools are used wisely and effectively. THECB could help build institutions' capacity to identify workforce needs by providing training and workshops on how to use available workforce datasets, how to solicit pertinent workforce information and how to interpret the resulting data.

To track graduate job placement. Finally, THECB could require institutions to track student job placements during the programme review to see if the graduate programmes have placed students in the labour market as intended. This requirement will signify to institutions the expectation to track this information and to invest in efforts to analyse labour market data more systematically. Institutions are likely to need additional resources to be able to track graduate student placement, especially at the master's level. The state could explore options for providing resources to the institutions.

8.5 Student Demand

Appropriately using student demand information to inform the expansion of programmes is challenging for institutions when there is no agreed-upon measurement metric.

8.5.1 Recommendations

To identify best practices for measuring student demand. THECB could identify best practices and provide institutions guidelines on how to measure student demand.

To provide THECB guidance on balancing student and labour market demands. THECB could also clarify for institutions how to balance the needs measured by student demand and labour market demand, especially in instances when such needs are misaligned.

8.6 *Emerging Multi-Disciplinary Fields*
Certain fields need graduates with multi-disciplinary skills, but whether the best way to develop those skills is through a master's degree or certification is likely to vary by field and proposed programme.

8.6.1 Recommendation
To require institutions to demonstrate a need for multi-disciplinary programmes. When institutions propose new multi-disciplinary programmes, THECB could require them to conduct more rigorous analyses of labour market needs than they would normally do. THECB could set standards by requiring institutions to articulate the benefits of the multi-disciplinary programme in terms of the breadth and depth of the programme, the skills it promotes, and why the need being met by the proposed multi-disciplinary programme cannot be satisfied by restructuring existing programmes in the main field through the addition of new courses or certificates.

8.7 *Professional Degree Upgrading*
Graduate programmes in nursing, physical therapy and other fields propose new graduate degrees to respond to professional associations. These associations advocate for advanced, often doctoral, degree programmes as entry to practice, usually to support and justify a greater level of professional responsibility for practitioners. The departments that we interviewed emphasized that their responsibility is to meet employer demand and make sure their graduate students are well placed; therefore, they see a need for such programmes.

8.7.1 Recommendation
To consider professional association standards when they are likely to shape employer demand. When evaluating new graduate programmes, THECB should take into account changes in professional association standards, where they exist, to the extent they are likely to shape student and employer demand.

9 Systemic and Process Aspects of Graduate Programme Development

In this section, we examine the pipeline of students entering science and engineering graduate programmes, the state funding approach for graduate programmes, the proposal development process, and ongoing programme review processes.

9.1 Strengthening the Pipeline of Domestic Students into Science and Engineering Graduate Programmes

While major structural factors contribute to the low enrolment of domestic students in science and engineering graduate programmes, institutions, systems and the state could all adopt programmes to strengthen this pipeline and increase the representation of domestic students in Texas graduate programmes. Because minority groups, especially Hispanics, are under-represented in Texas graduate degree awards, efforts to attract more domestic students should also aim to increase the number of under-represented students entering these graduate programmes.

9.1.1 Recommendations

Institutions and systems should consider programmes to strengthen the pipeline of domestic students, including underrepresented minorities, into science and engineering graduate programmes. We think institutions and systems have opportunities to collaborate to strengthen the exposure of domestic students, including under-represented minorities, to graduate study in science and engineering. Institutions could formally collaborate by developing pipelines through articulation agreements to transition students from undergraduate to graduate degrees.

THECB should examine plans for student stipends in new research graduate programmes. Stipends are important for supporting students, especially domestic students, in research graduate programmes. THECB should continue to examine proposed stipend levels and plans to fund them to ensure that stipends are adequate and competitive with other quality research graduate programmes.

The state (or other funders) should consider funding special stipends for domestic students in science and engineering doctoral programmes. The state, or perhaps other funders like foundations, could provide special stipends for domestic students beyond what the institutions or departments could provide. Since domestic students have options to pursue a master's degree during their career, we suggest that any special stipends be targeted specifically to domestic students in doctoral science and engineering programmes (either concurrent with a master's programme or following one). A portion of state research funding could be devoted to funding these additional stipends to make doctoral study more attractive.

9.2 Funding

Stakeholders have little interest in fundamental changes to the formula funding methodology, although the state should consider increases to fund the ambitious student growth goals of the 60x30 plan.

9.2.1 Recommendations

Consider increases in general fund appropriations to support growing enrolments and use the current formula funding method to allocate them. To meet the ambitious 60x30 goals of increased student enrolment and completions, institutions will require resources. If the state provides increased general fund appropriations that keep pace with student enrolment growth, these increases will reduce the chance that students will become burdened with escalating fees. Whatever the level of general fund appropriations, we recommend that THECB continue to use the current formula funding methodology to allocate them, although it may be prudent to monitor whether highly scalable online master's programmes are attracting an increasing share of formula funding over time and, if so, consider adjustments to the formula.

9.3 *Proposal Development and Review Process*

The proposal process could be improved through several strategies, focusing on providing earlier, informal reviews and sharing the practices that result in successful proposals.

9.3.1 Recommendations

Institutions should conduct their own pre-proposal reviews. Since proposal development takes significant time, institutions should conduct internal pre-proposal reviews to direct proposal development efforts in the most productive directions.

Institutions should consult informally with THECB staff early during proposal development. Similarly, institutions should seek early, informal consultation with THECB staff to understand the experiences of other similar proposal efforts and receive guidance on which aspects of a proposal are likely to receive the greatest scrutiny.

Provide guidance on the characteristics of successful proposals. To generalize and extend the consultation function, THECB could compile guidance on the aspects associated with the most successful proposals. This guidance could help institutions and departments as they prepare future proposals.

9.4 *Ongoing Programme Review Processes*

THECB generally has limited powers to review programmes after they have been approved, with two major exceptions: periodic doctoral programme reviews and low-producing programmes. Doctoral programmes are required to report to THECB annually for five years and then at least every seven years after that. Under the recent revisions to its mandate, THECB no longer has the authority to order the closure of degree programmes with low enrolment or production. Instead, the state now relies on an annual report from THECB on low-producing programmes that identifies degree programmes at each institution that have been operating at least five years and where the number of graduates has fallen below a specified threshold over a five-year period (25 for undergraduate, 15 for master's, and 10 for doctoral).

9.4.1 Recommendation

Continue policies and practices for programme review and low-producing programmes; review consolidation proposals closely. The doctoral programme review and low-producing programmes report seem to be helpful in managing graduate programmes. One area we recommend for further scrutiny is proposed consolidations of graduate programmes. Further scrutiny could prevent the funding of consolidations that do not entail meaningful integration of the academic programmes.

10 Conclusion

Texas's higher education ecosystem is large and complex. Because Texas depends very heavily on its public universities to train graduates, produce research and spur innovation, policies that affect the public university sector are even more important for maintaining and enhancing competitiveness in Texas than in other states that benefit from prestigious private universities.

Texas's 60x30 strategic plan and our analysis of labour market projections point to a continuation of the past 10 years of strong growth in graduate education in the state. Generally, Texas has been increasing its production of graduate degrees in fields corresponding to the occupational groups that are expected to have the most job openings: business, healthcare, education, computers and engineering. However, because growth in graduate engineering degrees has been slow compared to other states and to projected demand, THECB and institutions should consider expanding graduate programmes in engineering. In addition, THECB and institutions should expand efforts to recruit domestic students and provide adequate financial support to motivate those with a bachelor's degree to pursue graduate education.

To be competitive, Texas needs to compare favourably to other states and countries. The number of research universities in Texas is increasing rapidly compared to other states, but too few of these institutions are ranked at the highest levels internationally. Texas's institutions also do not attract the same share of federal R&D funding as other states, especially California. To further increase the competitiveness of its universities, Texas will likely need to make additional public investments in research capacity for institutions at several stages of development. However, these investments must be focused on institutions that have shown at least some capability to develop research programmes.

As Texas explores ways to increase graduate education production, it can look at increasing enrolment to existing programmes, but new programmes will likely be necessary as well. Developing new programmes presents the state and institutions both opportunities and challenges. Proposals for new programmes must be evaluated carefully to ensure that they maximize the benefits to Texas and the United States. While expanding graduate programmes and research is an opportunity to build institutional prestige, it can also be unproductive if institutions expand in areas not related to state economic needs. Institutions may also seek to develop large-scale online programmes to increase operating margins in the face of constrained state funding. These programmes may expand access and increase revenue, but they may also dilute quality.

If an institution seeks to shift to a research-intensive mission, it must make a widespread, sustained commitment, starting with developing a thoughtful strategic plan and then aligning its graduate programme proposals with that strategic plan. Other universities may choose to focus on specific niches by proposing graduate degree programmes that match their specific capabilities or context and that may not be available at other institutions.

Expanding graduate programmes is important for meeting the goals of THECB's 60x30 plan and for improving Texas's state competitiveness. However, this expansion must be managed well to ensure that the programmes are high quality. While institutions are responsible for monitoring the quality of their graduate programmes, THECB and accrediting agencies can support quality through their programme approval and review processes. The recommendations presented in this chapter are intended as guidance for THECB on how to strengthen its current review and approval process and how to help institutions determine whether there is a need to expand their graduate education programmes. Some of the recommendations also provide guidance for institutions and systems on how to manage competition and promote quality in graduate programmes.

References

Brewer, D. J., Gates, S. M., & Goldman, C. A. (2002). *In pursuit of prestige: Strategy and competition in US higher education*. New Brunswick, NJ: Transaction Press.
Salmi, J. (2009). *The challenge of establishing world-class universities*. Washington, DC: World Bank.
Texas Higher Education Coordinating Board. (2015). *60x30TX, Texas higher education strategic plan: 2015–2030*. Austin, TX: Texas Higher Education Coordinating Board.

CHAPTER 10

World-Class Universities' Contribution to an Open Society: Chinese Universities on a Mission?

Marijk van der Wende

Abstract

How can world-class universities continue to contribute to the global common good, when support for open borders, multilateral trade and cooperation is being weakened, globalization is criticized, and nationalism is looming? Can they compensate for the inequalities resulting from globalization, and if so, how? The pressure on the sector is two-faceted: the push to compete at the global level and a growing critique of local commitment and delivery. The pursuit of global positioning on rankings especially is being criticized for jeopardizing universities' national and local mission and for making them footloose from their society as a cosmopolitan project. How can they overcome these tensions in the context of a backlash against globalization and growing scepticism to internationalization in Europe and the US? And what will be the meaning and impact of the rise of China with its New Silk Road project, which could potentially span the Eurasian continent?

Keywords

Globalization – internationalization – inequality – higher education – China

1   Introduction: Waking up in a New World

Recent geopolitical events and intensified populist tendencies are promoting a turn away from internationalism and away from an open society. Support for open borders, multilateral trade and cooperation is being weakened, globalization is criticized, and nationalism is looming. The United Kingdom's 2016 vote for Brexit, questions around the (dis)integration of the Europe Union (EU), the United States (US) turning its back on the world, and attacks on universities in, for instance, Turkey and Hungary create waves of uncertainty in higher education regarding international cooperation, the free movement of students, academics, scientific knowledge and ideas. At the same time, China is launching new global initiatives such as the New Silk Road (or One Belt One Road) project, which could potentially span and integrate major parts of the world across the European and Asian continents, but likely on new and different conditions, also for higher education.

The backlash against globalization in the West may have surprised many, but had been foreseen by others for more than two decades (e.g. Rodrik, 1997; Castells, 2000; James, 2002; Stiglitz, 2002; Gray, 2002). Yet, the results of globalization in terms of both growing and shifting economic inequalities, had for too long not been fundamentally understood for their social consequences. Through the scholarly work of Piketty (2014) and Milanovic (2016) (among others) we have gained more insight into the complex and paradoxical effects of decreasing global inequality (mostly caused by China's rise) combined with increasing inequality within certain countries and regions (particularly in the West).

The discourse on globalization in higher education has been divided between on the one hand those who view higher education as an active part of the globalization process in terms of the speeding up of worldwide interconnectedness and growing interdependence (Held et al., 1999), logically resulting in the convergence of higher education models and systems between countries and regions (e.g. the Bologna Process). It is a view often connected to the global knowledge economy paradigm, in which higher education is a producer of human capital (talent, skills) and innovation as key requirements for economic growth and cross-border competition between corporations, public organisations and nations, and among higher education institutions, world-class universities in particular, as spurred by global rankings in their competition for global talent, reputation and financial resources (Marginson & van der Wende, 2007, 2009; van der Wende, 2008, 2011a).

On the other hand, those who view globalization as only adding to the perverse effects produced by 'academic capitalism' (a critical discourse that has been ongoing since the 1990s (Slaughter & Leslie, 1997; Slaughter & Taylor, 2016), through competition for international students, institutional income, and global reputation, resulting in increasing global stratification. A critique that coheres to a certain extent with the somewhat milder debate about world-class universities versus national flagships (Douglas, 2016; Douglass & Hawkins, 2017) and that on world-class universities versus world-class systems (see f.i. Salmi, 2014; van der Wende, 2014; Marginson, 2016a).

A recent review of future scenarios for higher education that were developed a decade ago by OECD (van der Wende, 2007, 2017) revealed that the one scenario that forecasted a backlash against globalization, described as 'caused by terror attacks, immigration, outsourcing, and the perception of threatened national identity, alongside heightened geopolitical conflicts' (OECD, 2006), was a decade ago not seen as very likely or probable by leaders in the sector. The higher education sector's faith in the inevitability of internationalization as a cosmopolitan project (Ziguras, 2016) was supported by definitions of globalization that were inherently progressive.

Yet, the shifting socio-economic inequalities at the global level have to a large extent been mirrored in higher education, while its potential to compensate for increasing inequalities within rich countries, i.e. its meritocratic role, is being called into question. The resulting pressure on the sector is two-faceted: enhanced competition at the global level and a growing critique of local commitment and delivery. This critique seems to concern world-class universities in particular. Their pursuit of global positioning may jeopardize their national mission and local relevancy (Douglas, 2016), risking them to become 'footloose', by turning to global markets of disproportionately privileged international students while failing to include 'others' from, for instance, local disadvantaged minorities (Rhoades, 2017). Hence the current scepticism and criticism of internationalization (or even 'anti-internationalization') as an elite cosmopolitan project, which only increases the benefits of higher education for an even smaller numbers of the happy few.

The present global context is provoked by Western leaders who denounce global citizenship: 'If you believe you are a citizen of the world, you're a citizen of nowhere' (Theresa May, 2016); 'There is no global flag, no global currency, no global citizenship' (Donald Trump, 2017). At the same time, China presents itself as willing to take the lead in economic globalization, as expressed by President Xi Jinping in his opening speech at the 2017 World Economic Forum. China is even willing to lead in the 2015 Paris Agreement on climate change. It is determined to restore its central place in the world by major initiatives such as building a New Silk Road (NSR) or One Belt, one Road (OBOR) initiative that is designed to logistically reconnect and also potentially integrate the Eurasian continent economically.

The NSR will carry more than just consumer goods. In line with the historical version(s) of the Silk Road, people, ideas, and knowledge will travel along this New Silk Road with mutual influence. And just as previous major geopolitical trends and events, for instance (the end of) World War II, the integration of the EU, the fall of the Berlin Wall, etc., have impacted international cooperation in higher education (for better or for worse), this can also be expected to result from the NSR. But how and under which conditions? China-EU cooperation is being established along the NSR through research hubs and higher education agreements, and China's impact on the global higher education landscape is growing. How will China's values impact higher education, and do we actually understand these values at all?

It is in this new global context that I will focus on world-class university's contributions to the global common good: (how) can they compensate for the inequalities resulting from globalization, while support for open borders, multilateral trade and cooperation is being weakened, globalization is criticized, and nationalism is looming? How can they overcome the tensions related to the backlash against globalization and growing scepticism to internationalization in Europe and the US? And how can they contribute to an open, democratic and equitable society, based on values addressing fundamental human rights and the rule of law, while these are increasingly under pressure in important parts of the world? What will be the meaning of the rise of China in this respect? In particular, what will be the impact of its New Silk Road project for higher education and research in Europe?

2   Globalization, Inequality and Higher Education

The empirical works of Thomas Piketty (2014) and Branco Milanovic (2016) underline the paradoxical outcomes of globalization, especially regarding its impact on inequality. While economic and social inequality has decreased at the global level, mostly due to the growth of Asian economies, notably China's, it has increased within certain countries and regions, especially in the West.

These patterns are to a large extent reflected in higher education and research. UNESCO (2015a) confirms that for research, global imbalances are generally decreasing as the North–South divide in research and innovation is narrowing, with a large number of countries moving towards knowledge economies and cooperation increasing between the regions. A very large share of the re-balancing effect is due to China's rise on the global higher education and research scene. China has the largest higher education system in terms of student numbers, second in terms of its share in world expenditure on R&D and is expected to have the world's largest R&D budget by the end of the decade (see the section on China's rise, below). The EU's R&D workforce is (still) the largest and is increasingly mobile, driven on the one hand by increasing disparities between countries that increase public funding and those that reduce investment in higher education, and facilitated on the other hand by growing EU funding with competitive mechanisms, such as the ERC. Consequently, the European R&D workforce is concentrating more and more in fewer hubs, thus creating bigger inequalities within Europe and contributing to the further stratification of the European higher education landscape (van der Wende,

2015). National policies to spur excellence (e.g. in Germany and France) may further enhance such stratification, funding gaps between countries are still increasing since the 2008 financial crisis (Pruvot et al., 2017) and it is still an open question what the effects of Brexit will be.

UNESCO reports that global inequality also decreases for higher education, as student numbers are exploding globally, with most growth observed, again, in Asia. The numbers of students studying abroad have increased at an even greater rate, to over four million today, and these flows are still clearly in favour of the OECD countries. But as they still represent only some two per cent of the student population, this brain drain is not seen to represent a threat to the development of national systems. At the same time, public financial support for higher education is under pressure in many countries (OECD, 2016) and average graduate debt is rising fast as private contributions become more important, e.g. in the UK and the US, where this shift in funding is being strongly criticized for issues of equity and decreasing value for money (The Economist, 2015). The meritocratic role of higher education is waning in these societies that have become significantly more unequal in terms of income from labour and notably from capital. Its importance in explaining income differences is diminishing and family background and social connections may matter more, especially when the upper limit of educational participation is approaching (Marginson, 2016b; Milanovic, 2016).

Global inequality in higher education and research may be expected to decrease further with the recent uncertainties that have occurred in the UK and the US. The vote for Brexit and the Trump administration are feared for weakening the public funding available for R&D, and for hampering the flows of international students and researchers due to stricter visa regulations. The US State Department have already announced a reconsideration of H1B visa for foreign students and researchers, and the Brexit negotiations have so far created uncertainties regarding the status of EU students. A decline in international applications is reported for both countries as important global higher education providers. Meanwhile, 'China stands to gain as its universities advance in global visibility' (Postiglione, 2017) and is becoming more successful in its aim to attract global talent (back). This is already visible in the growing return ratio of Chinese students that studied abroad, mostly in the US, from one third a decade ago to 82 per cent over the past years (Maslen, 2017). Moreover, China is attracting hundreds of thousands of foreign students to its shores.

It seems less certain at what speed global inequality at the level of doctoral education could reduce. It is most prevalent at this level, with 24 per cent of PhD students on average in OECD countries being international, against an average of nine per cent in all levels (OECD, 2016). In fact the bulk of doctoral education is provided by relatively few institutions globally, notably in the US and the UK which host over 50 per cent of all international doctoral students (UNESCO, 2015a). China's growth in R&D is impressive and two decades of restructuring of China's doctoral education has resulted in some adoption of the US model in relation to for instance the role of coursework. But many challenges remain in Chinese doctoral education, regarding government control, quality assurance mechanisms, and the quality of full-time faculty (Huang, 2017a). For decades, Chinese PhD students undertook their studies in the US and the UK in particular. The US relies heavily on such immigrants for its R&D and aimed to improve 'stay rates', especially for degree holders in STEM (Science, Technology, Engineering, Mathematics). Scholars pointed to the US' vulnerability in this respect (Proudfoot & Hoffer, 2016) and internally questions were raised in previous years as to whether this reduces job opportunities for US researchers. In 2015 the US Council on Foreign Relations asked in a report on 'Balancing China', more precisely whether the US should continue to help build the competitive advantage of its main competitor, China, by training so many Chinese graduate students. The Trump administration has expressed new views on the US-China relationship, so far mostly focusing on trade (imbalances), employment, and manufacturing, but with little promise for the future of its open doors policy for higher education. It remains to be seen whether the US can maintain its R&D performance without immigrant scientists. In fact, the changing global relationships and stricter visa policies, could speed up the global rebalancing of doctoral education over time, i.e. reduce inequalities also at this level.

Whether inequality in higher education and research will continue to increase within certain countries and regions could be related to the same trends, notably the UK's vote for Brexit and the new US Presidency. In both countries, reductions in institutional income from public research funding and international student fees could have unintended consequences, as they are likely to harm institutions in the second and third tiers of the system more than those in the first tier, i.e. world-class universities that rely more on their ability to attract, retain and accumulate financial and human capital from global sources. This effect could concur with policy trends in a range of countries that intend to enhance the visibility of world-class university's through differentiation policies, such as the Excellence Initiative in Germany (now in its third round) and other examples of such policies in for instance France, Russia, Japan, and obviously in China (see below). Intended or not, these trends would likely further increase the vertical differentiation, stratification, and thus inequality, within these systems.

3   Global Positioning, Local Commitment, Inclusive Internationalization and the Global Public Good

While global inequalities in higher education tend to decrease, inequalities in higher education and research within certain rich countries have been increasing. As said above, this reflects the general outcomes of globalization in inequality, while higher education's potential to compensate for these increasing inequalities, i.e. its meritocratic role, is being called into question. UNESCO (2015b) notes that even in countries with high enrolment rates, the participation of minorities continues to lag behind the national average. Critics see higher education under conditions of globalization even as a contributor to widening inequalities (Unterhalter & Carpentier, 2010; Slaughter & Taylor, 2016).

The pressure resulting from globalization on the higher education sector is thus two-faceted: on the one hand a push to compete and perform at global level, while on the other a growing critique of local commitment and delivery. The pursuit of global positioning in rankings is especially criticized for 'jeopardizing universities national mission and relevancy in the societies that give them life and purpose' (Douglas, 2016), and for 'creating a divide with local, regional, and national responsibilities' (Hazelkorn, 2016).

National and local stakeholders in particular are challenging research universities with global ambitions regarding this imbalance between global prestige and domestic commitment. Populist parties in the Netherlands and elsewhere in Europe ask critical questions of the costs and benefits of international students, spreading concerns about reduced opportunities and access for domestic students. Also in the US, universities are being criticized for having neglected their contribution toward redressing inequality and are called to recognize problems of their past and present. Many have a long history of exclusion by gender, ethnicity and social class, and remain best at serving elites, nationally and globally (Rhoades, 2017). This critique also seems to concern world-class universities in particular:

> Most elite universities would be diversified culturally at least as much by expanding access to low-income students of various ethnic and national backgrounds in their city, as by recruiting yet more relatively privileged international students. (ibid., p. 2)

Hence the current scepticism and criticism of internationalization, which is in this light now considered as another space for academic capitalism.

International educators' awareness of the issues is growing and the 2017 Conference of the European Association for International Education (EAIE) focused on how higher education is adjusting to rising opposition to globalization. Accompanying press reported that experts find little cause for optimism in the European future of internationalization and concluded that bridges need to be built, since across the world the political winds are blowing against internationalization and higher education in general (THE, 13 September 2017).

Academics outside these internationalization circles may voice critique as well. In the Netherlands some rail against internationalization as an elite cosmopolitan project; against the use of English as a second language for teaching and learning; and, of course against global rankings. Some academics now list internationalization, among such trends as massification and underfunding, as causes of higher education's current problems. Arguments that students are to be primarily trained for domestic labour markets are being heard, and the local and national mission and relevance of public higher education is being (re-)emphasized, alongside pleas for teaching in the national language. Student unions and councils in some institutions are reluctant to adopt English as their working language and some elite student clubs and fraternities are found to be resisting international participation.

Although these voices do not necessarily represent the dominant perspective, or formal policy or discourse, they do raise questions about whether and to what extend academia's internal debate is developing conservative traits that may result in tendencies towards academic nationalism, protectionism, or indeed isolationism?[1] Not only would this be in contrast with the strive for global reputation and impact (as possible features of academic capitalism), but also counter to the concept of higher education as a global public or common good, contributing to global development goals and creating opportunity for many. In other words, as recently formulated by Peter Scott (2017): 'Is the rise of populism a wake-up call, is the academy on the wrong side of history?'.

I previously argued (van der Wende, 2007, 2011b) that in order to rebalance the effects of globalization, higher education institutions should broaden their missions for internationalization, not only to respond to the profitable side of globalization (i.e. benefitting from the global flows of talent and capital), but also to address the challenges of globalization, such as migration and social exclusion; to be more open and inclusive; to balance economic and social responsiveness; in fact to (re)define their 'social contract' in a globalized context.[2] A key step in doing this is to widen access for migrant and local minority students; to support the integration of student groups with different cultural, ethnic and religious backgrounds, and to embrace diversity as the key to success in a global knowledge society, in order to become truly international and intercultural learning communities where young people can effectively develop the competences needed for this society and become real global citizens.

Martha Nussbaum (2012) phrased these arguments in 'Not for Profit', in favour of cultivating the humanities for world citizenship. Economic growth cannot be the only rationale for education. Higher education institutions have to contribute to 'a public response to the problems of pluralism, fear, and suspicion our societies face' (p. 125).

We are now facing such problems, indeed more so than we could have imagined in our optimism during the heyday of internationalization. In Europe, these characterized the 'happy nineties' that followed the fall of the Berlin Wall (1989), the signing of the European Treaty in Maastricht (1992), and the ensuing rapid expansion of the EU. EU policies for higher education developed quickly, following the popular academic exchanges supported by the ERASMUS programme and became increasingly economically oriented, aimed at making European higher education more responsive to the labour market and to global economic competitiveness (i.e. the so-called Lisbon Agenda).

In Europe the backlash against globalization was driven by the 2008 financial crisis, the 2011–2013 Euro crisis and the 2015 refugee crisis. Subsequent populist sentiment and the ongoing internal political tensions have urged the EU to also reconsider its policy directions for higher education. Its strong economic focus on employability became paralleled by an agenda for a more inclusive Europe, which was motivated by a Council Resolution stating:

> With regard to recent tragic events related to radicalization in parts of Europe, a particular focus on civic, democratic, intercultural competences and critical thinking is even more urgent. (EU, 2016a)

Consequently, the EU competency framework was enriched with more attention for social and civic competences in higher education, including 'personal, interpersonal and intercultural competence' and covering 'all forms of behaviour that equip individuals to participate in an effective and constructive way in social and working life' (EU, 2016b).

I remain convinced that higher education institutions, especially world-class universities, have to come to grips with their role and contribution to the global public or common good. As said, they need to (re)define their social contract in the global context, including a consideration of the global-local nexus. After all, 'all politics is local' for universities as well (Douglass, 2005). The current anti-globalization sentiments urge institutions to take even more responsibility for addressing the growing inequality between the 'winners' and 'losers' of globalization. A world-class university needs to be relevant to both groups, whether they come from faraway or from nearby, as the best place to bridge what divides them, and to stimulate them to form new networks across socio-economic, ethnic and gender lines. This is certainly not accomplished by treating internationalization and diversity as two separate policy themes or areas of action, as has been the case in certain national policies and in higher education institutions in recent decades. As argued above, internationalization needs to be inclusive, i.e. to embrace diversity in all its dimensions, including the cultural diversity associated with ethnic minorities represented at local level.

The fact that some global leaders now denounce the concept of global citizenship should not discourage our pursuit of a diverse and inclusive academic community, as was emphasized by various US university presidents in campus-wide statements responding to unrest following the US elections in November 2016, and even more so after the announced travel bans.

> As a community, we must use this moment to reaffirm our own values of respect and inclusion, while working together to preserve academic freedom, fearless inquiry, and diversity. Together we have both the will and the ability to rise above the rancor, to embody the best of what a free, open, and inclusive society should be. (Nicholas B. Dirks, Chancellor, Berkeley News, November 9th 2016)

At the same time, it should be recognized that the required contribution from world-class universities at local, national, and global levels, through a mix of both competition and cooperation mechanisms, seriously broadens their range of strategic options and thus the level of complexity and risk taking involved in their decision-making. They therefore may need time to experience how internal diversity can enrich such decision-making processes, and it implies engaging with more external stakeholders, having more accountability, and likely more risk. In many cases, these efforts will require more strategic capacity, stronger leadership and more autonomy than many of them possess at present. Yet world-class university's contribution to an open society is mostly at stake in those parts of the world where inherent democratic values regarding equality, human rights, and the rule of law, are increasingly under pressure. Astonishing enough this includes parts of Europe, such as Hungary where the future of the Central European University, a model institution with a mission based on the concept of an open society, is uncertain at this point.

4   China's Rise in Global Higher Education

China's higher education system has developed at an unprecedented scale and pace. It has the largest higher education system in terms of student numbers (around 33 million) and comes second in terms of its share in world expenditure on R&D. China's Gross Domestic Expenditure on R&D (GERD) is 19.6% compared to 28.1% for the US and 19.1% for the EU, putting it second in position for in the world's largest R&D budget in Purchasing Power Parity (PPP). It is also second for its world share of researchers (19.1%, compared to 22.2% for the EU and 16.7% for the US). China's growth is greatly contributing to the increase in the number of researchers worldwide (21% since 2007 to 7.8 million in 2013), which is again mostly observed in STEM fields (all data for 2013 in UNESCO, 2015a). China is ready to offer researchers in these fields very attractive packages if needed (South China Morning Post, 27 April 2016).

This focus on STEM seems to result in a rather skewed development of China's higher education system, concentrating in particular on progress in some particular fields in engineering and computer sciences. Clearly global competition is most fierce in these fields and of both economic and geopolitical importance. The Shanghai Ranking reported in 2015 an established number of 39 top engineering schools in Asia, 42 in the US, and only 19 in Europe. China's top engineering schools started to dominate those in its region and ranked in the world's top 10 for engineering and top 25 for computer sciences (ARWU, 2015). This trend is confirmed in the 2017 Shanghai academic subject ranking, in which China leads in four subfields of engineering with a Chinese university as number one combined with an above 20% presence on places in the global top 50 for the field (Table 10.1). And in another seven subfields on one of these criteria (Table 10.2).

The picture is confirmed by data from the Leiden ranking 2017, in which China leads on impact in math and computer sciences and physics and

TABLE 10.1   Subject fields in which China holds number 1 position and >20% of global top 50

Subject field	Highest position	Number of institutions in global top 50
Instruments Science and Technology	1	15
Metallurgical engineering	1	15
Mining	1	13
Telecom engineering	1	11

SOURCE: BASED ON ARWU 2017 GLOBAL RANKING OF ACADEMIC SUBJECTS

TABLE 10.2   Subject fields in which China holds number 1 position or >20% of global top 50

Subject field	Highest position	Number of institutions in global top 50
Civil engineering	1	8
Remote sensing	1	7
Mechanical engineering	8	10
Marie/ocean engineering	8	1
Chemical engineering	10	4
Energy Science and Engineering	10	13
Nano Science and Engineering	14	6

SOURCE: BASED ON ARWU 2017 GLOBAL RANKING OF ACADEMIC SUBJECTS

engineering with an almost 50% dominance in the global top 50, almost completely filling the top 10 in each (Table 10.3).

There is clearly scope for improvement in terms of impact as the percentage of publications in the top 10 per cent. This is also demonstrated by the fact that China has, despite its strong foothold in a few STEM fields, a much smaller size in terms of citations received from abroad than would be expected from its overall publication volume (Figure 10.1). But the performance in terms of volume and growth in these fields underlines the enormous potential of Chinese institutions for further development into global top league.

TABLE 10.3   Scientific impact per field

Field	Impact (number of publications)		Impact (number of top 10% publications)		Impact (percentage of publications in top 10%)	
	Number of institutions in top 50	Highest position	Number of institutions in top 50	Highest position	Number of institutions in top 50	Highest position
Math and computer sciences	23	1–8	16	1	1	10
Physics and engineering	25	1–5	17	3	0	-

SOURCE: BASED ON LEIDEN RANKING (CWTS, 2017)

FIGURE 10.1   China's position in international citations network 1996–2013

However, it is very much the question whether this could also be expected more broadly, beyond these STEM fields. It should also be noted that China's progress in humanities and social sciences is much less compelling. For these fields, it is absent in the top 100 of either rankings.

These rather uneven achievements reflect the significant share (43 per cent) of China's R&D that has been dedicated to development and building of science and technology infrastructure and relatively little (4 per cent) to basic research, as the OECD observed in 2015. This seems to be strategically motivated in relation to China's technological innovation, as needed for economic growth and geopolitical and strategic positioning.

Prior research (van der Wende & Zhu, 2016) indicates that Chinese academics recognize that in order to grow from good to great in research, systemic change is required to support a truly excellent research culture. This would especially involve changes in faculty evaluation, reward and funding structures, as well as a shift by individual researchers from extrinsic motivation (indicators, funding, publications) to intrinsic motivation (intellectual curiosity) and university administration, to a model with more autonomy, less governmental intervention, healthy competition and a more rationalized system for performance evaluation. A comprehensive international report on China's performance in science (Nature Publishing Group, 2015) made similar recommendations on structures for funding, conducting and sharing research, and on training and hiring practices, in order to improve the quality and impact of its scientific output.

It occurs that the growth in STEM fields is much more successful under the current university governance system than that in the social sciences and humanities. Government policies put a striking emphasis on science and engineering. These constitute 49 per cent of the disciplines selected to become world class, followed by 22 per cent for medical science and agriculture and forestry. Social sciences and humanities represent only 18 per cent and 11 per cent respectively and are expected to construct 'systems of philosophy and social science with Chinese characteristics, style and spirit' (Huang, 2017b).

Such an uneven development could jeopardize the growth of Chinese world-class universities as truly comprehensive universities, as well as their potential for progress in interdisciplinary fields, requiring cross-fertilization between (applied) sciences, social sciences and the humanities. It could also have a potentially skewing effect on developments in the sector globally. The new 'Double World-Class Project' that builds on the previous 211 and 985 projects aims for China to have around 40 world-class university's by mid-century and to generate significant global impact (ibid.).

The volume and rapid growth of Chinese higher education confirm our findings from prior research on China's role in global higher education, when we concluded that:

> It is time to view China not just as a follower, but also look at its (potential) role as a global leader in higher education. (van der Wende & Zhu, 2016)

It also confirms that it is appropriate to view China's higher education development from both perspectives, i.e. as an object and subject of globalization. This is in line with expert arguments regarding the way in which China's emerging role as a global leader should be analyzed:

> After three decades during which observers have watched how the world impacted China, it is now necessary to understand how China is impacting the world. (Shambaugh, 2013, p. 5)

> With China and globalization, we should not choose between thinking of the Chinese state as only either being reshaped by international forces or itself reshaping the global structure. We are instead better off drawing from all of these perspectives at once. (Wasserstrom, 2014, p. 167)

At the same time, we should realize that:

Whether the 21st century can be the Chinese century in higher education is a question that wouldn't have been asked even a decade ago and it is a comparative question: who leads whom and for how long will the US still be leading? (Kirby, 2014)

The present relevance of this question could not have been imagined perhaps even only two years ago. But the US turning its back on international markets, trade and cooperation, accelerates China's options to reposition itself as a world player. Higher education and scientific research are important elements of this geopolitical strategy with the New Silk Road as it major carrier.

5   The New Silk Road: Early Steps and Looming Perspectives[3]

The New Silk Road (NSR), also dubbed as the 'One Belt and One Road' (OBOR, or Belt and Road Initiative), was announced in 2013 by President Xi Jinping as a major new vehicle for China's global influence through both economic and soft power. A mega project with a land-based Silk Road and maritime Silk Road creating together a massive loop linking three continents, Asia, Europe, and Africa, reflects China's ambitions to reclaim its place as the 'Middle Kingdom' and linking it to the world by trade and cultural exchanges. Railroads are a main feature of the land-based Silk Road connecting major manufacturing cities in Western China to Europe via Central Asia, Iran, Turkey, the Balkans, and the Caucasus across the 11,000-kilometre-long Eurasian continent and potentially including over 60 countries.

The NSR is supposed to create more than a trade infrastructure, reviving the historical and cultural meaning of it. Through this 'infrastructure diplomacy', China also hopes to gain closer cultural and political ties with (especially its neighbouring) countries along the New Silk Road – resulting in a new model of 'mutual respect and mutual trust', a community with 'common interests, fate, and responsibilities', guided by China's principles for an 'open world economy and open international relations', according to the President. Its aim to contribute to global public goods is inextricably linked to the Silk Road in China's past as a source of goods and information for the rest of the world.

The NSR quickly became popular throughout 2014 as the key instrument of China's foreign policy, diplomacy and soft power. However, in the deliberately open (or ambiguous) formulation of the policy, details on implementation remained scarce. Which countries will precisely be included? NSR maps on the internet show intriguing differences, depending on the geographic position and interests of the country in which they are produced. Some of these may be strategically important for China's foreign relations, but represent territories that are quite challenging to navigate for businesses, researchers or students (Kaczmarski, 2015).

Higher education cooperation entered the agenda when President Xi announced in 2015 cultural exchange and cooperation in training and education to be important elements of NSR, both in terms of soft power and in order to address the region's yawning skills gap, which invariably stands in the way of its economic ambitions. It figured as a theme at the 2015 Euro-Asia Economic Forum, where the focus was primarily set on China's neighbouring and mostly developing countries, which usually still have, unlike China, an abundant young labour force, yet a low level of higher education infrastructure. Students from these developing countries are less interested in Chinese language learning than those from developed countries and more in degree courses in applied fields, such as engineering and medicine. This opened a market of educational services connected to China's development in high-end manufacturing and connected higher professional education, both by attracting students to mainland China as well as by building programmes in these countries. Higher education also had to ensure that Chinese professionals gain more knowledge of the developing world. China has been so much focused on the US and Europe that Chinese people, especially younger generations, should be encouraged to more closely study the histories, cultures, economies and religions of the developing countries along the NSR (Zhao, 2015).

The NSR inspired the Chinese Higher Education Association to adopt a new vision for internationalization. Training in infrastructure, finance and management, engineering and political sciences should ensure that Chinese graduates will become familiar with local political, economic and geographic situations in the NSR countries. The common mindset and focus in China on English-speaking developed countries should shift to a more diversified internationalization process, including curricula that address the role of international trade in developing countries and related issues of inequality, cultural differences and sustainability (Qu, 2015).

Leading Chinese universities started to establish Belt and Road Institutes, think tanks, and conferences to explore new alliances inspired by the NSR. Examples are the One Belt One Road Economic Research Institute at Renmin University, the Silk Road Institute at the Beijing Foreign Studies University, the China Academy of One Belt One Road Strategy at the Beijing International Studies University, the Road Research Center at Beijing Jiao Tong University, the Maritime Silk Institute at Huaqiao University, and also the University Alliance of the New Silk Road at Xi'an Jiao Tong University, which invited 60 universities from 22 potential NSR countries to explore opportunities for cooperation. These institutions see that NSR presents great opportunities and will further Chinese higher education's impact on these countries, for instance by establishing branch campuses, exchange programmes, and offering scholarships. But also that it presents challenges to produce talents who can understand the context and the situation of the NSR countries.

The NSR was also presented as an opportunity to re-balance China's unfavourable deficit in students going to the West to study versus incoming international students. Europe was the second largest receiver of (mainly undergraduate) Chinese students, after the US (with mainly graduate students). It could become a new epistemic road, with the large Chinese knowledge diaspora in Europe, including thousands of highly qualified Chinese researchers, acting as bridge builders between the two research communities (Welch, 2015).

The potential of the NSR for the European Higher Education (EHEA) and Research Area (ERA) seems positive. Higher education in Europe is, like in China, mostly public and more affordable than in the US, and European higher education has much to offer. Besides the growing range of bilateral Europe-China collaborations, joint programmes, branch campuses and scholarship programmes, Europe has a strong record of open approaches and frameworks for multilateral cooperation in higher education and research, supported with large-scale programmes, such as ERASMUS+ for education and Horizon 2020 for research. China participates already in ERASMUS Mundus (as the largest provider of non-EU students) and has access to the European Research Council funding facility. Mutual recognition is a well-established principle in Europe and the successful ECTS scheme is built out to the Academic Credit Transfer Framework for Asia (ACTFA). Another example is the project 'Tuning EU-China', in which EU countries and China collaborate in defining higher education learning outcomes.

Europe has also much to gain from cooperation with China as it needs a substantial amount of foreign talent to face the substantial skills shortage and mismatch in relation to its ambitious knowledge economy growth strategy (Morehouse & Busse, 2014; van der Wende, 2015). The strategic interest of European Higher education institutions for Asia is strong and on the rise, while other areas including North America are losing ground, as reported by the EUA. This seems to be accelerating since 2016 when the UK voted for Brexit and the new US Presidency have started to create high levels of uncertainty for international cooperation with these countries, which have for so long dominated the global higher education scene. A growing range of cooperation agreements on higher education, research and innovation have been signed by China with partners in Europe, both at the EU and individual member country levels, for instance, on academic recognition and exchange during a ministers' conference on 'Building a China-EU education Silk Road towards the future' in October 2016 (Morgan, 2016). A third EU-China Innovation Co-operation Dialogue explored enhanced cooperation under H2020 in June 2017. Even open access, open science and principles of mutual access to scientific results were discussed, but no concrete agreements have been reached so far.

Yet it is not simply a situation of mutual benefits only. In the first place because of potentially conflicting interests in the higher education market, for instance in the delivery of transnational education and in competition for talent. Traditionally, transnational higher education has been uniquely delivered by Western institutions in China (e.g. the University of Nottingham's Ningbo China campus). But China is now also expanding its own transnational higher education provision abroad (e.g. the recent investment by Peking University in setting up a business school in Oxford) (Montgomery, 2017). UK institutions especially seem to be concerned about these trends as transnational delivery has been an important strategy for its universities, and it is likely to become even more important as a result of the vote for Brexit. More generally, institutions in Europe and China could be competing more for the same sorts of students.

China is opening its higher education market to the world and aims to attract 500,000 international students to China, by making full degree programmes at Chinese universities more attractive and by providing additional scholarships. It seems successful with 442,773 international students studying in China in 2016, although a quite large proportion of these are enrolled in non-degree courses. The success is attributed in large part to the NSR, as nearly half of China's foreign enrolment derived from Silk Road countries, which outperformed the overall growth trend in inbound mobility for China and is expected to continue to drive further enrolment growth in the years ahead. Notable growth was also reported from Africa (ICEF, 2017). However, so far only 10 per cent came from Europe against 24 per cent of all Chinese overseas students going to Europe (a quite uneven 1:6 ratio in absolute numbers).

Secondly, there are questions around China's long term and political intensions driving this agenda. The recently established Asian University Alliance, led by Tsinghua University with full support from the Chinese government, underpins the aim to develop world-class universities based on an Eastern educational philosophy and heritage. Improving their position in regional and global rankings would enable these institutions to attract the best academics and students and mitigate the brain drain from Asia to Western universities, and could challenge the dominant 'Western voices' in the globalization of higher education. Not only would this affect Western higher education systems that have benefited for decades from the influx of full-fee paying foreign students, it also presents itself as a tool for advancing China's soft power, i.e. shaping the future of higher education across the region and also globally on Chinese terms and on conditions favourable to China (Gunn & Mintrom, 2017; Huang, 2017b).

Soft power is the ability to attract and co-opt rather than coerce, use force or give money (hard power) (Nye, 2004). China's soft power is clearly linked to its NSR policy, but is held back when it is generated by non-state actors over which the Chinese government has limited control and may be critical of its ideology (Nye, 2015). It is not undisputed in educational and cultural sectors. Since 2013, concerns have been rising over the Confucius Institutes regarding its hiring policy, non-disclosure of contracts and the lack of academic freedom in its curriculum, which is seen as infused with propaganda and political influence. The Braga incident led in 2014 to the banning of Confucius Institutes from some Western university campuses. The discussion of 'Western values' in Chinese classrooms has been curbed by governmental guidelines launched in 2013, and which were tightened in 2015. The Central Committee of the Communist Party of China placed 29 top Chinese universities under tighter control in 2017.

These ideological issues catch much attention in Western debate and media, where the common view is that academic freedom, faculty involvement in governance and institutional autonomy are essential conditions for academic excellence. Many see the restrictions of academic freedom not as an isolated move, but an extension of policies that have narrowed the space for public engagement and discussion across Chinese society. It is argued, however, that Chinese notions of academic freedom should be considered as distinctively different from those in the West (Marginson, 2011; Postiglione, 2015a). A clash of academic values erupted when the General Administration of Press and Publication in China urged Cambridge University Press in August 2017 to withdraw over 300 articles and reviews about sensitive topics such as the Tiananmen Square protests, the Cultural Revolution, Tibet, Xinjiang, Hong Kong and Taiwan. The publisher initially agreed, but returned this decision when more than 600 scholars from around the globe signed a petition threatening it to boycott all its journals. Discussions continue around free and open access to the internet, propaganda, (self-)censorship and freedom of publication.

6 The New Silk Road: Challenges and Implications for Higher Education and Research Cooperation

The geopolitical context for the NSR builds on the EU as China's largest trading partner (although the picture at the sub-EU level is very diverse) and as politically more open than the US to recognize China's role in the creation of new global institutions. This was for instance demonstrated in 2015 by the range of European countries that quickly joined the Asian Infrastructure Investment Bank (AIIB), launched by China as one of the main investment vehicles for the NSR.

But there are also significant challenges. The EU's mostly absent foreign policy, consequent weak coordination capacity over its member countries' diverging foreign policy interests and fragmented immigration policies. Tensions in Europe's border regions; the Middle-East, North Africa, and Russia's disputed territories, heightened in 2016 after the failed coup in Turkey. Security issues are on the rise following the vote for Brexit and the US's changing relationships with Europe and China. The precise itinerary of the Silk Road will therefore be an issue of geopolitical meaning, guided by Europe's concerns about refugees, security, terrorism, energy supplies, and issues of international legal order and human rights.

Yet it is time for Europe to come to grips with China's role in the next phase of globalization. Besides China's drive to exert global leadership in infrastructure projects and in the digital world, it can direct its considerable research capacity to shared scientific challenges, and thus contribute to generating global public goods (MGI, 2017). But while China hopes to lead a sustainable and inclusive version of globalization which could lead to further re-balancing global inequality, Western countries are still digesting the political backlash from the growing inequalities spawned by globalization within their borders. Moreover, big questions regarding the future of the EU require their attention. Several scenarios were presented in March 2017 on the occasion of the 60th anniversary of the signature of the Treaties of Rome. This may explain why government leaders from Europe were mostly absent (instead they sent representatives and observers) at the Belt and Road Summit hosted by President Xi in Beijing in May 2017. Despite the announcement of major extra investments from the Chinese side, concerns seem to persist. Hesitations may relate to issues in China or at home and requires time for individual countries to consider their position regarding the NSR.

The importance of strengthening relations with China is being recognized, but for many it is still unclear how this new reality can conform to current Western criticism of China concerning the lack of human rights and the rule of law. More specifically; how can such cooperation contribute to an open society, which is based on the belief of addressing inequalities across race, class, gender, sexual orientation and citizenship, and based on the belief in fundamental human rights, dignity and the rule of law as key values?

Experts argue that it is crucial to learn to understand China better and to have an open eye at how its rise and changing international position concerns

Europe. They stress that it is important that Europe refrains from looking at China from a solely Western viewpoint, because China can only be understood through its own history and culture. Only then does Europe have a chance to remain relevant in the global economy of which the centre of gravity is shifting ever more to the east (Jacques, 2017). They point to the integration of Eurasia as the main project for the 21st century, with China in the lead, while Europe is still hesitating. 'It is not about rights or cultural differences, but about real political and strategic interests. The main task is to design co-existence of very different systems' (Dufraine, 2017).

7 Questions for Further Research

Higher education and scientific cooperation will play a key role and further research should explore how the NSR could affect European higher education and research. Key questions are: what types of academic flows and activities emerge along the NSR, how do universities respond, under what conditions are these activities taking place, who defines these, and based on what values? How will China's values impact higher education (e.g. regarding academic freedom, scientific integrity, and the model and mission of the university)? Do we actually understand these values at all? And what will be the impact of these developments on the US higher education sector and its role in the global higher education landscape?

As has been argued in this chapter, these questions are relevant, as we can assume that:

– China's rise is among the most important geo-political trends that will characterize the (early) 21st century. And like all previous major geopolitical trends and events, that have impacted international cooperation in higher education (for better or for worse), this can also be expected to result from the NSR project.
– China's transformative shift is happening fast and it is a challenge to understand its size; the NSR project is estimated to be twelve times bigger than the Marshall plan (Woetzel et al., 2017).
– The New Silk Road will carry more than consumer goods alone. As before, along its old versions, people, ideas and knowledge will travel along with mutual influence.
– The size of China's higher education and R&D system and the speed at which it develops both to global standards will impact that of its major competitors globally, not least as it actively seeks to cooperate with academic partners along the New Silk Road.

As argued before, studying China requires us to draw from both the perspective of China being reshaped by international forces and itself reshaping the global structure at the same time. Or, as argued by Frankopan (2015), we need to enrich our vision and understanding of the world, to widen our focus from being predominantly or even exclusively Western, to open it towards a new history of the world.

Consequently, we will need to improve our understanding of globalization. Globalization in the East diverges from globalization in the West. As economic globalization becomes more Eastern-led, Easternization could become a force in international higher education, especially if a quarter of the world's best universities become Asian (Postiglione, 2015b).

We know that in higher education research, an international comparative perspective is insufficient to grasp the dynamics and impact of globalization, flows and dynamics, and that we need to overcome the limitations of methodological nationalism (van der Wende, 2002, 2017). More generally, we need to realize that if global collaboration is to be taken forward in social sciences, the time of separated 'mono-national' and 'mono-cultural' views has passed. The potential for a hybrid approach needs to be explored, i.e. what theories and methods can we use to understand these developments; and especially, how can we establish ways of seeing in higher education research that comprehend the world using the sensibilities, the perspectives, of both East and West – whether by blending the differing viewpoints, or by establishing a position external to all (Marginson & van der Wende, 2017).

We need to further our understanding of the similarities and differences in politics between globalization East and West, in processes of regional integration (e.g. EU, ASEAN), how they interact along the NSR in terms of both cooperation and competition in higher education and research, and how they relate to the contribution of higher education and research to the global common good, and to an open society.

Notes

1 These trends were discussed extensively during an international conference on New Nationalism and Universities, held at the Center for Studies in Higher Education, University of California, Berkeley, in November 2017.
2 This argument was also later made by UNESCO (2015b): 'The social contract that binds higher education institutions to society at large needs to be redefined in a context of increased global competition' (p. 52).
3 This section is partly based on van der Wende and Zhu (2016).

References

ARWU. (2015). *Discovering world-class*. Shanghai: Academic Ranking of World Universities.

ARWU. (2017). *Global ranking of academic subjects 2017*. Shanghai: Academic Ranking of World Universities.

Berkeley News. (2016, November 9). *Chancellor reaffirms campus values of respect and inclusion*. Berkeley, CA: University of California Berkeley. Retrieved May 1, 2018, from http://news.berkeley.edu/2016/11/09/chancellor-election-message-to-campus/

Castells, M. (2000). *The rise of the network society* (2nd ed.). Oxford: Blackwell.

CWTS. (2017). *Leiden ranking 2017*. Retrieved May 1, 2018, from http://www.leidenranking.com/ranking/2017/list

Douglass, J. A. (2005). How all globalization is local: Countervailing forces and their influence on higher education markets. *Higher Education Policy, 18*(4), 445–473.

Douglass, J. A. (Ed.). (2016). *The new flagship university: Changing the paradigm from global ranking to national relevancy*. London: Palgrave Macmillan.

Douglass, J. A., & Hawkins, J. N. (2017). *Envisioning the Asian new flagship university: Its past and vital future*. Berkeley, CA: Institute of Governmental Studies Press.

Dufraine, P. (2017, July 2). Speech at the China-EU Conference on Human Rights, VU University Amsterdam, Amsterdam.

EU. (2016a, December). Council resolution on a new skills agenda for an inclusive and competitive Europe (2016/C 467/01). *Official Journal of the European Union*.

EU. (2016b). *EU competency framework*. Retrieved May 1, 2018, from https://ec.europa.eu/education/policy/strategic-framework/expert-groups/citizenship-common-values_en

Frankopan, P. (2015). *The silk roads: A new history of the world*. London: Bloomsbury Publishing.

Gray, J. (2002). *False dawn: The delusions of global capitalism*. London: Granta.

Gunn, A., & Mintrom, M. (2017, June 2). The changing shape of global higher education geopolitics. *University World News*. Retrieved May 1, 2018, from http://www.universityworldnews.com/article.php?story=20170529151430202

Hazelkorn, E. (2016, October 14). Lessons from brexit. *University World News*. Retrieved May 1, 2018, from http://www.universityworldnews.com/article.php?story=20161011123810165

Held, D., McGrew, A., Goldblatt, D., & Perraton, J. (1999). *Global transformations: Politics, economics and culture*. Stanford, CA: Stanford University Press.

Huang, F. (2017a, January). *From the former Soviet patterns towards the US model? Changes in Chinese doctoral education* (Working Paper Series No. 12). London: Centre for Global Higher Education, UCL Institute of Education.

Huang, F. (2017b, September 29). Double world-class project has more ambitious aims. *University World News*. Retrieved May 1, 2018, from http://www.universityworldnews.com/article.php?story=2017092913334471

ICEF. (2017). *Foreign enrolment surging in China*. Retrieved May 1, 2018, from http://monitor.icef.com/2017/03/foreign-enrolment-surging-china/

Jacques, M. (2017, February 9). *Frozen Europe and fast changing China*. Keynote Speech at the Opening Conference of the Leiden Asia Centre, Leiden. Retrieved May 1, 2018, from http://www.martinjacques.com/media-archive/frozen-europe-and-fast-changing-china-martin-jacques-on-the-sino-european-dilemma/

James, H. (2002). *The end of globalization: Lessons from the great depression*. Cambridge, MA: Harvard University Press.

Kaczmarski, M. (2015, February 10). The new silk road: A versatile instrument in China's policy. *OSW Commentary*. Retrieved May 1, 2018, from http://www.osw.waw.pl/en/publikacje/osw-commentary/2015-02-10/new-silk-road-a-versatile-instrument-chinas-policy

Kirby, W. C. (2014). The Chinese century? The challenges of higher education. *Daedalus, 143*(2), 145–156.

Marginson, S. (2011). Higher education in East Asia and Singapore: Rise of the Confucian model. *Higher Education, 61*(5), 587–611.

Marginson, S. (2016a). Towards world-class systems: World-class universities in high participation systems of higher education. In N. C. Liu, Y. Cheng, & Q. Wang (Eds.), *Matching visibility and performance: A standing challenge for world-class universities*. Rotterdam, The Netherlands: Sense Publishers.

Marginson, S. (2016b). Global stratification in higher education. In S. Slaughter & B. J. Taylor (Eds.), *Higher education, stratification, and workforce development* (pp. 13–34). Dordrecht: Springer International Publishing.

Marginson, S., & van der Wende, M. C. (2007). To rank or to be ranked: The impact of global rankings in higher education. *Journal on Studies in International Education, 11*(3–4), 306–330.

Marginson, S., & van der Wende, M. C. (2009). Europeanisation, international rankings, and faculty mobility: Three cases in higher education globalisation. In *Higher education to 2030, volume 2: Globalisation*. Paris: OECD.

Marginson, S., & van der Wende, M. C. (2017, November 13). *Hybrid approach needed for global academic collaboration*. Paper presented at Research Institute for Higher Education, Hiroshima University, Higashihiroshima. Retrieved from http://www.researchcghe.org/news/2017-11-18-hybrid-approach-needed-for-global-academic-collaboration/

Maslen, G. (2017, May 30). Number of mobile students out of, and into, China soars. *University World News*. Retrieved May 1, 2018, from http://www.universityworldnews.com/article.php?story=20170530122432533

McKinsey Global Institute. (2017). *China's role in the next phase of globalization*. Retrieved from https://www.mckinsey.com/featured-insights/china/chinas-role-in-the-next-phase-of-globalization

Milanovic, B. (2016). *Global inequality: A new approach for the age of globalization.* Cambridge, MA: Harvard University Press.

Montgomery, C. (2017, May 26). China's higher education megaproject. *University World News.* Retrieved May 1, 2018, from http://www.universityworldnews.com/article.php?story=20170523001225119

Morehouse, C., & Busse, M. (2014). *How can the EU keep a competitive edge in the talent game? Lessons from China and the US* (Report of the CEPS Task Force on the Quantity and Quality of Human Capital in Higher Education: Comparing the EU, the US and China). Brussels: Center for European Policy Studies.

Morgan, J. (2016, October 18). China and EU aim to create 'education silk road to future'. *Times Higher Education.* Retrieved May 1, 2018, from https://www.timeshighereducation.com/news/china-and-eu-aim-create-education-silk-road-future

Nature Publishing Group. (2015). *Turning point: Chinese science in transition.* Retrieved November 26, 2015, from http://www.nature.com/press_releases/turning_point.pdf

Nussbaum, M. C. (2012). *Not for profit: Why democracy needs the humanities.* Princeton, NJ: Princeton University Press.

Nye, J. S. (2004). *Soft power: The means to success in world politics.* New York, NY: Public Affairs.

Nye, J. S. (2015, April 7). *Is the American century over?* (Lecture in the Program on US-Japan Relations in the Weatherhead Center for International Affairs). Cambridge, MA: Harvard University Press.

OECD. (2006). *Four futures scenarios for higher education.* Retrieved from https://www.oecd.org/edu/ceri/38073691.pdf

OECD. (2015). *Science, technology and industry scoreboard.* Paris: OECD Publishing.

OECD. (2016). *Education at a glance 2016: OECD education indicators.* Paris: OECD Publishing.

Piketty, T. (2014). *Capital in the twenty-first century.* Cambridge, MA: Belknap Press.

Postiglione, G. A. (2015a). Research universities for national rejuvenation and global influence: China's search for a balanced model. *Higher Education, 70*(2), 235–250.

Postiglione, G. A. (2015b, April 27). Asian universities are rising in the ranks. *The Washington Post.*

Postiglione, G. (2017, January 30). Trumpism and universities: Advantage China? *University World News.* Retrieved May 1, 2018, from http://www.universityworldnews.com/article.php?story=20170130231734559

Proudfoot, S., & Hoffer, T. B. (2016). Science and engineering labor force in the US. In L. Gokhberg, N. Shmatko, & L. Auriol (Eds.), *The science and technology labor force.* New York, NY: Springer International Publishing.

Pruvot, E. B., Estermann, T., & Kupriyanova, V. (2017). *Public funding observatory report 2017.* Brussels: European University Association.

Qu, Z. Y. (2015, August 13). The building of 'one belt and one road' and the new mission of national education. *Guangming Daily*. Retrieved May 1, 2018, from http://epaper.gmw.cn/gmrb/html/2015-08/13/nw.D110000gmrb_20150813_1-11.htm

Rhoades, G. (2017). Backlash against 'others'. *International Higher Education, 89*, 2–3.

Rodrik, D. (1997). Has globalization gone too far? *California Management Review, 39*(3), 29–53.

Salmi, J. (2014). *World-class universities or systems?* Retrieved May 1, 2018, from http://tertiaryeducation.org/2014/07/world-class-universities-or-systems/

Scott, P. (2017, March 24). Populism: Is the academy on the wrong side of history? *University World News*. Retrieved May 1, 2018, from http://www.universityworldnews.com/article.php?story=20170321131230967

Shambaugh, D. (2013). *China goes global: The partial power*. Oxford: Oxford University Press.

Slaughter, S., & Leslie, L. L. (1997). *Academic capitalism: Politics, policies, and the entrepreneurial university*. Baltimore, MD: Johns Hopkins University Press.

Slaughter, S., & Taylor, B. J. (Eds.). (2016). *Higher education, stratification, and workforce development: Competitive advantage in Europe, the US, and Canada*. Dordrecht: Springer International Publishing.

South China Morning Post. (2016, April 27). *The rise of China's millionaire research scientists*. Retrieved May 1, 2018, from http://www.scmp.com/news/china/policies-politics/article/1939032/rise-chinas-millionaire-research-scientists

Stiglitz, J. E. (2002). *Globalization and its discontents* (Vol. 500). New York, NY: W.W. Norton & Company.

The Economist. (2015, March 26). *Excellence v equity: Special report universities*. Retrieved May 1, 2018, from https://www.economist.com/special-report/2015/03/26/excellence-v-equity

Times Higher Education. (2017, September 12–15). *A mosaic of cultures*. Paper presented at 29th Annual Conference, EAIE 2017, Seville.

UNESCO. (2015a). *UNESCO science report towards 2030*. Paris: UNESCO.

UNESCO. (2015b). *Rethinking education: Towards a global common good?* Paris: UNESCO.

Unterhalter, E., & Carpentier, V. (Eds.). (2010). *Global inequalities and higher education: Whose interests are you serving?* Basingstoke: Palgrave Macmillan.

Wasserstrom, J. (2014). China and globalization. *Daedalus, 143*(2), 157–169.

Welch, A. (2015). A new epistemic silk road? The Chinese knowledge diaspora, and its implications for the Europe of knowledge. *European Review, 23*(S1), S95–S111.

van der Wende, M. C. (2002). *Hoger Onderwijs Globaliter: Naar nieuwe kaders voor beleid en onderzoek (oratie)* [Higher Education Globally (inaugural lecture)]. Enschede: Twente University Press.

van der Wende, M. C. (2007). Internationalization of higher education in the OECD countries: Challenges and opportunities for the coming decade. *Journal of Studies in International Education, 11*(3–4), 274–289.

van der Wende, M. C. (2008). Rankings and classifications in higher education: A European perspective. In J. C. Smart (Ed.), *Higher education: Handbook of theory and research* (Vol. 23). Dordrecht: Springer International Publishing.

van der Wende, M. C. (2011a). Global institutions: The organisation for economic co-operation and development. In R. King, S. Marginson, & R. Naidoo (Eds.), *Handbook on globalization and higher education*. Cheltenham: Edward Elgar.

van der Wende, M. C. (2011b). The role of higher education institutions in globalization. In *New horizons for the international university*. Bonn: DAAD.

van der Wende, M. C. (2014). On mergers and missions: Implications for institutional governance and governmental steering. In Q. Wang, Y. Cheng, & N. C. Liu (Eds.), *Global outreach of world-class universities: How it is affecting higher education systems*. Rotterdam, The Netherlands: Sense Publishers.

van der Wende, M. C. (2015). International academic mobility: Towards a concentration of the minds in Europe. *The European Review, 23*(S1), S70–S88.

van der Wende, M. C. (2017). *Opening up: Higher education systems in global perspective* (Working Paper Series No. 22). London: Centre for Global Higher Education, UCL Institute of Education.

van der Wende, M. C., & Zhu, J. (2016). *China a follower or leader in global higher education?* (Research and Occasional Papers Series CSHE 3.16). Berkeley, CA: University of California Berkeley, Centre for Studies in Higher Education.

Woetzel, J., Lin, D.-Y., Seong, J., Madgavkar, A., & Lund, S. (2017). *China's role in the next phase of globalization*. Retrieved May 1, 2018, from https://www.mckinsey.com/featured-insights/china/chinas-role-in-the-next-phase-of-globalization

Zhao, K. (2015, May 23). People factor key to 'belt and road'. *China Daily*. Retrieved from http://usa.chinadaily.com.cn/opinion/2015-05/23/content_20798229.htm

Ziguras, C. (2016, October 14). The five stages of brexit grief for universities. *University World News*. Retrieved May 1, 2018, from http://www.universityworldnews.com/article.php?story=20161012113345281

CHAPTER 11

World-Class Universities and the Global Common Good: The Role of China and the US in Addressing Global Inequality

Gerard A. Postiglione and Ailei Xie

Abstract

Contemporary discourse on university reform, especially in the West, has moved more toward addressing the notion of 'the common good'. While this idea can be traced back to Adam Smith's *The Theory of Moral Sentiments*, and to Confucius' *Analects*, much of its contemporary usage is rooted in demands for greater accountability. Many aspects of higher education have become targeted, including wider access, student fees and graduate employment. As different stakeholders and interest groups vie for agency, there is a lack of coherence about how universities should be serving the common good. Moreover, what is less clear is the formal agent of interpretation for the common good in the global context in which world-class universities operate. This chapter provides a comparison of Chinese and American perspectives on the 'common good' and how they apply to world-class universities. It also examines world-class university cases of access to learning, including both academic performance and social development, by students who come to university from rural and urban areas.

Keywords

Common good – world-class universities – Chinese and American perspectives

1   Introduction: A Shifting Centre of Gravity

The global common good is a big order, even for World-Class Universities (WCUs). Still, WCUs have made highly significant contributions to the global common good, especially through research output (Cole, 2016). An abbreviated list includes: discovery of recombinant DNA, transistors, bar codes, the cervical pap smear, lasers, magnetic resonance imaging, global positioning systems, improved weather forecasting, methods of surveying and measuring public opinion, the algorithm for Google searches, DNA fingerprinting, foetal monitoring, scientific cattle breeding, facial recognition system, big data analytics, machine-to-machine technology, new product development, development of bioengineering, new pharmaceuticals and medical devices, the nicotine patch, antibiotics, the Richter scale, buckyballs, nanotechnology, discovery of the insulin gene, cures for childhood leukaemia, scientific agriculture, the electric toothbrush, the self-fulfilling prophecy, heart catheterization, the Heimlich manoeuvre, concepts of congestion pricing, and human capital theory. Some of these contributions have not always contributed to the global common good in the ways intended. Some have had unintended consequences. WCUs try to ensure that their discoveries and innovations are used in ethical ways. Some WCUs invest their endowments in ways that may not always be viewed as being in the interest of the global common good.

The discoveries and innovations referred to above occurred at US WCUs. That equation may not change in the short term, due in part to a century of momentum, favourable migration policies for recruiting talented scientists, and laws that help preserve university autonomy. (The latter two factors also explain how China's Hong Kong with only 0.7 per cent of Gross Domestic Product for Research and Development (R&D) can have more WCUs than any other city in the world (i.e. two best business programmes in the world (Financial Times), as well as 4th (Times Higher Education) and 7th (Quacquarelli Symonds (QS)) in the world in education field.)

Major changes are under way in China where more universities continue to enter the WCU rankings than from any other country (Postiglione, 2015a). China is fast becoming an innovation nation. It has filed more patents than any other country. It is a global leader in green technology, super computers (with the world's fastest computer), digital payments systems, and teleporting subatomic particles into outer space. The visionary one-trillion-yuan 'One Belt, one Road' (OBOR) initiative, Asian Infrastructure Development Bank and an economy that is still growing at more than seven per cent, sends a message best encapsulated in the words of Henry Kissinger that 'the world's centre of gravity is shifting' (Delaney, 2017).

In the years ahead, WCUs in the world's two largest economies are expected to contribute much more to the global common good through research, teaching and knowledge exchange that addresses climate change, health crises, economic inequality and other pressing world problems. WCUs in China and the US will have an inordinate influence on the interpretation of, and service to, the global common good. Their 'positionality' gives them the potential to build the most extensive WCU collaborative networks in history, including those on the 'One Belt, one Road' as well as Western industrialized countries. This means that they have a responsibility, through research and teaching, as well as academic and educational exchanges, to work more closely together to remove obstacles to improvement of the global common good.

This chapter argues that the global common good, as defined by what is shared and beneficial for all or most members of the global community and achieved by collective action, will rest more heavily on WCUs in two countries – China and the US – and how they build productive networks of academic collaboration in the next fifty years that address urgent global problems. It especially requires that they pay much more attention to the growth in social and economic inequality as well as unequal access and equity in their own institutions.

2   No Alternative: Building Collaborative Networks toward 2050

At the September 27th 2017 US-China University Presidents Forum: Relations Over the Next 50 Years, held at Columbia University, Vice Premier Madame Liu Yandong said China and the United States should enhance people-to-people exchanges to build stronger ties where the two countries 'have the least disagreements and the most consensus' (Columbia University Programs, 2017). This includes academic exchanges through collaborative research, as well as education exchanges that help students in both countries to develop a commitment to the global common good. Academic and educational exchanges among WCUs in both countries, have continued to expand over the past 35 years. Madame Liu asserted that: 'China-US ties have become warmer, more resilient and more dynamic'. She went a step further: 'We hope that universities and think-tanks of the two countries will carry out strategic and forward-looking research and jointly cultivate high-quality talents so as to make positive suggestions for the development of China-US relations' (Liu, 2017).

While the enhancement of the global common good inevitably depends upon relations among all countries, the relationship between the US and China currently constitutes the world's most important bilateral link. At the same Forum, Henry Kissinger, the architect of US-China relations that led to normalization in 1979, said: 'the only alternative to positive relations between Washington and Beijing is global destruction' (Kissinger, 2017). Such a statement must give pause to WCUs in any consideration of their role in advancing and safeguarding the global common good. In a similar light, former Yale University President Richard Levin, a frequent visitor to

China, highlighted the transformation of contemporary WCUs in historical perspective: 'As never before in their long history, universities have become instruments of national competition as well as instruments of peace [...] a powerful force for global integration, mutual understanding and geopolitical stability' (Levin, 2006).

WCUs obviously deserve the confidence and support of their governments to address global obstacles to sustainable social and economic development, as well as global peace and security.

For this to happen, WCUs have had to promote open enquiry and trust, widespread communication of ideas, and inclusive educational and academic exchanges. They also have to attract the best minds from around the world and integrate them into their universities. They have to ensure that impersonal criteria is used for establishing scientific facts, as well as ensure that scientists and scholars do not profit financially from their research. To be effective they must go beyond providing a state of the art infrastructure of laboratories, libraries, and IT by using peer-review systems to ensure arguments are tested by the best. Academics have to be given a significant voice in running their universities, and academic communities have to work for the growth of an enlightened public. Finally, WCUs have to be more attuned to the value of diverse types of intelligence in recruitment of students and staff from men and women from different regional, racial and ethnic communities.

3   Reforming WCUs for Global Significance

It is an opportune time for China's WCUs them to take an expanded global role. China's many years of reform and opening to the outside world have prepared its WCUs for this role. In the words of Ezra Vogel, Ford Professor of Asian Studies of Harvard University, 'The result of China's opening and reform for higher education has been an intellectual vitality that may be as broad and deep as the Western Renaissance' (Vogel, 2003). As they take on more confidence for an expanded role in the world, WCUs will become better positioned to take on a new kind of reform trajectory for the changing global circumstances.

One area where China's universities have been signalling greater attention to the global common good has been in curriculum reform. Leading universities have begun to engage in developing a model of liberal arts and general education curriculum (Postiglione, 2016). This has the potential to strengthen innovation for economic restructuring and sustainable development in an academic atmosphere of open dialogue and intercultural communication. A China WCU general education core curriculum is a potential long-term asset for engaging with the significant diversity of other leading research universities located in countries encompassed by the OBOR initiative. These include Russia's 13; Southeast Asia's 14 (Singapore, Indonesia, Malaysia, Thailand, Philippines), India's 9, the Middle East's 34 (Iran, Saudi Arabia, United Arab Emirates, Bahrain, Qatar, Oman, Lebanon, Israel, Turkey, Cyprus and Egypt), Eastern Europe and Central Asia's 16: Poland, Czech, Hungary, Estonia, Lithuania, Belarus, Ukraine, Slovenia, Serbia, Croatia and Kazakhstan. Sixty-four OBOR universities also have excellence initiatives (Liu, 2017).

With respect to a common core curriculum that highlights and interprets key issues such as inequality for the advancement of the global common good, WCUs in both countries have a unique opportunity to be deepen their engagement, China WCUs especially with selected OBOR WCUs, and US WCUs with selected WCUs in Western Europe.

4 Closing the Gap: Divergent Concepts

An American executive president of a Sino-foreign campus in China who spoke at the recent Columbia University Forum noted: 'The gathering always is useful because it highlights certain key elements [...] Like the huge gap in US understanding of China versus Chinese understanding of the US' (2017). It is bemusing that after many decades, there is still a staggering ignorance about China by Western elites. This sentiment has become increasingly common. First, Jean Pierre Lehmann, Professor at Switzerland's International Institute for Management Development (IMD), Founder of the Evian Group, and visiting professor at the University of Hong Kong, stated '...it is dispiriting and indeed alarming to see how ignorant the West is about China, and, from what I can see, intends to remain so' (Lehmann, 2017). He finds unfathomable why his MBA students at IMB do not want to look at China's history to see how Chinese view it, even though 88 per cent of the next billion middle class people are likely to come from Asia Pacific (AP/Brookings).

Second, Diego Gilardoni, author of Decoding China, a geopolitical analyst and specialist consultant in global business expresses a similar concern: 'Unfortunately in the West, many political and business leaders are facing the challenges of the future with an intellectual toolbox of the past. [...] rare are those who make a serious effort to understand China and try to see the world through its cultural prism' (Gilardani, 2017). He points out three familiar fundamental historically rooted differences: Short- versus long-term vision, focusing on the parts rather than the whole, and one truth versus a synthetic integration of reconcilable opposites.

Third, Daniel Bell in his recent book, The China Model, published by Yale University Press caused quite a stir among Western Sinologists. Bell points out that while China studies the West, the reverse is far less true and much needed. He discusses the advantages and pitfalls of political meritocracy, distinguishes between different ways of combining meritocracy and democracy, and argues that China has evolved a model of democratic meritocracy that is morally desirable and politically stable (Bell, 2015).

In short, Chinese and American core ideas represent different views about the common good, which can be extrapolated to their respective views of the global common good. This does not mean the fundamental conceptual differences are incompatible. China's universities were deeply influenced by US universities in much of the 20th Century. China's influence on America occurred even earlier at a critical stage in the establishment and development of the United States. Many of the key figures of the American Revolution gave special recognition to Chinese civilization and Confucian ideas. Thomas Paine considered Confucius to be in the same category as Jesus and Socrates. Thomas Jefferson, the principal author of the Declaration of Independence, promoted Chinese moral principles in his inaugural speech in 1801. Benjamin Franklin and other founders such as John Adams and Benjamin Rush regarded Confucius highly in their efforts to make a blueprint for the new nation. Benjamin Franklin and others urged the citizens of the United States to adopt positive elements from Chinese moral philosophy to cultivate and advance their own virtues (Wang, 2014).

Chinese thinking about the common good is grounded the principle of datong (大同) – a utopian vision of the world in which everyone and everything is at peace. It is an idea that contrasts with the less utopian and more practical xiaokang (小康) that finds itself part of the current government arsenal of strategies for economic development. The concept of tianxia (天下, literally, 'all under heaven') denotes the entire geographical world or the metaphysical realm of mortals, later to become associated with Chinese sovereignty.

These themes embed themselves in the advanced economies and university systems of the Asian region, and may also add to a better understanding of Easternization as a force in international higher education for the global common good (Shin, Postiglione, & Huang, 2015). As economic globalization becomes more Eastern-led, Asia's WCUs may be ready to take more of a lead, especially if a quarter of the world's best universities become Asian by 2040. China would most probably have the largest slice of that one-quarter (Postiglione, 2015b). The newly established Asian University Alliance (AUA) is an indication of this. On 29 April 2017, the AUA was established at Tsinghua University, marking a new milestone in Asian higher education. AUA brought together 15 universities from 13 countries across Asia to form a creative partnership with a mission 'to jointly address regional and global challenges, specifically related to higher education and economic, scientific and technological development, by strengthening collaboration among member institutions' (AUA, 2017).

5   Closing the Gap: WCUs and National Inequality

Inequality is anathema to the global common good (Li, 2016). China's government has highlighted the widening wealth gap in the world as a global challenge. While declaring it will uphold the international order, it noted that no country can handle such a challenge alone. The World Economic Forum (WEF) put widening inequality on record as 'one of the key challenges of our time' (WEF, 2015, 2017). This is because many global issues are associated with widening inequality, including a weakening of social networks, a rise in crime and weaker democracies. Widening inequality also has worrying implications for sustainable development, such as climate change, health catastrophes, and global economic instability.

The S&P Global Ratings cites the gap in income as a long-term threat to economic growth in the US (Standard and Poor's, 2014). To combat the wage gap, economic nationalists would risk a winner-less trade war. Inequality also remains a challenge for China, especially between rural and urban incomes, with the latter three times the former (Zhuang, 2016). For the first time in seven years, the Gini Coefficient increased from 0.462 in 2015, to 0.456 in 2016 according to data released by the National Bureau of Statistics (Li, 2016).

Due in part of economic globalization, China and the US share certain similarities with respect to inequality. Alvaredo, Chancel, Piketty, Saez, and Zucman (2014, 2017) note that both countries have witnessed an extreme rise in income inequality since the 1970s. Earners in the top one percent in the US take down about 20 per cent of pre-tax national income. The top one per cent in the US owns one-third of all the wealth and the top 10 per cent own three-quarters (Xie, 2017). The corresponding figure in 1978 was 12 per cent. They calculate that over the same period, the top one per cent in China doubled their share of income, which rose from six per cent in 1987 to 12 per cent now. After bringing more than a half a billion people (640 million) people out of poverty in 30 years (1981–2010) China plans to eliminate poverty by 2020 (Economist, 2013). China also restores stability to the global economy because 800 million Chinese workers have become as productive as their Western counterparts, but are not close in terms of consumption (Xie, 2017).

It is not surprising that economic globalization would make both countries experience a rise in economic inequality in tandem. The main difference is that the US' bottom 50 per cent of income earners were cut out of the country's economic growth. Alvaredo and his colleagues call it 'a complete collapse of the bottom 50 per cent income share in the US between 1978 to 2015'. But they note, 'In contrast, and in spite of a similar qualitative trend, the bottom 50 per cent share remains higher than the top one per cent share in 2015 in China' (Alvaredo et al., 2014).

The incomes of about 117 million American adults stagnated at about $16,200 per year before taxes and transfer payments. But, China's economic growth made it possible that the incomes of the bottom 50 percent have grown markedly. The poorest half of Chinese workers experienced an average income growth of over 400 percent from 1978 to 2015. For Americans, it decreased by one percent.

The Gini Coefficient for inequality in China is one of the highest in the world. The US Gini Coefficient rose by 20 per cent from 1979 to 2010. However, the income growth experienced by the poorest half of Chinese workers is likely to make rising inequality much more acceptable in China. In contrast, in the US there was no growth left at all for the bottom 50 per cent (Picchi, 2017).

If WCUs in both countries want to address this dimension of the global common good, then they must begin with addressing unequal access and equity that is embedded within their own institutions. Of all the dimensions of the global common good, the rapid growth of inequality poses the greatest risk and undergirds other global problems, such as sustainable development and social stability (Piketty, 2015).

How Chinese and American WCUs deal with issues of access to the national wealth and WCU credentials is indicative of how well or poorly they address the global common good. The privileges associated with WCU elite credentials are now widely acknowledged. Yet, access to these positional goods remains restricted and is 'determined in accord not with absolute, but relative income' (Hirsh, 1997). Rather than being innocent victims, WCUs have become active participants in the construction of a hierarchically differentiated status system (Bastedo & Bowman, 2010, 2011). Evidence suggests that 'best' universities are the worst at widening participation (Leonhardt, 2017).

6   Closing the Gap: Access and Equity in US WCUs

Students at elite universities in the US are from far wealthier families than most citizens realize. According to a study by Chetty et al. (2017) based on millions of anonymous tax filings and tuition records, 38 universities in the US, including five in the Ivy League – Dartmouth, Princeton, Yale, Penn and Brown – have more students who come 'from the top 1 percent of the income scale than from the entire bottom 60 percent'. The study tracked about 30 million students born between 1980 and 1991. They linked anonymized tax returns to attendance records from almost all universities in the US. 'At elite colleges, the share of students from the bottom 40 percent has remained mostly flat for a decade. Access to top colleges has not changed much, at least when measured in quintiles. The poor have gotten poorer over that time, and the very rich have gotten richer' (Chetty et al., 2017).

A number of other studies have examined unequal access to top tier universities from an historical perspective. Though too numerous to discuss in this brief chapter, some of the most notable works include: The Chosen: The Hidden History of Admission and Exclusion at Harvard, Yale and Princeton Universities by Jerome Karabel (2005); Student Diversity at the Big Three: Changes at Harvard, Yale, and Princeton Since the 1920s by Marcia Synnott (2013); and The Qualified Student: A History of Selective Admissions in the US by Harold Wechsler (1977). Other studies of a similar but more contemporary nature are The Price of Admission by Daniel Golden (2006), and The Flow of the River by Douglas Massey et al. (2008). These studies point to the root of unequal access, especially at elite universities, and how it is sustained throughout the transition from elite to mass higher education.

With the continued growth of economic inequality, elite universities tend to adopt practices which arguably accentuate a socially-uniform student cohort as competitive and comparative ranking rewards elite institutions. Financial rating agencies, such as Moody's or Standard and Poors, study application outcomes. It is more of a concern now than in the past if an institution is not becoming more selective (Hoover, 2010). For WCUs, this is because selectivity is often used as an indicator of the capacity to attract wealthy high fee paying students or philanthropists\investors or to spawn well-placed and influential graduates/alumni.

Global rankings promulgate deeper inequalities (Hazelkorn, 2014; Bastedo & Jaquette, 2011). For example, WCUs tend to admit more international students who can bring in more cash than low income locals. In this sense, the issue is not about widening access, per se, but rather about the degree of increasing stratification within the system; in other words, not simply 'access to what' but 'who gets access'. Finally, WCUs have led in rising tuition fees out of reach of the poor. How the two top economies in the world address this problem of equalizing access by way of their WCUs, now and in the future, has the potential to globally influential to other WCUs in other parts of the world, whether in OBOR countries or Western industrialized countries. In short, these two countries have a responsibility to do more to address this issue.

With respect to university access and equity, both countries share similarities and differences. Both have policies and laws to improve access. China uses quotas for ethnic minorities and increased quotas for improving access for students from impoverished areas to enter top tier (Project 211) universities. The US has legal precedents that encourage universities to institute 'affirmative action' policies to ensure diversity. Both countries provide various levels of financial support to students unable to afford tuition and fees. Policies and laws have not resulted in more equal access, but rather an intense struggle over what constitutes merit.

7   Closing the Gap: Access and Equity in China's WCUs

China now produces twice as many college and university graduates a year as the US does. In 2017, China graduated more than double the number of students who will graduate this year in the US (World Economic Forum 2017, China National Bureau of Statistics and US Department of Education). Admission rates to China's WCUs risk mirroring the US pattern, especially during the transition to mass higher education. The top tier is increasingly dominated by students from high income urban areas in a nation that is still half rural. Fortunately, and to some extent because of the one child policy, women access higher education in far higher proportions than women did in the US at a similar stage of economic development. Systematic study of access to university in China had a later start than in the US but several book length studies have been published, including Meritocracy and Inequality in China by Liu Ye (2016) and Impacts of Cultural Capital on Student College Choice in China by Gao Lan (2011). There are an increasing number of empirical studies in the journals.

Despite the fairness of the national exam, one that takes precedence in admission to elite universities, there has been a growing disparity in admission to top tier research universities between students from urban and rural regions (Li, 2015). Liu et al. (2012) focused specifically in Peking University and how there has been a shift in enrolments over time toward advantaging urban students over rural students. Xie and Li (2000) did a study of 37 colleges and universities that sorted China's universities into four categories (national top, regular top, regular and local). Their results 'showed that the proportion of rural children in schools decreases as the rank of the school in question rises' and the proportion of children of party members, government cadres, business managers and professionals increases. In another study, Liu (2007) surveyed 19 colleges and universities and found similar results, with farmers' children attending vocational colleges more than those of other families. In a study of women's access, Xie, Wang, and Chen (2010) also found similar results for rural women in higher education.

Some parents have protested when the cut-off points on the national examination scores are reallocated among different provinces. For example, the chances of a test taker in Shandong province being admitted to college, especially to first tier universities, is lower that of students from some other provinces. Three students from Shandong province took their case to court and claimed that if they were in Beijing, they would have been admitted to university with those scores (Zhang, 2010). The conundrum for many rural students is that they may have to attend private universities which are more costly and less prestigious. Yu and Ertl (2010) examined this in terms of the role of public and non-public institutions. Yang Dongping (2011) has pointed out how elites take advantage of the admission system.

8 Closing the Gap: Student Experience

Xie and Postiglione (2017) are currently studying access and equity in selected WCUs. The aim is to examine access and experience of rural students in China to top tier universities. We selected students who represent typical first-tier, large, public and Project 985 universities. The approximately 2,000 participants were selected by using a two-stage cluster sampling strategy. We contacted the registrars of four of the Project 985 universities for the full class lists of the year 2013 class and then classified all schools/faculties into three groups in arts/humanities and social sciences, sciences and engineering, medicine and biology. A number of classes were then selected randomly in each of the group. Students in each selected class were invited to attend the survey. Five hundred participants were targeted for each of the universities. For the follow-up interviews, participants were selected purposively. We categorized all rural participants into four groups according to their origins, academic performance and social success achieved (based on high/low for each achievement). Twelve participants in each of the group were selected in each of the four universities.

Our survey instrument was an adjusted survey questionnaire, similar to the Survey of College Life and Experience used by a group of social scientists from universities in the US. We translated, tested and piloted the instrument to assess its reliability. We used forward-translation and expert panel consultations to achieve a Chinese version of the English instrument that is conceptually equivalent in the Chinese social and cultural context. A small pilot test (n = 50 students) was also conducted in 2014, with encouraging results. For the pilot test, the Cronbach's alpha reliability for most of the items was + .75, suggesting appropriate instrument internal consistency. This result indicated that the instrument can be applied to a larger sample of participants with varying academic and social experiences. The data we use for analysis are collected from the first round of the survey in 2014.

To our surprise and in contrast to studies of top tier elite university students in the US, we found no significant difference between rural and urban students in academic performance measured by their Grade Point Average (GPA) ranks. However, we found that rural students are left behind socially. They are less likely to be appointed/selected as class monitors or committee members. They are less likely to be appointed/selected secretary of the faculty/university branch of the Youth League/Students Union. The data also suggest that compared to their rural counterparts, urban students are more likely to get access to cultural capital investment measured by parental participation in their development, pre-college cultural activity participation and material resources. In fact, our Ordinary Least Squares regression suggests that pre-college cultural activity participation have significant positive effects on the GPA ranks that students achieved while in university. Both family economic capital and cultural capital have an effect on their participation of extra-curriculum activities measured by their appointment as class monitors or committee members, or secretary of the faculty/university branch of the Youth League/students unions.

9 Closing the Gap: WCUs out Front for the Global Common Good

It is incumbent upon WCUs to reconsider their positioning as the world's centre of gravity continues to shift. As inequality becomes the greatest challenge to the global common good, with implications for climate change, health crises and global economic instability, WCUs from the world two largest economies can increase cooperation and become more strategic in strengthening research collaboration. To maximize their contribution to the global common good by the mid-century, WCUs can begin by addressing unequal access and inequity within their own institutions.

Shifting world circumstances will surely test the autonomy of WCUs universities in both countries. The potential of their academic communities to be a force for rational communication and strengthen networks of collaborative research for the global common good will also hinge upon the extent to which overseas they are well integrated into their WCUs (Postiglione & Xie, 2017). This is an opportunity for WCUs to distinguish themselves not only as an instrument of national competition but also as institutions for international peace. Universities in both countries may not be able to address all of the challenges in store as the world's centre of gravity continues to shift, but there is much they can do to sustain and improve the global common good in the coming 50 years by reducing inequality.

References

Alvaredo, F., Chancel, L., Piketty, T., Saez, E., & Zucman, G. (2014). *Global inequality dynamics: New findings from WID.world* (Working Paper No. 23119). Cambridge, MA: National Bureau of Economic Research. Retrieved February 6, 2018, from http://www.nber.org/papers/w23119

Alvaredo, F., Chacel, L., Piketyy, T., Saez, E., & Zucman, G. (2017). Global inequality dynamics: New findings from WID.world. *American Economic Review: Papers and Proceedings, 107*(5), 404–409. Retrieved February 6, 2018, from https://doi.org/10.1257/aer.p20171095

Asian University Alliance. (2017). *Asian higher education outlook 2017: Creation and direction of the Asian universities alliance* (Internal document).

Bastedo, M. N., & Bowman, N. A. (2010). The U.S. news and world report college rankings: Modeling institutional effects on organizational reputation. *American Journal of Education, 116*, 163–184.

Bastedo, M. N., & Bowman, N. A. (2011). College rankings as an inter-organizational dependency: Establishing the foundation for strategic and institutional accounts. *Research in Higher Education, 52*, 3–23.

Bastedo, M. N., & Jaquette, O. (2011). Running in place: Low-income students and the dynamics of higher education stratification. *Educational Evaluation and Policy Analysis, 33*(3), 318–339.

Bell, D. (2015). *The China model: Political meritocracy and the limits of democracy*. Princeton, NJ: Princeton University Press.

Chetty, R., Friedman, J., Saez, E., Turner, N., & Yagan, D. (2017). *Mobility report cards: The role of colleges in intergenerational mobility*. Retrieved February 6, 2018, from http://www.equality-of-opportunity.org/papers/coll_mrc_paper.pdf

Cole, J. (2016). *Toward a more perfect university*. New York, NY: Public Affairs.

Columbia University Programs. (2017). *U.S.-China university presidents forum: Relations over the next fifty years*. Retrieved February 6, 2018, from http://universityprograms.columbia.edu/us-%E2%80%93-china-university-presidents-forum-relations-over-next-fifty-years

Delaney, R. (2017, September 27). *Kissinger urges greater cooperation with China as 'the world's centre of gravity' shifts.* Retrieved from http://www.scmp.com/news/china/policies-politics/article/2112957/kissinger-urges-us-boost-cooperation-beijing-massive

Economist. (2013). *Toward the end of poverty.* Retrieved February 6, 2018, from https://www.economist.com/news/leaders/21578665-nearly-1-billion-people-have-been-taken-out-extreme-poverty-20-years-world-should-aim

Gao, L. (2011). *Impacts of cultural capital on student college choice in China.* New York, NY: Rowman & Littlefield.

Gilardoni, D. (2017, September 2). Chinese lessons. *South China Morning Post.* Retrieved from http://www.scmp.com/comment/insight-opinion/article/2109172/learning-china-three-lessons-ignorant-west

Golden, D. (2006). *The price of admission: How America's ruling class buys its way into elite colleges – and who gets left outside the gates.* New York, NY: Random House.

Hazelkorn, E. (2014). The effects of ranking on student choice and institutional selection. In B. Jongbloed & H. Vossensteyn (Eds.), *Access and expansion post-massification: Opportunities and barriers to further growth in higher education participation.* London: Routledge.

Hirsh, F. (1997). *The social limits to growth.* London: Routledge.

Hoover, E. (2010, November 5). Application inflation. *Chronicle of Higher Education.* Retrieved February 6, 2018, from https://www.chronicle.com/article/Application-Inflation/125277

Karabel, J. (2005). *The chosen: The hidden history of admission and exclusion at Harvard, Yale and Princeton universities.* Cambridge, MA: Harvard University Press.

Lehmann, J. P. (2017, August 8). Why the world has to study China. *South China Morning Post.* Retrieved from http://www.scmp.com/comment/insight-opinion/article/2105912/why-world-has-study-chinese-history-and-how-china-views

Leonhardt, D. (2017, May 26). College access index methodology. *New York Times.* Retrieved February 6, 2018, from https://www.nytimes.com/2017/05/25/opinion/sunday/the-assault-on-colleges-and-the-american-dream.html

Levin, R. (2006, August 21–28). Universities branch out. *Newsweek.* Retrieved February 6, 2018, from https://law.yale.edu/system/files/documents/pdf/Public_Affairs/PresidentLevinArticle.pdf

Li, C. L. (2015). Trends in educational inequality in different eras (1940–2010): A re-examination of opportunity inequalities in urban-rural education. *Chinese Education and Society, 48*(3), 63–82.

Li, S. (2016). *Recent changes in income inequality in China* (World Science Report). Paris: UNESCO. Retrieved February 6, 2018, from http://unesdoc.unesco.org/images/0024/002459/245943e.pdf

Liu, H. Z. (2007). Shehui jieceng fenhuayu gaodeng jiaoyu jihui jundeng [Social Class Disunion and Higher Education Access, in Chinese]. *Beijing Shifandaxue Xuebao* [Journal of Beijing Normal University], *1*, 17–22.

Liu, N. C. (2017, March 28). *World-class universities and excellence initiatives in 'one-belt-one-road' countries*. Lecture at University of Hong Kong, Hong Kong.

Liu, Y. (2016). *Higher education, meritocracy and inequality in China*. Singapore: Springer.

Liu, Y., Wang, Z. M., & Yang, X. F. (2012). Selecting the elite: Status, geography and capital – Admission of rural students to Peking university (1978–2005). *International Journal of Chinese Education, 1*(1), 19–53.

Liu, Y. D. (2017, September 27). Quoted in 'China, US have least discord on people-to-people exchanges'. *China Daily*. Retrieved February 6, 2018, from https://www.chinadailyasia.com/articles/49/118/189/1506508247156.html

Massey, D., Charles, C. Z., Lundy, G., & Fischer, M. J. (2008). *The source of the river: Freshmen at America's selective colleges and universities*. Princeton, NJ: Princeton University Press.

Picchi, A. (2017). *US vs China: Whose income inequality is worse?* Retrieved February 6, 2018, from https://www.cbsnews.com/news/usa-china-income-inequality-economic-research/

Piketty, T. (2015). *The economics of inequality*. Cambridge, MA: Belknap Press.

Postiglione, G. A. (2015a). Research universities for national rejuvenation and global influence: China's search for a balanced model. *Higher Education, 70*(2), 235–250.

Postiglione, G. A. (2015b, April 27). Asian universities are rising in the ranks. *The Washington Post*. Retrieved February 6, 2018, from https://www.washingtonpost.com/posteverything/wp/2014/10/05/asian-universities-are-rising-in-the-ranks-but-opposition-to-foreign-scholars-could-hold-some-back/?noredirect=on&utm_term=.bacb8892ebe9

Postiglione, G. A. (2016). China's search for its liberal arts and sciences model. In W. Kirby & M. C. van der Wende (Eds.), *Experiences in liberal arts and science education from America, Europe and Asia*. New York, NY: Palgrave Macmillan.

Postiglione, G. A., & Xie, A. L. (2017). International faculty in two top tier Chinese universities: One country, two types of internationals. In M. Yudkevich, P. G. Altbach, & L. E. Rumbley (Eds.), *International faculty in higher education: Comparative perspectives on recruitment, integration, and impact*. New York, NY: Routledge.

Shin, J. C., Postiglione, G. A., & Huang, F. T. (Eds.). (2015). *Mass higher education development in East Asia: Strategy, quality, and challenges*. Dordrecht: Springer.

Standard and Poor's. (2014). *How increasing income inequality is dampening U.S. economic growth, and possible ways to change the tide*. Retrieved February 6, 2018, from https://www.globalcreditportal.com/ratingsdirect/renderArticle.do?article Id=1351366&SctArtId=255732&from=CM&nsl_code=LIME&sourceObjectId=8741 033&sourceRevId=1&fee_ind=N&exp_date=20240804-19:41:13

Synnott, M. (2013). *Student diversity at the big three: Changes at Harvard, Yale, and Princeton since the 1920s*. New York, NY: Routledge.

Vogel, E. (2003, December 5). China's intellectual renaissance. *The Washington Post*. Retrieved February 6, 2018, from https://www.washingtonpost.com/archive/opinions/2003/12/05/chinas-intellectual-renaissance/95e43774-0378-46c7-a354-103f88633b4b/?utm_term=.91eb5e91c5f1

Wang, D. (2014). Confucius in the American founding. *Virginia Review of Asian Studies, 16*, 11–26.

Wechsler, H. (1977). *The qualified student: A history of selective admissions in America*. London: Routledge.

World Economic Forum. (2015). Retrieved February 6, 2018, from http://reports.weforum.org/outlook-global-agenda-2015/top-10-trends-of-2015/1-deepening-income-inequality/

World Economic Forum. (2017). Retrieved February 6, 2018, from https://www.weforum.org/agenda/2017/04/higher-education-in-china-has-boomed-in-the-last-decade

Xie, A. (2017, October 9). No more fool's gold. *South China Morning Post*.

Xie, A., Hong, Y., Postiglione, G. A., & Zhang, L. (2017, May 1). *Rural students in China's elite universities: Understanding their first year of academic and social success*. Paper presented at American Education Research Association Annual Meeting, San Antonio, TX.

Xie, W. H., & Li, X. L. (2000). Gaodeng jiaoyu gongpingxing de diaocha yu yanjiu baogao [Report on a survey and study of equality in higher education]. In M. C. Zeng (Ed.), *Jiaoyu zhengce yu jingji fenxi* [An economic analysis of educational policy]. Beijing: Beijing People's Education Press.

Xie, Z. X., Wang W. H., & Chen, X. W. (2010). A study of women's access to higher education in rural and urban China. *Chinese Education and Society, 43*(4), 32.

Yang, D. P. (2011). An empirical study of higher education: Admission opportunities in China. *Chinese Education and Society, 43*(6), 59.

Yu, K., & Ertl, H. (2010). Equity in access to higher education in China. *Chinese Education and Society, 43*(6), 36–58.

Zhang, R. (2010). Media, litigation, and regional discrimination in college admission in China. *Chinese Education and Society, 43*(4), 60–74.

Zhuang, J. Z. (2016, November 8). Reducing inequality remains a challenge. *China Daily*. Retrieved February 6, 2018, from http://usa.chinadaily.com.cn/opinion/2016-11/08/content_27305374.htm

CHAPTER 12

What Are the Benefits and Risks of Internationalization of Japanese Higher Education?

Futao Huang

Abstract

The purpose of this study was to analyse the vice presidents' views on the benefits and risks of the internationalization of Japanese higher education based on major findings from a national survey in March 2017. The study begins with a brief introduction to recent policies to internationalize Japanese higher education. It then focuses on the discussion of the benefits and risks of the internationalization of higher education by employing different variables. The final section summarizes the main findings and offering implications for research, policy and institutional practices.

Keywords

Internationalization of higher education – benefits and risks – Japan – survey

1   Introduction

Since the 1990s, with a growing impact of globalization, internationalization has increasingly become an integral part of reforming and improving national higher education systems worldwide. There is little doubt that it has both benefits and risks. Previous studies have pointed out that the risks of internationalization of higher education include commercialization or the commodification of higher education, brain drain, and the increasing dominance of the cultural values and ideologies of the US, the UK and other English-speaking countries that are actively exporting their English products or ideas (Abdullahi et al., 2007; Brandenburg and de Wit, 2011; Cheung et al., 2011). Furthermore, according to earlier global surveys administered by the IAU (2017), on one hand, the internationalization of higher education has obviously benefitted students' increased international awareness and engagement with global issues, and improvement of quality of teaching and learning. On the other hand, respondents from their survey in 2017 also perceive as the most significant risk of internationalization for institutions, that international opportunities will be available only to students with financial support, followed by the difficulty of local regulations, the quality of foreign programmes and by excessive competition among higher education institutions.

The purpose of this study was to analyse the vice presidents' views on the benefits and risks of the internationalization of Japanese higher education based on major findings from a national survey in March 2017. The study begins with a brief introduction to recent policies to internationalize of Japanese higher education. It then focuses on the discussion of the benefits and risks of the internationalization of higher education by employing different variables. The final section summarizes the main findings and offering implications for research, policy and institutional practice.

In terms of methodology, the national survey was implemented in 744 universities and colleges. The target population of the survey was vice presidents or institution-level administrators who are responsible for international affairs or internationalization in all national, local public and private universities. Altogether 744 questionnaires were sent out. By April 2017, 173 respondents (23.3 per cent) had been received.

2 Research Background

Contemporary Japanese higher education basically consists of three major types of institution: universities, junior colleges (Tanki Daigaku in Japanese) and colleges of technology.[1] In some cases, specialized training colleges (Sensyuu Gakkou)[2] are also considered a part of higher education. The number of students being officially enrolled in the Open University of Japan, the University of the Air until October, 2007) and those pursuing their higher education learning through television or radio in other regular universities and junior colleges are included in the data of Japan's post-secondary education as well. Compared to many Western countries, especially the US and European countries, the notable characteristics of Japanese higher education can be identified as follows:

Firstly, because the 'national' and 'public' universities are mainly established, funded and administered by local and national government respectively, while school corporations are established by the private sector. The three different types of institution are expected to play different roles and fulfil diverse functions. There is a clear division of labour between the national and private sector institutions. Except for a very few private universities with a long history, the vast majority of private sector institutions focus on teaching. In contrast, in addition to teaching activities, the national universities are more engaged in basic, applied, and large-scale scientific research. The local public sector which is established and funded by local authorities focuses on the production of graduates for the regional economic development and engages in service activities for local community. In contrast, the vast majority of private sector is involved in educational activities in humanities and social sciences at an undergraduate level. They have provided more vocational and practical educational programmes. Moreover, as a huge amount of their revenue comes from tuition and fees, the operation and management of the private sector is more market-oriented than either national or local public sector.

Secondly, Japan's private sector accounts for a large share of all institutions. For example, in 2016, the private junior colleges and universities accounted for 95 per cent and 77.2 per cent of the total respectively. Moreover, the proportion of students in private universities and junior colleges comprises 73.5 per cent and 94.7 per cent of the total (MEXT, 2017).

In terms of internationalization of Japanese higher education, since the early 1980s, the Japanese government has implemented several national-level strategies of internationalization of higher education. By the late 1990s, most of these strategies focused on attracting international students to study in Japanese universities. In recent years, in order to enhance the global competitiveness of Japanese universities, the Japanese government has devoted more efforts and funding to internationalize Japanese universities and improve the quality of its teaching and learning activities and academic performance. For example, in 2001, the Japanese government set the goal of fostering the Top 30 universities towards attainment of top global standards. Later, the programme was changed into a scheme of cultivating 'Centers of Excellence in the 21st Century' (COE21). The central government chose to focus on and expand the budget for units in nine key disciplines. In 2009, the government launched a new Global 30 programme, aiming to accept 300,000 foreign students by 2020. In order to achieve the goal, 13 universities, including seven national and six private, were selected to play a central role in implementing the programme. In 2012, the Japanese government implemented the Global Human Resource project (also called Super Global University project). The project consists of two types. For Type A, the government selected 11 universities and required them to produce more graduates with global perspectives and competencies. 31 faculties and graduate schools were selected for Type B, focusing on producing global human resources in particular disciplines (MEXT, 2012). In 2014, the Japanese government started the Top Global University Project. There are two types in the project. Type A (Top Type, 13 universities) is for world-class universities that have the potential to be ranked in the top 100 world university rankings. Type B (Global Traction Type,

24 universities) is for innovative universities that lead the internationalization of Japanese society (JSPS, 2017). The implantation of the projects has resulted in the disclosure of more factual information on relevant universities, increasing transparency of their missions and activities, and creating a gap between different universities.

3   Findings

Regarding the benefits of internationalization in general (Figure 12.1), the top response from leaders is 'students' increased international awareness' (95.9 per cent), followed by 'staff's increased international awareness' (90.8 per cent), and 'promoting international collaboration and partnership' (89.6 per cent). The lowest response is 'revenue generation' (27 per cent).

By sector, as shown in Table 12.1, all national leaders emphasize the importance of 'promoting international collaboration and partnership', followed by 'strengthening research and knowledge creation' (99 per cent), and 'students' increased international awareness' (96.7 per cent). The highest response from the leaders belonging to local public universities is 'students' increased international awareness' (100 per cent), followed by 'staff's increased international awareness' (96 per cent), and 'promoting international collaboration and partnership' (96 per cent). Similarly to local public universities, the top and the second largest responses from the leaders of private universities are also 'students' increased international awareness' (94.9 per cent) and 'staff's increased international awareness' (89.6 per cent), although minor percentages of them admitted these. The third highest response from the leaders of local public universities is 'attracting domestic students through internationalization' (89 per cent). Interestingly, despite clear differences between the national sector and other two sectors, the lowest response of the leaders from all the sectors are 'revenue generation'.

By type, Table 12.2 presents benefits perceived by the leaders from all the universities which are included in 'Global Human Resource' project and other universities. Normally, the former is considered to be research-intensive universities in Japan and the latter refers to education-centred universities. Except for the responses to 'revenue generation' and 'equipping students with the quality of citizenship', it is evident that the leaders from research-intensive universities have much higher positive responses to the benefits of internationalization of higher education.

As for the risks of internationalization (Figure 12.2), 'growing gaps between universities within the country' appear as the most frequently mentioned risk

BENEFITS AND RISKS OF INTERNATIONALIZATION OF JAPANESE HE   235

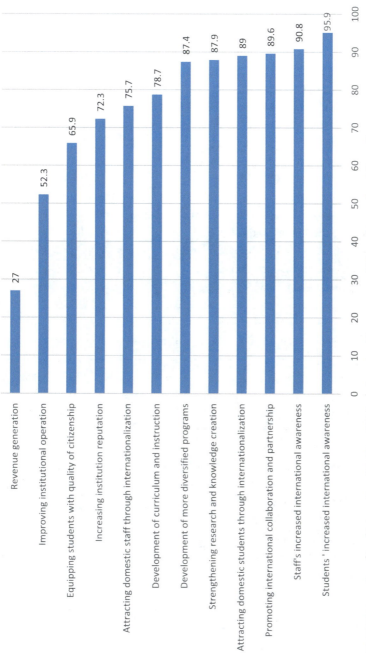

FIGURE 12.1 Benefits of internationalization of higher education (%, responses of "Strongly agree" and "Agree")

TABLE 12.1 Benefits of internationalization of higher education by sector-level of importance (%) (responses of 'strongly agree and agree')

Item	National	Local public	Private
Students' increased international awareness	96.7(3)	100(1)	94.9(1)
Staff's increased international awareness	90.3(4)	96(2)	89.8(2)
Promoting international collaboration and partnership	100(1)	96(3)	85.6(5)
Attracting domestic students through internationalization	90(6)	80(4)	89(3)
Strengthening research and knowledge creation	99(2)	88(5)	84.7(6)
Development of more diversified programs	93.5(5)	84(6)	86.5(4)
Development of curriculum and instruction	83.9(7)	76(7)	77.9(7)
Attracting domestic staff through internationalization	76.6(9)	84(8)	73.7(8)
Increasing institution reputation	86.7(8)	60(9)	71.2(9)
Equipping students with quality of citizenship	67.8(11)	60(10)	66.6(10)
Improving institutional operation	77.4(10)	36(11)	49.2(11)
Revenue generation	32.2(12)	16(12)	27.9(12)

TABLE 12.2 Benefits of internationalization of HE by type-level of importance (%)[a]

Item	SGU A & B[b]	Other
Students' increased international awareness	100	95.9
Staff's increased international awareness	100	90.5
Promoting international collaboration and partnership	100	89.3
Attracting domestic students through internationalization	100	88.7
Strengthening research and knowledge creation	100	87.6
Development of more diversified programs	100	87
Development of curriculum and instruction	80	78.8
Attracting domestic staff through internationalization	100	75
Increasing institution reputation	100	71.4
Equipping students with quality of citizenship	40	66.7
Improving institutional operation	60	52.1
Revenue generation	0	27.8

a. Responses of 'strongly agree and agree'.
b. SGU A and B refers to the universities of both Type A and Type B in 'Global Human Resource' project.

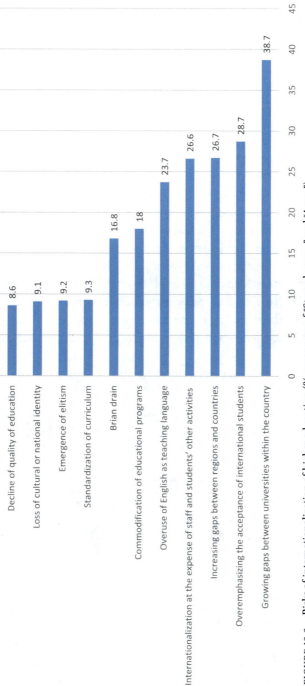

FIGURE 12.2 Risks of internationalization of higher education (%, responses of "Strongly agree" and "Agree")

(38.7 per cent), followed by 'overemphasizing the acceptance of international students' (28.7 per cent) and 'increasing gaps between regions and countries' (26.7 per cent). In contrast, the lowest response of leaders worries about 'decline of quality of education' (8.6 per cent).

Regarding sectorial stratifications (Table 12.3), 'growing gaps between universities within the country' is listed as the top risk across the three types of institution. The second most frequent response for the national universities is 'overemphasizing the acceptance of international students', followed by 'increasing gaps between regions and countries'. The second highest response of leaders from local public universities fears the 'increasing gaps between regions and countries', followed by 'overuse of English as teaching language'. Private universities worry particularly about 'internationalization at the expense of staff and students' other activities' and 'overemphasizing the acceptance of international students'.

By type (Table 12.4), the responses from both the research-intensive universities and other universities are noteworthy. They both see 'emergence of elitism' as the number one risk. In both types of universities, the second most frequent responses are also the same: 'growing gaps between universities within the country'. While the third highest response from the research-intensive universities includes both 'overemphasizing the acceptance of international students'

TABLE 12.3 Risks of internationalization of HE by sector-level of importance (responses of 'strongly agree and agree')

Item	National	Local public	Private
Growing gaps between universities within the country	1	1	1
Overemphasizing the acceptance of international students	2	4	3
Increasing gaps between regions and countries	3	2	4
Internationalization at the expense of staff and students' other activities	5	5	2
Overuse of English as teaching language	6	3	5
Commodification of educational programs	8	8	6
Brain drain	4	7	7
Standardization of curriculum	7	6	8
Emergence of elitism	9	9	9
Loss of cultural or national identity	11	11	10
Decline of quality of education	10	10	11

TABLE 12.4 Risks of internationalization of higher education by type-level of importance

Item	SGU A & B	Other
Growing gaps between universities within the country	50	37.9
Overemphasizing the acceptance of international students	41.7	27.8
Increasing gaps between regions and countries	41.7	25.5
Internationalization at the expense of staff and students' other activities	8.3	28
Overuse of English as teaching language	33.3	23
Commodification of educational programs	16.7	18.1
Brain drain	25	16.3
Standardization of curriculum	0	9.9
Emergence of elitism	75	74.5
Loss of cultural or national identity	8.3	9.3
Decline of quality of education	25	7.4

and 'increasing gaps between regions and countries', in the other universities, they fear 'internationalization at the expense of staff and students' other activities'. A special mention should be made that in both types of universities it appears that they do not worry about 'standardization of curriculum', despite differences in degree.

4   Sectorial Stratification and Type Differences

These findings suggest that functional stratification of three sectors of universities and also types of universities in Japan determines the benefits and risks of internationalization in individual universities. Several factors explain this. Firstly, except for a short period of time from the early 1930s to the end of the World War II, incorporating the standards and practices of Germany, France, the UK and the US into Japanese university systems the educational ideas has constituted an integral part of its internationalization and national higher education policies. In a major sense, internationalization has played a vital role in the emergence and development of Japan's universities. Secondly, although a large number of private universities need to recruit sufficient numbers of fee-paying international students to maintain their operation, since 1973 the central government has begun to provide public financial support to all private universities. For example, even as of 2010, public expenditure constituted more than 10 per cent of the total revenues of private universities. Thirdly, national universities are expected to facilitate the adcement of basic and applied scientific research, some of which is large-scale. A large number of national universities remain more prestigious and are the centres of most graduate work at the PhD level. By contrast, almost all private universities provide only vocational and practical educational programmes. Finally, increased academic competition worldwide has made Japan's universities realize the need to enhance their international competitiveness through internationalization, particularly teaching and research activities (Huang & Daizen, 2017).

As in other aspects of higher education, not only significant sectorial differences remain in many areas of benefits and risks of internationalization of Japanese higher education, but also variations can also be found in several areas between research-intensive universities and other universities.

However, it cannot be denied that in other sectorial comparisons and comparisons between research-intensive universities and teaching-centred universities, there is indeed a general consensus around both the top-ranked responses and lowest ranked responses. To illustrate, with regard to the benefits of internationalization of higher education, the lowest responses from all sectors and types of universities are 'revenue generation'. Further, in relation to the top responses to international risks to their institutions, there are not many differences between the sectors or types of universities, because they all rank 'growing gaps between universities within the country' as the top risk among 11 areas.

5 Conclusion

It appears that in most cases, institutional leaders' perceptions of benefits and risks of internationalization at their universities differentiate significantly from those of the US, the UK, Australia and other English-speaking countries, which have been increasingly affected by the market. In general, the internationalization of Japanese higher education is still highly valued and academically prioritized. They list higher responses of students/staff international awareness, international collaboration and partnership in research, and knowledge creation. This is especially different from those countries in which internationalization at an institutional level is primarily expected to generate more revenues.

It is obvious that the findings above also offer numerous implications for research, policy and institutional practice. As for research, since these findings are obtained from a national survey of institutional leaders' perceptions of relevant issues, it is necessary to undertake more comprehensive and in-depth research into what changes have occurred in Japanese universities and colleges at an institutional, departmental, programme, and even individual levels, while the recent policies for the internationalization of higher education internationalization were implemented. Further, how do faculty members and university students, as well as other stakeholders such as industry and business, view the benefits and risks of higher education internationalization in a Japanese context? In terms of implications for government policy-making, these findings and any future research in relation to the internationalization of higher education should provide hard evidences for the government to evaluate the outcomes or effectiveness of implementing national policies of higher education internationalization, and even to develop new policies in this regard.

More importantly, the government should pay more attention to the issues raised in the survey. They include the issues of the 'growing gaps between universities within the country', 'overemphasizing the acceptance of international students', and the 'increasing gaps between regions and countries'. For individual universities and colleges, more efforts are expected to be made by individual universities and colleges to redefine clear-cut missions and create their institutional policies or strategies for the internationalization of higher education which are of relevance and importance to their teaching and research goals, and other academic activities. Despite differences being confirmed between different types and sectors of Japanese universities and colleges mentioned above, the issue of how to maximize the benefits of internationalization and reduce or avoid the risks seems to be a common challenge facing all universities and colleges. Individual universities and colleges should consider finding appropriate solutions to solving the problem according to their characteristics, role and functions being played in the national higher education system, and especially the financial schemes and situation. Further, individual universities and colleges should be fully aware of the benefits and risks of their own strategies and activities that internationalization would produce in terms of the quantitative expansion and qualitative improvement of their academic activities, and especially to their students, faculty members and administrative staff, etc. Finally, it is important for Japanese universities and colleges to bear in mind that internationalization is merely a means of cultivating quality graduates, improving the quality of research, and helping them to be more closely involved in the activities of facilitating the development of regional economy and services for society at large.

Notes

1   A higher education institution which offers a unified five-year education (five years six months for mercantile marine studies) aimed at nurturing technical experts. It requires graduation from lower secondary schools or equivalent academic ability for admission. A minimum of 167 credits are required for graduation (147 credits for mercantile marine studies). Graduates are awarded the title of Associate.
2   A higher education institution which provides practical and technical learning and skills in a wide variety of disciplines such as medical care, technology, culture and general education, business, personal care and nutrition, education and welfare, fashion and home science, agriculture and much more. Graduates are conferred with Certification.

References

Abdullahi, I., Kajberg, L., & Virkus, S. (2007). Internationalization of LIS education in Europe and North America. *New Library World, 108*(1–2), 7–24.

Brandenburg, U., & de Wit, H. (2011). The end of internationalization. *International Higher Education, 62*, 15–17.

Cheung, C. K., Yuen, W. W., Yuen, Y. M., & Cheng, Y. C. (2011). Strategies and policies for Hong Kong's higher education in Asian markets, lessons from the United Kingdom, Australia, and Singapore. *International Journal of Educational Management, 25*(2), 144–163.

Huang, F., & Daizen, T. (2017, August 18). How do university leaders view internationalisation? *University World News*, p. 470.

IAU. (2017). IAU 4th global survey report. *Internationalization of Higher Education: Growing Expectations, Fundamental Values*, 9–10.

JSPS (Japan Society for the Promotion of Science). (2017). *Top global university project*. Retrieved May 1, 2018, from https://www.jsps.go.jp/english/e-tgu/index.html

MEXT. (2012). *Global jinzai ikusei suishin jigyou* [Promoting Global Human Resource project]. Retrieved July 29, 2017, from http://www.mext.go.jp/b_menu/houdou/24/09/attach/1326084.htm

MEXT. (2017). *Statistical abstract*. Tokyo: National Printing Bureau. [in Japanese]

CHAPTER 13

State and World-Class Universities: Seeking a Balance between International Competitiveness, Local and National Relevance

Isak Froumin and Mikhail Lisyutkin

Abstract

The role of the governments in the development and operation of universities in the emerging countries is being significantly transformed by the global agenda. There are a lot of evidences that governments' aimed at the establishment of the world-class universities increase their interference in higher education systems and even in the operation of particular institutions. Governments set tasks for universities related to the accelerated increase of their global competitiveness by launching so-called excellence-initiatives in higher education. Consequently, the matter of the changing autonomy of the higher education institutions participating in excellence initiatives arises.

There are academic and expert discussions arguing that the implementation of excellence initiatives is in large degree irrelevant to national and local challenges. The question arises whether governments should specifically set national and local objectives for world-class universities, or whether the growth of global competitiveness brings benefits for national and local challenges. Through the analysis of excellence initiatives, this chapter shows that in most cases governments do not specify the objectives related to national and local contribution. This chapter presents a study that examines the implementation of the Russian excellence initiative, Project 5-100, which aims to have at least five universities participating in the project in the top 100 world rankings by 2020. This initiative ignores potential direct national and local contribution. At the same time, the experience of the Russian initiative shows that participating universities purposefully develop nationally and locally relevant activities while they move towards global competitiveness without government pressure. The chapter discusses why these objectives are interrelated.

Keywords

Excellence initiative in higher education – multiversity – university autonomy – Project 5-100 – Russian Federation

1   Introduction

Evidence suggest that the overwhelming majority of governments aiming to establish world-class universities launch excellence initiatives in higher education (Sadlak & Liu, 2009). They mostly set tasks for particular universities related to the accelerated increase of their global competitiveness. Such policies became prior considerations in many countries when world universities rankings have joined the range of the top issues in the higher education policy agenda. Started in a few countries, excellence-driven policies and initiatives have become frequent practice in recent years.

Recent scholarly debates on the phenomenon of the excellence initiatives in higher education largely concentrate on two key issues. The first one proceeds from the fact that governments increase their interference into the higher education system and even into the operation of particular universities while implementing excellence initiatives (Froumin & Lisyutkin, 2015). Consequently, the matter of the changing autonomy of the higher education institutions participating in the excellence initiatives arises. The second one relates to the balance of the objectives of both governments implementing excellence initiatives and the excellence-driven higher education institutions between global competitiveness and local commitment. Academic discussions arguing that the implementation of the excellence initiatives is in large degree irrelevant to the national and local challenges make the abovementioned problem challenging (Benneworth et al., 2017). Therefore, a basic research question of the study is how higher education institutions change while participating in the implementation of the excellence initiatives in relation to the abovementioned discussion points. Do they focus on the global competitiveness agenda only while moving toward world-class university model? Does the level of their autonomy increase or decrease in practice?

This chapter presents a study that examines the implementation of the Russian excellence initiative, Project 5-100, which aims to have at least five universities participating in the project in the top 100 world rankings by 2020. It explores the transformations of excellence-driven universities. The researchers surveyed professors and administrators at these universities and statistical analysis shows that the level of the autonomy of higher education institutions and its nature has changed during the project implementation. It also reveals that while being pushed by the government toward the global research university model, Higher education institutions have also become more responsive to local and national needs. The chapter argues that while being pushed by governments to become internationally competitive, the universities move towards the so-called 'multiversity' model. Interviews with the leaders of excellence initiatives from eight countries allowed to suggest that these transformations (with some features) are peculiar to other countries.

The growing role of the international competitiveness agenda in higher education and the expansion of excellence-driven policies and initiatives in higher education around the globe are described in the first part of the chapter. The second part analyses the Russian excellence initiative, Project 5-100, in terms of the rationale for its launch, the design and implementation of the policy. The methodology of the study and empirical research base are described in the next part. The transformations of the universities participating in the Project 5-100 are identified as the results of the study in the fourth part of the chapter. In the concluding part of the text, some questions for further research are discussed.

2 Excellence-Driven Policies and Initiatives in Higher Education around the Globe

The global agenda has an increasing influence on shaping the priorities of governments (especially typical of the developing countries) in the development of higher education systems and even particular universities. Many countries have launched specific projects aimed at the establishment of the world-class universities (mainly called excellence initiatives) requiring universities to achieve globally significant results, mostly as a result of world universities rankings being turned into one of the top issues in higher education policy agenda (Froumin & Lisyutkin, 2015). Such policies have changed the focus from comprehensive higher education policy to support of a limited groups of the universities.

Specifying in more detail what is meant by the excellence initiative in the chapter, we follow Barbara Kehm and Jamil Salmi definitions of such policies. It is claimed by Kehm that excellence-driven policy is an initiative aimed to promote top-level research and to improve the quality of universities and research institutions in general, making the country more attractive research location, making it more internationally competitive (Kehm & Pasternack,

2009). Salmi and Froumin (2013) understand excellence initiatives as a large injection of funding by a national government aimed at financing the development of world-class universities in an accelerated fashion. It should be stressed that in our approach we consider top-down governments' initiatives (which come from the very high levels of the government mostly) as the excellence policies.

The growing interest of the national governments in achieving international competitiveness in higher education is evidenced by the fact that 13 excellence initiatives were launched from 1989 to 2004 in different countries. Afterwards their number has increased dramatically. Nearly 40 excellence initiatives were launched from 2005 to 2015 around the globe (Salmi, 2016). Additional financial resources came from the public accounts (with some features in a few countries) to support higher education institutions through the excellence initiatives mechanism. The substantial amount of money was invested in such projects. Their total costs approximately equals to more than US$60 billion. In most cases, the universities which participate in the excellence initiatives receive additional funding of US$20–100 million for the implementation of the development programme (ibid.).

It is important to separate the key characteristics, similarities and differences of the excellence initiatives for s better understanding of the basic concepts behind such policies. Comparative analysis of the excellence initiatives launched by different countries allows us to single out some particular rationales for their implementation (Froumin & Lisyutkin, 2015). Governments consider the development of higher education institutions as the key to the nation's prosperity and economic advancement. Some of them solve the need for their legitimation by showing global quality and global competitiveness. Governments implementing excellence policies think that the universities could play significant role in the development of globally competitive innovation-based economies and/or in global political and cultural competition, and they want universities to bring the fruits of an innovative economy as fast as possible.

Some governments consider the universities (especially world-class ones) as the entities having direct economic impact, producing significant part of the national gross domestic product by selling the educational services (also internationally) (e.g. education is among the top Australia's exports, most of which are in higher education). The rationale for excellence initiatives in many instances is that the world-class universities (WCUs) attract foreign students and best professors as future cadres of innovative economy and make a great contribution to development of the human capital. However, all governments follow the growing focus on global research and development as the part of public policy by launching excellence initiatives in higher education (Froumin & Lisyutkin, 2015). Reasoning from this fact, we join Mohrman, Ma, and Baker (2008) who argue that excellence initiatives promote a more or less universal model of global research university.

A government's rationale for implementing a policy to a large extent determines the particular development directions of excellence-driven universities. In a large number of instances, the universities which participate in the excellence initiatives are expected to take actions that directly or indirectly lead to the improvement of the indicators used by the most influential world university rankings. Methodologies of the Academic Ranking of World Universities (ARWU), the Times Higher Education World University Rankings (THE), and the Quacquarelli Symonds World University Rankings (QS) show that research productivity (quantitatively and qualitatively) generally has the greatest role in their calculations.

The thesis that universities participating in excellence initiatives are pushed by governments in certain directions is confirmed by a series of national cases. Canada had set research and development priorities for its higher education institutions; France pushed universities to merge; German excellence initiatives have determined a PhD programmes' model. In most of the cases, universities are forced to attract foreign students and faculty and to publish in English. In some countries, governments assign universities a responsibility for the development of specific sectors of the economy to international standards.

Governments allocate special development grants to universities participating in the excellence initiatives, as mentioned previously. Resource allocation per university by excellence initiative differs significantly from country to country (Salmi, 2009) but the way higher education institutions can spend additional funding is determined by specific objectives set by governments and is mainly related to the research productivity. Allocation of additional public money requires governments to build complicated instruments to steer selected universities. Alongside the indicators counted by the rankers, governments evaluate various performance criteria reflecting the university's global position (e.g. the number of incoming international students, international academic partnerships and joint educational programmes).

Cumulatively, it could be argued that the objectives for the development of the universities set by governments are related to the idea of bringing education and research activities of the participating universities to the global level. The basic characteristics of the excellence-driven policies and initiatives prove that governments promote a global research university model. They make focused efforts to orient selected universities on the global competitiveness issues. On the one hand, it makes assertions that the challenges related to local development are beyond the scope of excellence initiatives. On the other hand, the fact that governments introduce KPIs and direct recommendations for the development of universities suggests that the autonomy of the excellence-driven universities is being limited.

Nevertheless, the analysis of the excellence initiatives' design is only one side of the coin. Another (and even more important) subject to be studied is the actual transformation of the universities within the race for international competitiveness. The case of the universities participating in Russia's Project 5-100 brings these transformations to light.

3 Russian Excellence Initiative in Higher Education – Project 5-100

The design of the Russian excellence initiative in higher education Project 5-100 should be discussed carefully to gain a greater understanding of the intentions for its implementation. Project 5-100 is an initiative by the Russian federal government to foster the transformation of top tier national universities to world-class level launched in 2012. The basic goal of the project is that at least five Russian leading universities which participate in the initiative will enter the group of world's top 100 universities according to the most influential international rankings (ARWU, THE, QS) by 2020. The main point of this initiative is federal support to increase research excellence and global competitiveness of the leading Russian higher education institutions to the level of the best universities of the world.

The basis for the Project 5-100 to be launched was formed by the previous higher education policy implemented by the Ministry of Education and Science of the Russian Federation. A series of large-scale federal projects supported the development of the leading universities in Russia over the past 10 years. Most of the Project 5-100 universities participated in these initiatives.

The 'Federal Universities' project was launched in 2006 aimed at the establishment of a group of higher education institutions substantially contributing to socio-economic, cultural and innovation-driven development of the macro-regions in their locality (Romanenko & Lisyutkin, 2018). The basic managerial mechanism used for the formation of the federal universities was the merger of various universities located in the same region. The main group of the federal universities was formed during the period from 2006 to 2009. Three more federal universities were established by the year 2014.

The next initiative was to form a group of National Research Universities, to which 29 higher education institutions currently belong. It was launched

FIGURE 13.1 Geographical distribution of the Project 5-100 universities

in 2008 (Froumin & Povalko, 2014). Active internationalization and project management approach are among the key priorities of these universities also.

The Project 5-100 was a logical follow-up to the previous higher education policies against the background of the increasing role of the global agenda in higher education. The design of the Project 5-100 was based on an in-depth analysis of best global practices of excellence initiatives, primarily the German and Chinese projects. The Russian Federation (as with most other countries) used an open competition to select particular universities to be provided with additional support for the improvement of their international competitiveness. Currently 21 Russian universities located in 13 regions of the Russian Federation participate in the Project 5-100.

Competitive selection was based on the previous records of the universities and their development plans. Universities submitted so-called development road-maps to enter the competition. The evaluation of the universities' proposals involved international expertise. The work of the selection committee was highly appreciated both by the government and the universities because of the quality and transparency. As a result, all members of the selection committee were invited to join the Project Implementation Oversight Committee, which was to monitor the implementation of the strategic development plans of the 5–100 universities regularly (Froumin & Povalko, 2014).

Federal government funding for the project amounts to about US$180 million annually by 2020 for the university participants as a whole. It is important that the funds are distributed among the Project 5-100 universities on a competitive basis also. Universities participating in the Project 5-100 do not receive equal sums of money from the government to increase their international competitiveness. Instead, better performance is rewarded with additional government funding. Participating universities are expected to aspire to become among the best universities that adhere to the indicators established by the government. These indicators include not only rankings positions but also indicators measuring universities' performance and progress, such as entrants' average scores in the Russian Unified State Examination, the proportion of non-budgetary funding, the proportion of the foreign students, etc. Universities are also allowed to include additional specific indicators in their strategic development roadmaps (Froumin & Lisyutkin, 2018).

TABLE 13.1 The areas of the activities which could be funded by the universities from the Project 5-100 grant (subsidy)

Activity	Description
International research and education projects	New educational programmes conducted jointly with leading foreign and Russian universities and research institutions
	R&D projects jointly conducted with international and leading national companies
	World-class or breakthrough fundamental and applied research
	Implementation of research projects and development of subdivisions or centers of excellence headed by leading international and national experts
International recruitment	Recruitment of top university management and young faculty with experience in leading foreign and national universities and research institutions
	Recruitment of international students
Professional development	Development of programmes supporting international and national academic mobility and faculty professional development
	Development of support for initiatives of young faculty and promising students

SOURCE: DECREE OF THE GOVERNMENT OF THE RUSSIAN FEDERATION N 211 (2013)

The areas of the activities which could be funded by the universities from the Project 5-100 grant are defined by the special government's decree (Government Decree No. 211 of 16 March 2013).

Table 13.1 illustrates the way the government perceives international competitiveness of the higher education institutions. It also shows that the issue of the internationalization of research and education as well as of the faculty and students body of the Russian universities is at the top of the project agenda. Therefore, it could be argued that the priorities are placed on the challenges related to the enhancement of the global competitiveness by the government – the Russian government consistently promotes global research university model or world-class university model while implementing Project 5-100. Activities related to the regional and local development are not supported within the Project 5-100 framework.

After the rationale for and the design of the Project 5-100 is described it is possible to move onto the discussion of the actual transformations and particular initiatives of the Russian excellence-driven universities.

4 Empirical Data

The Empirical study which allowed identifying the actual transformations of the Project 5-100 universities included data analysis and qualitative research. The data from the Universities' performance monitoring conducted by the Ministry of Education and Science of the Russian Federation annually since 2012 was analyzed to trace the dynamics of the different characteristics of the Project 5-100 universities (Monitoring, 2017). The database includes more than 50 indicators characterizing nearly 500 Russian public universities (including excellence-driven higher education institutions) in terms of their educational, research, international, financial activities.

The results of the survey of professors and administrators at the universities, participating in the Russian excellence initiative (seven universities, nearly 2000 respondents) conducted by the Centre for Strategic Research and the Centre for Strategic Research North-West were analysed to consider the transformations which the Project 5-100 universities have been (or are going) through, during the implementation of the project (Center for Strategic Research 'North-West', 2016). The survey included questions related to the major changes in the universities after the Project 5-100 was launched; the focus and priorities for the universities' development; as well as the university model towards which the universities moved.

Strategic development programmes of the Project 5-100 universities, roadmaps for their implementation, as well as the progress reports on how these planning documents are being implemented and target indicators are being achieved were studied also to uncover particular actions made by the participating universities.

A series of interviews with the leaders of the excellence initiatives from eight countries were also conducted during the International Conference on Excellence Initiatives in Saint-Petersburg in 2016.

5   More or Less Autonomy?

Since the early works by Jamil Salmi (2009, 2011), Kathryn Mohrman (2008) and Barbara Kehm (2009), it has been assumed that all excellence-driven policies promote the world-class university model or global research university model, the basic features of which are talents, resources, and smart governance (including primarily a high level of autonomy). So, the main question for this part of the chapter is, has the level of the Project 5-100 universities' autonomy increased during the project's implementation?

It is arguable that one of the main peculiarities of the Russian excellence initiative is the significant role of the government in the development of the participant-universities – the basic goals are set and critical decisions are made outside of the universities by the government. The government requires excellence-driven universities to define their development priorities and ensures that they are being fulfilled through the systematic monitoring. An international council is convened twice a year to control the progress of the Project 5-100 universities. The council's evaluations are one of the key criteria when decisions on financing of the universities' development programmes are being made. It should be stressed again that the activities that the Russian excellence-driven universities could fund from the Project 5-100 grant are limited by the government decree.

Of course, there are other examples of direct interventions of the government into the development and operation of the universities within the excellence-driven policies and initiatives. Merger of leading French universities with the research organizations and the transformation of the graduate education within German excellence initiative or hiring international faculty in Chinese 985 programme are good examples. But, we argue that the Russian Project 5-100 illustrates almost extreme example of government intervention in the universities development which makes the issue of universities' autonomy significantly challenging.

Despite the fact that the Project 5-100 universities were allowed to create curricula according to their own standards, and were given more freedom to manage funds from income-generating activities, their autonomy over operational management was limited (Froumin & Povalko, 2014). Their accountability to the government on some issues increased in frequency (e.g., by 10 times: from one report every five years to one report twice a year). The survey has shown that 85 per cent of the administrators complained about the increased accountability and direct administrative pressure from the Ministry of Education and Science and the Project 5-100 implementation agency.

The survey of professors and administrators at the Project 5-100 universities educed that not only the autonomy of the selected group of the Higher education institutions is being limited by the government, but also internal academic freedom is being limited by the excellence-driven universities by themselves. All Project 5-100 universities introduced complex internal evaluation systems (including evaluations of professors and researchers) tracing the implementation of the plans recorded in the roadmaps. Thus, 70 per cent of the professors reported the increased administrative pressure from the university leadership. Based on the abovementioned facts we can argue that managerialism is growing within the Project 5-100 universities under the external pressure of the government. An additional point is that the interviews with the leaders of the excellence initiatives (including Project 5-100) has shown that universities leadership may complain about their limited autonomy but ultimately agree with it because it allows them to claim for additional resources, as well as to shift part of the responsibility for their universities' performances to the government.

Consideration of the abovementioned facts through the theoretical framework of the corporate actor (Coleman, 1974, 1990), which assumes that the corporate actor combines two functions – the object self (principal) and the acting self (agent) – allows us to argue that the excellence initiatives in higher education represent a transition to a situation where the principal (goal-setting) functions are being taken on by the government to a large extent – it is demonstrated by the Project 5-100 perfectly. The government's actions are contradictory in the long term from this point of view: while introducing elements of competition, and explicitly demanding initiative and entrepreneurial behaviour from the universities, it determines the directions of the development and intervenes in the management of the universities. The challenge for governments is to find the right instruments to ensure that enough principal functions are being performed by the universities and not usurped by the government.

Proceeding from the disputed issues related to the changing autonomy of the universities being pushed for excellence, it could be argued that a new theoretical model is needed to consider autonomy in higher education from a dynamic perspective. We believe that it could be based on the framework of the corporate actor.

6 Global and Local

The analysis of the rationale for and design of the Russian excellence initiative Project 5-100 has shown that the global research university model is being promoted by the government, and the majority of the participant-universities have made a strategic move towards this model, as the survey has also identified. Theoretical discussions criticizing the WCU (or the global research university model) are hinged on the thesis that WCUs focus mostly on their research mission, tending to ignore their third mission and local and national needs (Douglass, 2016; Benneworth et al., 2017). Having decided to test this statement, we used the Project 5-100 as a case study in order to make an attempt to answer the following question: do the universities participating in the excellence initiative tend to ignore or decrease the third mission and focus on research and global issues only?

Needless to say, Project 5-100 universities invest a great deal of their resources to initiatives related to research and internationalization. Project 5-100 universities create international research centres and laboratories, and support joint international research teams and projects. Russian excellence-driven universities introduce research-intensive graduate and postgraduate programmes in English, they fund international faculty development programmes, make major efforts to attract the most qualified (and research-productive) international faculty, and promote education programmes to attract more foreign students.

However, the case of Project 5-100 has shown that despite the strong external push for the global research university model, coupled with internal efforts aimed at the implementation of this model, excellence-driven universities have become more responsive to local and national needs. The evidence from the development roadmaps of the Project 5-100 universities show that many of them independently take on the role and the obligations related to the implementation of the regionally and even locally oriented initiatives, despite the fact that they do not get additional funding to do it.

The series of examples of the Project 5-100 universities' initiatives should be provided to illustrate the statement above. The case of one of the leaders of the Project 5-100 – the National Research University Higher School of Economics

(HSE University) in Moscow – is very illustrative. The HSE University is highly selective (among the top three Russian universities), and it has an annual budget of about US$240 million, nearly 40 per cent of which are from non-government sources (mainly from fee-paying education activities).

The HSE University development programme includes a specific section called 'University's Social Mission' (HSE Roadmap, 2017). This section stipulates the implementation of the measures related to the increase of the impact of university on the socio-economic and cultural development of the city where the HSE University is located. It also includes initiatives aimed at the development of the Russian education system, as well as national socio-economic and cultural development.

Being excellence-driven and research-oriented, the HSE University implements educational, cultural and social projects for Moscow citizens and develops a public expert platform at the University for the City. HSE University involves students and faculty in cultural and charity projects in Moscow, including socially-oriented projects aimed at improving students' professional skills. The HSE University also undertakes responsibility for the improvement of its local environment and the development of the City's cultural and historical environment. Concerning the initiatives of the HSE University related to national needs, it is worth noting that the university put its financial and intellectual resources into the support of other Russian universities, including regional higher education institutions, by sharing its best practices through a system of open learning resources. HSE University develops new teaching materials and methodologies for teaching social sciences and humanities at secondary schools and offers professional development for high school teachers.

Another example of the engagement of the excellence-driven universities from the Project 5-100 with regional and local development challenges is Tomsk State University (TSU) located in Siberia. More than 13,000 students study in TSU, nearly 1,500 of which are international students. TSU's annual budget equals to slightly more than US$75 million, more than a third of which is earned by research and development activities.

The development roadmap of Tomsk State University includes a specific section called 'Raising the attractiveness of the University and Tomsk city to improve competitiveness sustainability'. It includes the implementation of a series of locally and regionally oriented initiatives (TSU Roadmap, 2017). The University sets itself the task of raising the attractiveness of the University and Tomsk city by ensuring openness and responsibility for regional development, as well as by strengthening the educational, expert, and organizational role of the University in addressing regional problems. Tomsk State University also plans measures aimed at the involvement of its alumni in the process of development of the region and the development of social–professional University volunteer services. Implementation of programmes for the development of student entrepreneurship on a University basis, including social entrepreneurship, in the interest of regional development is also stipulated by the TSU development roadmap.

Additionally, partnership activities with local schools were put into the development roadmaps of the overwhelming majority of Project 5-100 universities: Kazan Federal University, National Research Nuclear University (MEPhI), Tomsk Polytechnic University, the National University of Science and Technology (MISiS), the leaders of the Project 5-100, are among these higher education institutions. It shows the strengthening of the performance of the third mission and reflects the inclusion of local needs to the priorities by excellence-driven universities while moving towards international competitiveness.

As can be seen from the cases above, Russian excellence-driven universities which participate in the Project 5-100 launch initiatives of local and regional importance independently, despite the fact that the government only sets the objectives related to the enhancement of international competitiveness, as well as despite the fact that only measures and activities related to global competitiveness are eligible for financial support, according to the design of the project.

The data also shows that, even mostly being research-intensive and globally-oriented, Project 5-100 universities increases admission (including undergraduate programmes), becoming more diverse, and do not close the units which are not research intensive but develops them. They actively develop innovation and entrepreneurship infrastructure and increase their flagship role within the education sector. Reasoning from the results of the analysis of the Russian excellence-driven universities, we argue that in actual practice Project 5-100 universities introduce a more complex model than that of the global research university model promoted by the government and which, following the ideas of Kerr (2011) and Marginson (2017), could be called a multiversity, or flagship university in some cases (Douglass, 2016).

International experts on the excellence initiatives have shown that excellence-driven universities in other countries to a large extent pursue a multiversity model also (interviews with the leaders of the excellence initiatives from different countries conducted by the authors). It has been affirmed by researchers and experts that the multiversity model provides a balance between all missions, between global research excellence and local and national relevance. Holding the focus on the agenda of the global competition, at the same time multiversities ensure their stability by comprehensive growth.

One possible interpretation of this tendency may be that the excellence initiatives in their full merits are just time-limited projects, so even excellence-driven universities establish broader and more solid ground for their long-term functioning by balancing their missions, and ensuring sustainable growth by moving towards the multiversity model. It is argued that multiversities have more resources with which to respond to global challenges, including global rankings (Marginson, 2017). Furthermore, the implementation of the multiversity model allows excellence-driven universities to gain greater local support, to establish tighter linkages with the innovative businesses, in other words, to build an ecosystem, maintaining their long-term and multifaceted development.

7 Concluding Remarks

It should not be unmentioned that within the framework of the limiting autonomy, and while implementing initiatives regarding the local, regional and national needs, Russian excellence-driven universities have demonstrated significant positive results in terms of the increase of their global competitiveness. During the four years of the Project 5-100, the participating universities demonstrated significant positive dynamics in terms of the promotion in institutional and especially in subject world universities rankings. For instance, according to the recent QS World University Rankings by Subject in 2018, five Project 5-100 universities ranked among the Top 100 in the world. Excellence initiatives implemented by other countries have led to the comparable results after 10–15 years.

In addition to the promotion in rankings, Russian excellence-driven universities demonstrate significant positive dynamics in terms of the research productivity and internationalization. The studies confirm that the dynamics of the total number of publications of the Project 5-100 universities significantly exceeds the overall publication trend of the Russian higher education institutions (Poldin et al., 2017). Project 5-100 has triggered internationalization of the participating universities in terms of the number of foreign students (up to 25 per cent of the student body in particular cases are international students), and expressed by the share of the international faculty (it almost tripled in the Project 5-100 universities). What is even more important is that the leading academic experts highly appreciate the potential for cooperation with the Project 5-100 universities. Therefore, the challenge in future years for the Russian excellence initiative implementation would be to retain and strengthen the results, balancing university autonomy and supporting their initiatives.

In conclusion we would like to argue that the fact that the excellence-driven universities (even being pushed by governments to only enhance their international competitiveness) implement initiatives related to local and regional challenges made the shift from the world-class or global research university model to the multiversity or flagship university model more visible (Douglass, 2016). The Russian case brings into sharp focus that excellence-driven universities move towards such model. Project 5-100 universities actively develop the territories of their localization, make a significant positive contribution to the local and regional socio-economic development, and implement important social and cultural initiatives. The study has found that the excellence-driven universities in other countries increase their third mission activities also.

The implementation of local initiatives at the same time as education and research is being developed according to international standards proves that even world-class oriented universities are becoming more diverse in terms of their basic functions to ensure sustainable development. We argue that the development of excellence-driven universities reflects the statement that the model of comprehensive multi-disciplinary and multi-functional research university is becoming dominant (Marginson, 2017). The Russian case shows that all three dimensions of action are in play: global, national and local (Marginson & Rhoades, 2002). Thus, a question arises whether governments should specifically set national and local objectives to universities aspiring for excellence within the design of the excellence initiatives, or whether the growth of global competitiveness itself brings benefits for national and local challenges. This issue is tightly bounded with the dilemma of the changing autonomy of excellence-driven universities also. Inasmuch as the discussion about the changing dominant university model has just started, more international research on the changing balance of the universities' missions as well as on the changing autonomy of the excellence-driven universities is needed.

References

Altbach, P. G., & Salmi, J. (Eds.). (2011). *The road to academic excellence: The making of world-class research universities*. Washington, DC: World Bank.

Benneworth, P., Zeeman, N., Pinheiro, R., & Karlsen, J. (2017). National higher education policies challenging universities' regional engagement activities. *EKONOMIAZ. Revista vasca de Economía, Gobierno Vasco/Eusko Jaurlaritza/Basque Government*, 92(2), 112–139.

Center for Strategic Research 'North-West'. (2016). The results of the survey 'Project 5-100: Some results and development potential – Assessment of the changes in higher education institutions, participating in the implementation of the program aimed at the improvement of the competitiveness of the Russian Higher Education institutions among leading research and education centers'.

Coleman, J. S. (1974). *Power and the structure of society.* New York, NY: Norton.

Coleman, J. S. (1990). *Foundations of social theory.* Cambridge, MA: Harvard University Press.

Decree of the Government of the Russian Federation N 211. (2013). O merah gosudarstvennoj podderzhki vedushhih universitetov Rossijskoj Federacii v celjah povyshenija ih konkurentosposobnosti sredi vedushhih mirovyh nauchno-obrazovatel'nyh centrov [On the measures of state support of the leading Russian universities in order to enhance their competitiveness among the world's leading research and education centers].

Douglass, J. (2016). *The New Flagship University: Changing the paradigm from global ranking to national relevancy.* London: Palgrave Macmillan.

Froumin, I., & Lisyutkin, M. (2015). Excellence-driven policies and initiatives in the context of bologna process: Rationale, design, implementation and outcomes. In A. Curaj, L. Matei, A. Pricopie, J. Salmi, & P. Scott (Eds.), *The European higher education area: Between critical reflections and future policies.* Heidelberg: Springer International Publishing.

Froumin, I., & Lisyutkin, M. (2018). The state as the driver of competitiveness in Russian higher education: The case of the Project 5-100. In A. Oleksiyenko, Q. Zha, I. Chirikov, & J. Li (Eds.), *International status anxiety and higher education: Soviet legacy in China and Russia.* Hong Kong: CERC-Springer.

Froumin, I., & Povalko, A. (2014). Top down push for excellence: Lesson from Russia. In Y. Cheng, Q. Wang, & N. C. Liu (Eds.), *How world-class universities affect global higher education: Influences and responses.* Rotterdam, The Netherlands: Sense Publishers.

Higher School of Economics Roadmap. (2017). *The development roadmap of the national research university higher school of economics.*

Kehm, B., & Pasternack, P. (2009). The German 'excellence initiative' and its role in restructuring the national higher education landscape. In D. Palfreyman & T. Tapper (Eds.), *Structuring mass higher education: The role of elite institutions.* New York, NY: Routledge.

Kerr, C. (2001). *The uses of the university* (5th ed.). Cambridge, MA: Harvard University Press.

Marginson, S. (2017). The world-class multiversity: Global commonalities and national characteristics. *Frontiers of Education in China, 12*(2), 233–260.

Marginson, S., & Rhoades, G. (2002). Beyond national states, markets, and systems of higher education: A glonacal agency heuristic. *Higher Education, 43*(3), 281–309. doi:10.1023/A:1014699605875

Ministry of Education and Science. (2018). *Results of the performance monitoring of the higher education institutions in the Russian Federation*. Retrieved June 20, 2018, from http://indicators.miccedu.ru/monitoring/

Mohrman, K., Ma, W., & Baker, D. (2008). The research university in transition: The emerging global model. *Higher education policy, 21*(1), 5–27.

Poldin, O., Matveeva, N., Sterligov, I., & Yudkevich, M. (2017). Publication activities of Russian Universities: The effects of Project 5-100. *Voprosy Obrazovaniya, 2*, 10–35.

Romanenko, K., & Lisyutkin, M. (2018). University mergers in Russia: Four waves of educational policy. *Russian Education and Society, 60*(1), 58–73.

Sadlak, J., & Liu, N. C. (2009). 'World-class': Aspirations and reality checks. In J. Sadlak & N. C. Liu (Eds.), *The world-class universities as part of a new higher education paradigm: From institutional quality to systemic excellence*. Bucharest: UNESCO-CEPES.

Salmi, J. (2009). *The challenge of establishing world-class universities*. Washington, DC: World Bank.

Salmi, J. (2016). Excellence initiatives to create world-class universities: Do they work? *Higher Education Evaluation and Development, 10*(1), 1–29.

Salmi, J., & Froumin, I. (2013). Excellence initiatives to establish world-class universities: Evaluation of recent experiences. *Journal of Educational Studies, 1*, 25–69.

Tomsk State University Roadmap. (2017). *The development roadmap of the National Research Tomsk State University*.

Printed in the United States
By Bookmasters